There is a lot of solid value in this hands-on, example-rich programming
cards using Java. The book describes step-by-step Java Card programm
cards with real-world explanations and has examples that help guide the
understand how to develop and implement applications. I would recommend that this
book be added to the smart card reading list for anyone developing smart applications.

—Henry N. Dreifus, President & CEO, Dreifus Associates, Ltd.

Java Card Technology for Smart Cards™ is an excellent book on Java Card technology
that will bring a whole new generation of users to smart cards and their applications.

—Dr. Bertrand du Castel, Chairman, Java Card Forum Technical Committee

Java Card technology, which is now mature, stable, and deployed, needs such a book
in this series. I am happy to see this book as the result of the work done over three
years by SUN and the smart card industry in the Java Card Forum. The arrival of
Java in an embedded system such as a card is just the beginning of the story. Many
other systems will benefit from the open platform technology and the change of para-
digm it introduces.

Many thanks to Zhiqun Chen for such a necessary book.

—Christian Goire, President of the Java Card Forum, and Director, Advanced
Research, Bull Smart Cards & Terminals

At last, a book shedding light on the secrets of smart card applications and Java
applied to these tiny environments. Java Card is a critical technology in support of
multi-application Open Platform cards. With Java Card and Open Platform, the
future of credit cards will not be the same. In this book, Zhiqun shares her hands-on,
first-class expertise to provide a clear, thorough, and exhaustive description of Java
Card technology.

—Marc Kekicheff, Vice President, Emergency Technologies, VISA International

Java Card technology provides a truly open platform that enables rapid development
of smart card applications. This book helps the existing and ever-growing Java devel-
oper community to expand their computing knowledge to smart cards. I wish all the
readers much fun in developing their first Java Card applet.

—Sabine Schilg, Marketing Manager, eApplications, Pervasive Computing
Division, IBM.

Java Card™ Technology for Smart Cards

Architecture and Programmer's Guide

The Java™ Series

Lisa Friendly, Series Editor
Tim Lindholm, Technical Editor
Ken Arnold, Technical Editor of The Jini™ Technology Series
Jim Inscore, Technical Editor of The Java™ Series, Enterprise Edition

www.javaseries.com

Eric Armstrong, Stephanie Bodoff, Debbie Carson, Maydene Fisher, Dale Green, Kim Haase
The Java™ Web Services Tutorial

Ken Arnold, James Gosling, David Holmes
The Java™ Programming Language, Third Edition

Cynthia Bloch, Annette Wagner
MIDP 2.0 Style Guide for the Java™ 2 Platform, Micro Edition

Joshua Bloch
Effective Java™ Programming Language Guide

Mary Campione, Kathy Walrath, Alison Huml
The Java™ Tutorial, Third Edition: A Short Course on the Basics

Mary Campione, Kathy Walrath, Alison Huml, Tutorial Team
The Java™ Tutorial Continued: The Rest of the JDK™

Patrick Chan
The Java™ Developers Almanac 1.4, Volume 1

Patrick Chan
The Java™ Developers Almanac 1.4, Volume 2

Patrick Chan, Rosanna Lee
The Java™ Class Libraries, Second Edition, Volume 2: java.applet, java.awt, java.beans

Patrick Chan, Rosanna Lee, Doug Kramer
The Java™ Class Libraries, Second Edition, Volume 1: java.io, java.lang, java.math, java.net, java.text, java.util

Patrick Chan, Rosanna Lee, Doug Kramer
The Java™ Class Libraries, Second Edition, Volume 1: Supplement for the Java™ 2 Platform, Standard Edition, v1.2

Kirk Chen, Li Gong
Programming Open Service Gateways with Java™ Embedded Server

Zhiqun Chen
Java Card™ Technology for Smart Cards: Architecture and Programmer's Guide

Maydene Fisher, Jon Ellis, Jonathan Bruce
JDBC™ API Tutorial and Reference, Third Edition

Li Gong, Gary Ellison, Mary Dageforde
Inside Java™ 2 Platform Security, Second Edition: Architecture, API Design, and Implementation

James Gosling, Bill Joy, Guy Steele, Gilad Bracha
The Java™ Language Specification, Second Edition

Doug Lea
Concurrent Programming in Java™, Second Edition: Design Principles and Patterns

Rosanna Lee, Scott Seligman
JNDI API Tutorial and Reference: Building Directory-Enabled Java™ Applications

Sheng Liang
The Java™ Native Interface: Programmer's Guide and Specification

Tim Lindholm, Frank Yellin
The Java™ Virtual Machine Specification, Second Edition

Roger Riggs, Antero Taivalsaari, Jim Van Peursem, Jyri Huopaniemi, Mark Patel, Aleksi Uotila
Programming Wireless Devices with the Java™ 2 Platform, Micro Edition, Second Edition

Henry Sowizral, Kevin Rushforth, Michael Deering
The Java 3D™ API Specification, Second Edition

Sun Microsystems, Inc.
Java™ Look and Feel Design Guidelines: Advanced Topics

Kathy Walrath, Mary Campione
The JFC Swing Tutorial: A Guide to Constructing GUIs

Seth White, Maydene Fisher, Rick Cattell, Graham Hamilton, Mark Hapner
JDBC™ API Tutorial and Reference, Second Edition: Universal Data Access for the Java™ 2 Platform

Steve Wilson, Jeff Kesselman
Java™ Platform Performance: Strategies and Tactics

The Jini™ Technology Series

Eric Freeman, Susanne Hupfer, Ken Arnold
JavaSpaces™ Principles, Patterns, and Practice

The Java™ Series, Enterprise Edition

Stephanie Bodoff, Dale Green, Kim Haase, Eric Jendrock, Monica Pawlan, Beth Stearns
The J2EE™ Tutorial

Rick Cattell, Jim Inscore, Enterprise Partners
J2EE™ Technology in Practice: Building Business Applications with the Java™ 2 Platform, Enterprise Edition

Mark Hapner, Rich Burridge, Rahul Sharma, Joseph Fialli, Kim Haase
Java™ Message Service API Tutorial and Reference: Messaging for the J2EE™ Platform

Inderjeet Singh, Beth Stearns, Mark Johnson, Enterprise Team
Designing Enterprise Applications with the Java™ 2 Platform, Enterprise Edition

Vlada Matena, Sanjeev Krishnan, Linda DeMichiel, Beth Stearns
Applying Enterprise JavaBeans™, Second Edition: Component-Based Development for the J2EE™ Platform

Bill Shannon, Mark Hapner, Vlada Matena, James Davidson, Eduardo Pelegri-Llopart, Larry Cable, Enterprise Team
Java™ 2 Platform, Enterprise Edition: Platform and Component Specifications

Rahul Sharma, Beth Stearns, Tony Ng
J2EE™ Connector Architecture and Enterprise Application Integration

Java Card™ Technology for Smart Cards

Architecture and Programmer's Guide

Zhiqun Chen

ADDISON-WESLEY

Boston • San Francisco • New York • Toronto • Montreal
London • Munich • Paris • Madrid
Capetown • Sydney • Tokyo • Singapore • Mexico City

Library of Congress Cataloging-in-Publication Data

Chen, Zhiqun, 1969-

    Java Card technology for smart cards : architecture and programmer's guide / Zhiqun Chen.

        p.   cm. — (The Java series)

    Includes bibliographical references and index.

    ISBN 0-201-70329-7 (alk. paper)

    1. Java (Computer program language)   2. Smart cards. I. Title. II. Series.

  QA76.73.J38 C478 2000

  005.13'3—dc21   00-036360

The publisher offers discounts on this book when ordered in quantity for special sales. For more information, please contact:

Pearson Education Corporate Sales Division
One Lake Street
Reading, Massachusetts 01867
(800) 382-3419
corpsales@pearsontechgroup.com

Visit us on the Web at www.awl.com/cseng

Text printed on recycled and acid-free paper.

ISBN 0201703297

2 3 4 5 6 7 DPC 07 06 05 04

2nd Printing   February 2004

To the Java Card Team

Contents

Foreword

The book you are holding in your hands is a milestone in the history of the smart card. It epitomizes a radical change in the industry: smart cards are no longer closed proprietary products that can be created and understood by only a handful of technical gurus. They have become full-fledged programmable objects that can be readily integrated inside information systems using publicly available interfaces and widespread programming languages.

And what is the impact? Is it about an industry playing catch-up with the rest of the world? Not quite: smart cards are not just any computing platform. They are intended to be trusted. Smart cards may contain a key to your bank account, your use-rights as a subscriber to pay-television channels, or your emergency medical data.

Here was the challenge the industry faced: how could smart cards be deployed rapidly, contain creative applications, keep up with the rapid pace of the Internet, yet remain trusted?

Enter the Java™ programming language, which brought trusted and reliable object-oriented programs to the Net. These attributes are even more essential to smart cards than they are to mainstream network applications. The Java platform provides this reliability and trust through three key attributes.

- *Simplicity:* Programmers become fluent in the language very rapidly, and their programs can be debugged more efficiently than with any other language.

- *Safety:* The language is both type-safe and memory-safe. This eliminates the mechanisms by which unwarranted access to data and boundary violations happen with other mainstream programming languages.

- *Security:* The platform comes with a built-in secure loading mechanism that can distinguish among various levels of trust in multiple external entities.

The smart card industry has been looking for a trusted and reliable software platform for quite some time. Perhaps the first commercial request for inventive and network-ready smart cards came in 1988, when News Group's BSkyB (then called SkyTV) in Great Britain sought a new generation of cards for its innovative satellite pay-television system. It needed the ability to change its subscription tiering system and the cryptography housed in the smart cards as often as it saw fit in order to adjust easily to new commercial requirements and to comply with changing regulations. At that time, and for years to come, the only tools available for smart card software developers were assembly language and oscilloscopes.

Over the course of the early 1900s slight improvements were made, with the introduction of C compilers capable of producing decent smart card programs without too much code expansion. However, there were no security features whatsoever built into those tools. Security was expected to come largely from the programmer's intuition, skills, and goodwill.

Research was conducted by various groups in France, Holland, and the United States to create interpretive structures inside smart cards, which would achieve basic memory-safety. Those developments laid the groundwork and established the momentum that led, at the end of 1996, to Sun Microsystems, agreeing to devise a version of the Java platform for smart cards. The industry promptly coalesced around this technology and collaborated with Sun to help create the Java Card standard.

To the smart card industry, Java Card technology represents the result of about 10 years of yearning for a better platform, on a par with what the rest of the desktop computing industry has been enjoying. This book comes right from the heart of the Java Card team at Sun Microsystems. It is not geared toward one particular vendor's products, yet it contains a lot of concrete examples of actual card applets. Of particular value to hands-on programmers will be the chapter devoted to applet optimization techniques, since today's smart cards still have extremely constrained resources.

I would like to thank the entire Java Card team for their long-term commitment and hard work. I would also like to thank the card industry itself, which has been very supportive of Sun's efforts and has already been instrumental in deploying the technology in tens of millions of products. Lastly, I am very grateful to Zhiqun Chen for her willingness to write this book and for contributing her impressive Java Card programming talents to this ground-breaking technology.

Patrice Peyret
April 2000
Cupertino, California

Preface

Audience for This Book

Java Card™ technology combines a subset of the Java programming language with a runtime environment optimized for smart cards and other memory-constrained devices. This book is intended for a wide technical audience with different needs of understanding Java Card technology.

First and foremost, it is written for Java Card applet developers. You will find a smart card tutorial, in-depth discussions on various Java Card features, helpful programming tips for applet development, and the reference to the Java Card APIs.

Second, this book is supplementary reading for Java Card platform implementors. It provides further discussion of many topics in the Java Card specifications and includes code examples to clarify those topics.

Third, this book is useful for technical managers or anyone who wants to gain an overall understanding of Java Card technology. In particular, the first three chapters are introductions to orient you within the technology from both a technical and marketing point of view.

Throughout this book, I assume that readers are familiar with the fundamentals of the Java language. For those who want to learn more about the Java language, the book by Arnold and Gosling is a good resource.

Organization of This Book

This book is written in a bottom-up fashion. Each chapter was a step to the next one, so it is best if you read the chapters in order.

Part 1: Introduction

- Chapter 1 introduces smart cards and Java Card technology—history, benefits, and applications.

- Chapter 2 discusses smart card basics as a foundation for exploring the rest of the book.

Part 2: Java Card Technology

- Chapter 3 gives an overview of Java Card technology—the system architecture and its components.

- Chapter 4 discusses the properties and the behavior of persistent and transient objects in the Java Card platform and how to create and use those objects.

- Chapter 5 explains what atomicity means in the Java Card platform and how to develop an applet using transactions to protect data integrity.

- Chapter 6 discusses exceptions in the Java Card platform and how applets throw and handle exceptions.

- Chapter 7 explains how applets run within the JCRE and demonstrates the techniques of applet writing.

- Chapter 8 describes the techniques of handling APDUs in an applet.

- Chapter 9 explains the behavior of objects, exceptions, and applets under the control of the applet firewall and discusses how applets can safely share data using object sharing mechanisms.

- Chapter 10 first introduces many important cryptographic concepts and algorithms. It then outlines the cryptographic APIs in the Java Card platform and demonstrates how to use these APIs through code examples.

- Chapter 11 describes the security features in the Java Card platform and discusses how these security features are enforced through a variety of mechanisms. Along with the discussion, this chapter summarizes the topics covered in Part 2.

Part 3: Programming Guide and Tips

- Chapter 12 walks you through a step-by-step process of creating a simple electronic wallet applet.

- Chapter 13 provides a number of recommendations for optimizing applets. In many cases, a discussion is provided with the recommendation to help you understand various design trade-offs.

- Chapter 14 discusses issues related to using the `int` data type when writing Java Card applets.

Part 4: Appendices

- Appendix A describes the subset of the Java programming language that is supported in the Java Card platform.
- Appendix B provides a comprehensive reference to the Java Card 2.1 APIs.

The Version Covered in This Book

This book is based on Java Card version 2.1, the latest release when the book was written. At the meantime, the next version 2.1.1 is underway. Version 2.1.1 will include minor enhancement updates to version 2.1. The contents and techniques covered in the book will continue to be relevant to future Java Card releases, and new things will be incorporated in future editions of this book.

Retrieving Additional Information On-line

You can get the latest on Java Card technology or the latest Java Card development kit from the Java Card web site at `http://java.sun.com/products/javacard`. For updated information about this book, visit `http://java.sun.com/books/series/javacard`.

Acknowledgments

Writing a book is so much more than putting words to paper, and this book especially benefited from the help and support of many people.

It was not possible to turn ideas of the book into reality without the management support of Andy Streich, Alan Brenner, and Patrice Peyret. I received full support from my manager, Andy Streich, who allocated time for me to concentrate on writing and rescued me whenever I encoutered obstacles. I would also like to thank Debra Dooley, who encouraged me to start this project and supported me along the way.

Lisa Friendly and Tim Lindholm, the Java Series editors, provided many invaluable suggestions and were instrumental in getting this book written and published. The team at Addison-Wesley was enormously helpful. I am indebted to

Mike Hendrickson and Julie DiNicola, who guided me through the writing process and rescued me whenever I encoutered obstacles. Diane Freed oversaw the production, from copyediting to final printing. Penny Hull copyedited the manuscript and Evelyn Pyle did the proofreading. Kim Arney and Jim Holliday did the typesetting and page composition.

A number of reviewers greatly improved the book through their careful reading and helpful suggestions. Li Gong, author of *Inside Java 2 Platform Security,* offered technical guidance on improving the structure and content of the book. Kirk Chen, Pieter Hartel, and Ravi Tanjore provided detailed comments. I especially benefited from many constructive discussions with them. Bertrand du Castel, Eric Vétillard, and Sebastian Hans thoroughly reviewed the book and generously offered their intimate knowledge from the field of deploying Java Card technology. Mitch Butler, Jerome Danville, Mike Eisler, Eduard de Jong, Danny Louie, Eric Nellen, Andy Streich, Jessica Wei, Jiang Wu, and Jennifer Yonemitsu all provided valuable comments to the book.

This book also benefited from the help of Peter Cattaneo, Karen Hsiang, Albert Leung, Moshe Levy, and Jennifer Yonemitsu, who gave me useful advice and helped me organize the project.

Finally, in the past several years, I have had the privilege of working with a group of talented and dedicated people in the Java Card team. This book is dedicated to them.

Zhiqun Chen
April, 2000

PART 1

Introduction

CHAPTER 1

From the Beginning

The explosion of the Internet and of wireless digital communication has rapidly changed the way we connect with other people. As the world has become more connected, the business model has evolved from the traditional face-to-face in-store transaction to the on-line transaction conducted with a few mouse clicks in our home or office. The rapid emergence of electronic business opens not only new avenues for commerce but also vast opportunities for an industry to reach out to its customers and to introduce value-added services.

The success of the electronic business market relies on the same level of trust that companies have built up over years of doing business face to face and relies on technology to help handle business easily. The security and portability of smart cards provide a safe, reliable, convenient, and effective way to ensure secure e-business and to enable a broad range of new applications.

1.1 Smart Cards

The same size as a credit card, a smart card (Figure 1.1) stores and processes information through the electronic circuits embedded in silicon in the plastic substrate of its body. A smart card is a portable and tamper-resistant computer. Unlike magnetic stripe cards, smart cards carry both processing power and information. Therefore, they do not require access to remote databases at the time of a transaction.

1.1.1 Brief History

The idea of incorporating an integrated circuit into a plastic card was first introduced by two German inventors, Jürgen Dethloff and Helmut Grötrupp, in 1968. Later they filed a German patent on their invention. Independently, Kunitaka Arimura of the

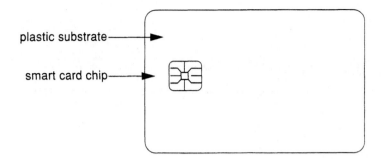

Figure 1.1   Smart card

Arimura Technology Institute in Japan filed a patent on the smart card in 1970. However, real progress came with Roland Moreno's 47 smart card–related patents filed in 11 countries between 1974 and 1979[1]. In the late 1970s, CII-Honeywell-Bull (now Groupe Bull) first commercialized smart card technology and introduced microprocessor cards.

The initial smart card trials took place in France and Germany in the early 1980s using smart cards as prepaid phone cards and secure debit/credit bank cards. These successful trials proved the potential of smart cards against tampering and flexibility.

Recently, with advances in chip technology and modern cryptography, smart cards have become more powerful. They are now used to store electronic cash, replacing paper money, to store and secure personal medical records, to prevent unauthorized access to cable and satellite broadcasts, and to improve wireless telephone security.

Already very common in Europe and Asia because of the widespread use of applications such as GSM and banking cards, smart cards began to make significant entries into the U.S. market in the late 1990s with the growing demand for security technologies in the e-business arena.

1.1.2   Benefits

The interest in smart cards is a result of the benefits they provide. One benefit, of course, is their built-in computational power. *Security, portability,* and *ease of use* are the other key advantages of smart cards.

The processor, memory, and I/O support of a smart card are packaged in a single integrated circuit embedded in a plastic card. A smart card is resistant to attack because it does not need to depend on potentially vulnerable external resources. Probing information in a smart card requires the physical possession of the card, intimate knowledge of the smart card hardware and software, and additional equipment. The security features in smart cards are further strengthened by cryptographic functions. Data stored in the card can be encrypted to safeguard its privacy in the physical memory, and data exchanged between the card and the outside world can be signed and encrypted. In addition, accessing a smart card usually requires the card holder to enter a PIN (personal identification number), which prevents the card from being used by an unauthorized person. Overall, it would be much more difficult to crack into a smart card than into a traditional desktop computer.

Another benefit of smart cards is their inherent portability. You can carry a smart card in your wallet in the same way you carry credit cards. Because of this characteristic, smart cards keep data available wherever needed, as the card holder moves from one location to another.

Smart cards are also very convenient to use. To begin a transaction, you insert the card into a card acceptance device, and you remove the card from the device when the job is done.

1.1.3   Applications

Smart cards are often used for secure data storage and to authenticate and ensure security of transactions. This section provides examples of applications for using smart cards.

In the *telecommunication industry*, prepaid phone cards offer a cash-free, low-maintenance, and antifraud mechanism for accessing public phones. Today, the wireless telecommunication industry is the largest market using smart cards for security. The most notable example is GSM (global system for mobile communication). A GSM wireless phone has a subscriber identity module (SIM) card, which is a smart card with a much smaller plastic substrate, that fits into a slot inside the phone. The SIM card identifies the user and provides encryption keys for digital voice transmission. It is very difficult to intercept telephone numbers and illegally program them into wireless phones. The key generated by the SIM card for encryption is temporary and is changed with each use. Therefore, even if a GSM transmission could be decrypted, it would be useless for the next transmission. Because the user's identity is programmed into the SIM card, the user can use not just one phone but any GSM-compatible phones that accept the SIM card. A subscriber gets a SIM card from the service provider and inserts it into a phone that can be purchased or leased separately.

As wireless communication gains wide acceptance, the role of wireless phones is going much further than voice transmission. To retain a competitive edge, telcom operators are competing to provide value-added services, such as mobile banking, mobile commerce, Web access, and so on, which all rely on smart cards to verify the subscriber's identity and ensure security in data transmissions.

In the *payment and banking industries*, smart cards are used as secure credit or debit bank cards. Their functions are similar to magnetic stripe cards. But because of the on-board computing power of smart cards, they can handle off-line transactions and verifications. Unlike magnetic stripe cards, data in a smart card cannot be easily copied and then misused. Smart card–based credit cards help to prevent credit card fraud that costs banks around the world billions of dollars a year.

Recently, the newer trends in the payment and banking area include the e-purse (or e-wallet) applications. The card stores electronic money, and the balance can be increased or decreased. Smart card–based electronic purses can reduce the cost of handling paper money; in particular, they provide an ideal payment mechanism for on-line microtransactions, where the overhead in using regular credit cards is too high for low-value transactions.

In a *retail loyalty scheme*, the card can help to promote cobranded retailer partnership and increase sales and customer satisfaction. The card stores loyalty points that are accumulated when the card holder purchases items from sponsoring retailers. The card holder can use the points for point-of-sale discounts, air miles, or other gifts. The data captured when the card is used can also help retailers to understand the customer's purchase preferences and behavior.

In a *mass-transit system*, smart cards can replace tokens and tickets. In the field of *automotive transportation*, smart cards can replace coins for parking and toll, in a way that is similar to the function of prepaid phone cards. The smart card solution provides many benefits in collecting fares, managing huge numbers of small transactions, and attracting customers with user-friendly and faster transactions.

In the *health care sector*, smart cards can help to reduce the complexity of managing information concerning patients' insurance coverage and medical histories. The card can store administration data to manage a patient's eligibility for benefits and to process claims. The card can also store a patient's medical records, providing up-to-date and reliable medical information and enabling the sharing of information among physicians, hospitals, and pharmacies.

On the *Internet*, user authentication and access control is an important motivation for choosing smart cards. There is increasing use of smart cards in the public key infrastructure. A smart card carries the card holder's private key and digital certificate—two components that verify the card holder's identity to the electronic world. In the public key encryption scheme, the private key, known only to you, is paired with a public key that is made widely available. The private key is used in conjunction with the public key to support digital signature signing and verification. The digital certificate is issued by a certificate authority that testifies to the authenticity of a public key. Applications using smart cards for authentication include Web site access control, digital signing of e-mail messages, and secure on-line transactions. Many other Internet applications can be envisioned.

In a *closed environment,* such as a corporation or a university, multiapplication smart cards can provide physical entrance to buildings and computer facilities, grant levels of network access to internal Web sites and servers, store and process administration data, and enable various financial transactions (paying for meals, purchasing snacks at vending machines, ATM withdrawals and deposits, and so on).

As smart card technology gains wider acceptance, smart cards are finding their way into everyone's wallet.

1.2   Challenges in the Development of Smart Card Applications

Developing a smart card application traditionally has been a lengthy and difficult process. Although the cards are standardized in size, shape, and communication protocol, the inner workings differ widely from one manufacturer to another. Most smart card development tools are built by the smart card manufacturers using generic assembly language tools and dedicated hardware emulators obtained from silicon chip vendors. It has been virtually impossible for third parties to develop applications independently and sell them to issuers. Therefore, developing smart card applications has been limited to a group of highly skilled and specialized programmers who have intimate knowledge of the specific smart card hardware and software.

Because there are no standardized high-level application interfaces available in smart cards, application developers need to deal with very low-level communication protocols, memory management, and other minute details dictated by the specific hardware of the smart card. Most smart card applications in use today have been custom developed from the ground up, which is a time-consuming process; it usually takes a year or two for a product to go to the market. Upgrading software or moving applications to a different platform is particularly difficult or impossible.

Further, because smart card applications were developed to run on proprietary platforms, applications from different service providers cannot coexist and run on a single card. Lack of interoperability and limited card functions prevent a broader deployment of smart card applications.

1.3   Applying Java to Smart Cards

Java Card™ technology offers a way to overcome obstacles hindering smart card acceptance. It allows smart cards and other memory-constrained devices to run applications (called applets) written in the Java programming language. Essentially, Java Card technology defines a secure, portable, and multiapplication smart card platform that incorporates many main advantages of the Java language.

1.3.1   Benefits of Java Card Technology

Smart card application developers can benefit from Java Card technology as follows.

Ease of application development—The Java language brings smart card programming into the mainstream of software development, relieving developers from going through the swamps of microcontroller programming, such as programming in 6805 and 8051 assembly languages. Smart card developers can also benefit from many off-the-shelf and integrated Java development environments from vendors such as Borland, IBM, Microsoft, Sun, and Symantec. Furthermore, Java Card technology offers an open platform that defines the standard application programming interfaces and runtime environment. The platform encapsulates the underlying complexity and details of the smart card system. Applet developers work with the high-level programming interfaces. They can concentrate most of their effort on the details of the application and leverage extensions and libraries that others have created.

Security—Security is always of paramount concern when working with smart cards. Java's built-in security features fit in well with the smart card environment. For example, the level of access to all methods and variables is strictly controlled, and there is no way to forge pointers to enable malicious programs to snoop around inside memory. In addition, applets on the Java Card platform are separated by the applet firewall. This way the system can safeguard against a hostile application's attempts to damage other parts of the system.

Hardware independence—Java Card technology is independent of the type of hardware used. It can run on any smart card processors (8 bit, 16 bit, or 32 bit). Java Card applets are written on top of the Java Card platform and thus are smart card hardware independent. Ready-to-use applets can be loaded into any Java smart card without recompilation.

Ability to store and manage multiple applications—A Java smart card can host multiple applets, such as an electronic purse, authentication, loyalty, and health care program, from different service providers. Because of the Java Card firewall mechanism, applets are not able to access each other unless explicitly permitted to do so.

Once the card is issued, its value is not fixed. More applets can be downloaded to the card. A Java smart card's functionality can be continually upgraded with new or updated applets, without the need for issuing a new or a different card.

Compatibility with existing smart card standards—Java Card technology is based on the smart card international standard ISO 7816, so it can easily support smart card systems and applications that are generally compatible with ISO 7816. Applets can interoperate not only on all Java smart cards but also with existing card acceptance devices.

1.3.2 Brief History of Java Card Technology

The Java Card APIs were first introduced in November 1996 by a group of engineers in Schlumberger's product center in Austin, Texas, working to bring smart card development into the mainstream while preserving smart card security. They soon recognized that the Java programming language was the solution. Schlumberger proposed the initial draft for the Java Card APIs and became the first licensed smart card company. A few months later, Bull and Gemplus joined Schlumberger to cofound the Java Card Forum, an industry consortium created for identifying and resolving issues of Java Card technology and promoting its adoption by the smart card industry.

Java Card 1.0 consisted of only specifications for APIs and is not an extensible platform that can easily be built upon. With wide industry support, Sun Microsystems, Inc. set out to develop Java Card technology as a Java technology platform for smart cards and other memory-constrained devices. Its first move was to acquire Integrity Arts, a spinoff of Gemplus that specialized in the development of virtual machine and operating system technologies for smart cards.

In November 1997, Sun Microsystems announced the Java Card 2.0 specification, which evolved from the work of Integrity Arts and was developed in collaboration with the industry and the members of the Java Card Forum, including smart card manufacturers, card issuers, and smart card associations. The Java Card 2.0 APIs differed significantly from the initial 1.0 version in providing an object-oriented way to write applets. In addition, Java Card 2.0 spelled out more fully the application runtime environment. However, the downloadable applet format was not specified.

Java Card version 2.1 was unveiled in March 1999. It consisted of three specifications: the Java Card 2.1 API Specification, the Java Card 2.1 Runtime Environment Specification, and the Java Card 2.1 Virtual Machine Specification. In version 2.1, APIs were updated but largely based on the previous 2.0 version, and applet runtime environment was further standardized. The most significant contribution of Java Card 2.1 was that it explicitly defined the Java Card virtual machine architecture and applet-loading format that makes true applet interoperability possible.

Since its inception three years ago, Java Card technology has been widely embraced by the smart card industry. It is licensed by all major smart card manufacturers and many more industry players—in all, more than 30 licensees. The list of Java Card technology licensees and partners can be found at the URL `http://java.sun.com/products/javacard/#partners`.

CHAPTER 2

Smart Card Basics

This chapter gives a quick tour of the smart card world. It introduces smart card basics as a foundation for exploring the rest of the book. For readers who want to learn more about smart card technology, two books, one by Rankl and Effing[1] and the other by Guthery and Jurgensen[2], are good resources. Readers who have a smart card background can skip or skim through this chapter.

2.1 Overview of Smart Cards

Smart cards are often called chip cards, or integrated circuit (IC) cards. The inte-

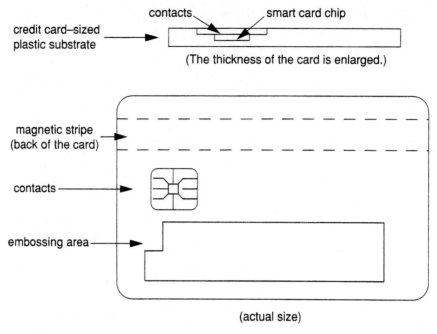

Figure 2.1   Smart card physical appearance

2.2.1   Memory Cards versus Microprocessor Cards

The earliest smart cards produced in large quantities were memory cards. Memory cards are not really smart, because they do not contain a microprocessor. They are embedded with a memory chip or a chip with memory and nonprogrammable logic.

Typically, memory cards hold up to 1K to 4K of data. They are used primarily as prepaid cards for public phones or other goods and services that are sold against prepayment.

Since a memory card does not have a CPU to process data, its data processing is performed by a simple circuit capable of executing a few preprogrammed instructions. Such a circuit has limited functions and cannot be reprogrammed. Therefore, memory cards cannot be reused. When the value in the card is spent, the card is disposed of.

Depending on the security requirements of the stored data, the data access can be protected by means of protected memory or secure logic. For example, prepaid phone cards can contain logic to prevent the value from being increased. However, memory cards can be counterfeited relatively easily.

The advantage of memory cards lies in the simple technology. Therefore, they are favored where low cost is a particular consideration.

By contrast, microprocessor cards, as the name implies, contain a processor. They offer greatly increased security and multifunctional capability. With a microprocessor card, data are never directly available to the external applications. The microprocessor controls data handling and memory access according to a given set of conditions (passwords, encryptions, and so on) and instructions from the external applications. Many current models of microprocessor cards feature built-in cryptographic support. Such cards are particularly useful for applications that need to address data security. Microprocessor cards are very flexible. They can be optimized for one application or can integrate several different applications. Their functionality is restricted only by the available memory resources and computing power.

Microprocessor cards are widely used for access control, banking applications, retail loyalty applications, wireless telecommunication, and so on, where data security and privacy are major concern.

As a result of mass production, the cost of microprocessor cards has fallen drastically since the early 1990s. Microprocessor cards typically cost between $1 and $20, depending primarily on the memory resources and the software functionality included in the card.

In general, the term smart card refers to both memory cards and microprocessor cards. However, some publications prefer to call only microprocessor cards smart cards, because of the intelligence provided by the embedded processor. The term chip cards is used for both memory cards and microprocessor cards.

Because a general-purpose programmable processor is required to support the Java Card environment, in this book the term smart card refers to microprocessor cards. Memory cards are not discussed further.

2.2.2   Contact Cards versus Contactless Cards

Contact cards must be inserted in a card acceptance device, and they communicate with the outside world by using the serial communication interface via eight contact points, as shown in Figure 2.1. Section 2.3.1 provides a detailed look at the contacts in a smart card.

Because a contact card must be inserted into a mechanical card acceptance device in the correct way and in an exact orientation, contactless smart cards are popular in situations requiring fast transactions. Public transport systems and access control for buildings are excellent applications for contactless cards.

Contactless cards do not need to be placed in a card acceptance device. They communicate with the outside world through an antenna wound into the card. Power can be provided by an internal battery or can be collected by the antenna. Contactless cards transmit data to a card acceptance device through electromagnetic fields.

Because the microcircuit of contactless cards is fully sealed inside the card, contactless cards overcome limitations of contact cards: there are no contacts to become worn from excessive use, cards do not need to be carefully inserted into a CAD, and cards do not have to be of a standard thickness to fit in a CAD card slot.

However, contactless cards have their own drawbacks. Contactless cards must be within a certain required distance to exchange data with the card acceptance device. As the card may move out of range very quickly, only limited data can be transmitted due to short duration of a transaction. It is possible for transactions to take place on a card or transmitted data to be intercepted without the card holder knowing it. Furthermore, contactless cards are currently more expensive than corresponding contact cards.

This book uses contact cards in the examples because they are more commonly used. Nevertheless, many discussions about contact cards apply equally well to contactless cards.

2.3   Smart Card Hardware

A smart card has contact points in the surface of the plastic substrate, an embedded central processing unit, and various kinds of memory. Some smart cards also come with coprocessors for math computation.

2.3.1   Smart Card Contact Points

A smart card has eight contact points; their functional assignments are shown in Figure 2.2. The dimensions and locations of the contacts are covered in part 2 of ISO 7816.

- The Vcc point supplies power to the chip. Vcc voltage is 3 or 5 volts, with a maximum deviation of 10 percent. Smart cards in mobile phones typically have the 3-volt Vcc range.

- The RST point is used for sending the signal to reset the microprocessor—this is called a *warm reset*. A *cold reset* is done by switching the power supply voltage off and on again. Taking the card out of the CAD and reinserting it results in a cold reset.

- Smart card processors do not possess internal clock generation. The CLK point supplies the external clock signal from which the internal clock is derived.

- The GND point is used as a reference voltage; its value is considered to be zero volts.

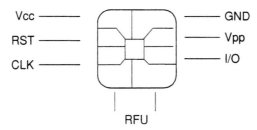

Figure 2.2 Eight contact points

- The Vpp point is optional and is used only in older cards. When used, it supplies the programming voltage with two levels. The lower voltage is called the *idle state*; it must be maintained by the CAD until the other voltage level (*active state*) is required. The voltage change is necessary to program EEPROM memory in some old smart card chips.

- The I/O point is used to transfer data and commands between the smart card and the outside world in half-duplex mode. Half duplex means that commands or data can be transmitted in only one direction at any particular time.

- The RFU points are reserved for future use.

2.3.2   Smart Card Central Processing Unit

The central processing unit in most current smart card chips is an 8-bit microcontroller, usually using the Motorola 6805 or Intel 8051 instruction set, and with clock speeds up to 5MHz. High-end cards very often include a clock multiplier (by 2, 4, or 8), which allows these cards to operate up to 40MHz (5MHz times 8).

Newer smart card chips have a 16-bit or 32-bit microcontroller, and smart cards with reduced instruction set (RISC) architecture are also available. In the future, 16-bit and 32-bit smart cards will likely become more common.

2.3.3   Smart Card Coprocessors

Smart card chips that are designed for use in security applications very often have a built-in coprocessor. A cryptographic coprocessor is a special integrated circuit for expediting calculations, particularly modular arithmetic and large-integer calculations. Such calculations are required by cryptographic operations, such as the RSA algorithm.

The inclusion of a coprocessor usually affects the cost of the chip.

2.3.4   Smart Card Memory System

Smart cards usually contain three kinds of memory: persistent nonmutable memory, persistent mutable memory, and nonpersistent mutable memory. ROM, EEPROM, and RAM are the most widely used memories, respectively, for the three kinds

- *ROM* (read-only memory) is used for storing the fixed program of the card. No power is needed to hold data in this kind of memory. However, as the name implies, it cannot be written to after the card is manufactured. A smart card's ROM contains operating system routines as well as permanent data and user applications. The process of writing a binary image (representing programs and data) into the ROM is called *masking*. It occurs during the chip fabrication process.

- *EEPROM* (electrical erasable programmable read-only memory), like ROM, can preserve data content when power to the memory is turned off. The difference is that the content in this kind of memory can actually be modified during normal use of the card. Therefore, it is used for data storage—the smart card's equivalent of the hard disk on a PC. User applications can also be written into EEPROM after the card is made. The important electrical parameters of EEPROM are the number of write cycles over the lifetime of a card, data retention period, and access time. EEPROM in most smart cards can reliably accept at least 100,000 write cycles and can retain data for 10 years. Reading from EEPROM is as fast as reading from RAM, but writing to EEPROM is 1,000 times slower than writing to RAM.

- *RAM* (random access memory) is used as temporary working space for storing and modifying data. RAM is nonpersistent memory; that is, the information content is not preserved when power is removed from the memory cell. RAM can be accessed an unlimited number of times, and none of the restrictions found with EEPROM apply.

ROM is the least expensive of these three kinds of memory. EEPROM is more expensive than ROM because an EEPROM cell takes up four times as much space as a ROM cell. RAM is very scarce in a smart card chip. A RAM cell tends to be approximately four times larger than an EEPROM cell.

Today, other memory technologies are also gaining popularity in smart cards. For example, flash memory is becoming more common. Flash memory is a kind of persistent mutable memory; it is more efficient in space and power than EEPROM. Flash memory can be read bit by bit but can be updated only as a block. Thus, flash memory is typically used for storing additional programs or large chunks of data that are updated as wholes.

2.4 Smart Card Communication

2.4.1 Card Acceptance Device and Host Applications

A smart card is inserted into a card acceptance device (CAD), which may connect to another computer. Card acceptance devices can be classified as two types: readers and terminals.

A reader is connected to the serial, parallel, or USB port of a computer, through which a smart card communicates. A reader has a slot into which a card is placed, or it can receive data carried through electromagnetic fields from a contactless card. In addition to supplying the card with power, a reader establishes a data communication pathway in which the smart card can talk to the computer connected to the reader. Though normally readers do not have the intelligence to process data, many have error detection and correction functions if transmitted data are not compliant with the underlying transport protocol.

Terminals, on the other hand, are computers on their own. A terminal integrates a smart card reader as one of its components. The most commonly seen terminals are devices used in gas stations and stores for payments and credit card transactions. Bank ATMs are another form of terminal. In addition to having the functionality of a smart card reader, a terminal has the ability to process data exchanged between itself and the smart card. For example, an ATM, if it accepts smart cards, can add or deduct money from an electronic purse application in the smart card.

For simplicity, this book does not draw the line between a reader and a terminal; they are both referred to as card acceptance devices, or CADs. The applications that communicate with the smart card—whether they reside in the computer connected to the reader or in the terminal—are called host applications. Host applications direct the process of communication with the smart card, as explained in Section 2.4.2.

2.4.2 Smart Card Communication Model

The communication pathway between the card and the host is half-duplexed; that is, the data can either be sent from the host to the card or from the card to the host but not both at the same time.

When two computers communicate with each other, they exchange data packets, which are constructed following a protocol, such as TCP/IP. Similarly, smart cards speak to other computers by using their own data packets—called APDUs (application protocol data units). An APDU contains either a command or a response message.

In the card world, the master-slave model is employed. A smart card always plays the passive (slave) role, waiting for a command APDU from a host. It then executes the instruction specified in the command and replies to the host with a response APDU. Command APDUs and response APDUs are exchanged alternately between a card and a host, as shown in Figure 2.3.

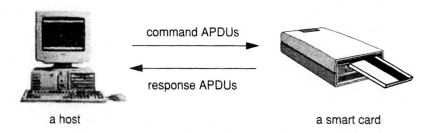

command APDUs

response APDUs

a host   a smart card

Figure 2.3   Smart card communication model

2.4.3   APDU Protocol

The APDU protocol, as specified in ISO 7816-4, is an application-level protocol between a smart card and a host application. APDU messages under ISO 7816-4 comprise two structures: one used by the host application at the CAD side of the channel to send commands to the card, the other used by the card to send responses back to the host application. The former is referred to as the *command APDU (C-APDU)* and the latter as the *response APDU (R-APDU)*. A command APDU is always paired with a response APDU. Their structures are illustrated in Table 2.1 and Table 2.2, respectively.

Table 2.1   Command APDU structure

Mandatory header				**Optional body**		
CLA	INS	P1	P2	Lc	Data field	Le

Table 2.2   Response APDU structure

Optional body	**Mandatory Trailer**	
Data field	SW1	SW2

The command APDU header consists of 4 bytes: CLA (class of instruction), INS (instruction code), and P1 and P2 (parameters 1 and 2). The class byte identifies a category of command and response APDUs. The instruction byte specifies the instruction of the command. The two parameter bytes P1 and P2 are used to provide further qualifications to the instruction.

The section after the header in a command APDU is an optional body that varies in length. The Lc field in the body specifies the length of the data field (in bytes). The data field contains data that are sent to the card for executing the instruction specified in the APDU header. The last byte in the command APDU body is the Le field, which specifies the number of bytes expected by the host in the card's response.

The response APDU, sent by the card in reply to a command APDU, consists of an optional body and a mandatory trailer. The body consists of the data field, whose length is determined by the Le field in the corresponding command APDU. The trailer consists of two fields SW1 and SW2, together called the status word, denoting the processing state in the card after executing the command APDU. For example, the status word "0x9000" means that a command was executed successfully and completely.

The data field is optional in both command and response APDUs. Therefore, APDUs can be further categorized as having the following four cases, based on whether a data field is contained in the C-APDU or R-APDU (Figure 2.4).

- In case 1, no data are transferred to or from the card, so the command APDU contains only the header, and the response APDU contains only the trailer status word.

- In case 2, no data are transferred to the card, but data are returned from the card. The body of the command APDU contains one byte—the Le field, which specifies the number of data bytes in the corresponding response APDU.

- In case 3, data are transferred to the card, but no data are returned from the card as a result of processing the command. The body of the command APDU includes the Lc field and the data field. The Lc byte specifies the length of the data field. The response APDU contains only the trailer status word.

- In case 4, data are transferred to the card, and data are returned from the card as a result of processing the command. The body of the command APDU includes the Lc field, the data field, and the Le field. The response APDU contains both the data and the trailer status word.

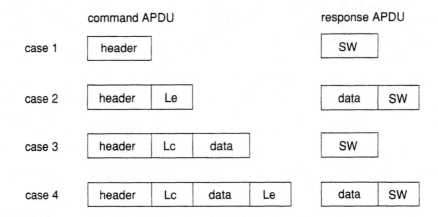

Figure 2.4   Command and response APDU cases

2.4.4   TPDU Protocol

APDUs are transmitted by the next-level protocol—the transport protocol, defined in ISO 7816-3. The data structures exchanged by a host and a card using the transport protocol are called *transmission protocol data units,* or *TPDUs.*

The two transport protocols that are in primary use in smart card systems today are the T=0 protocol and the T=1 protocol. The T=0 protocol is byte-oriented, which means that the smallest unit processed and transmitted by the protocol is a single byte. By contrast, the T=1 protocol is block-oriented; in other words, a block, consisting of a sequence of bytes, is the smallest data unit that can be transmitted between a card and a host.

The TPDU structures used in the T=0 protocol are quite different from those used in the T=1 protocol. For more information of the transport protocol, see ISO 7816-3.

2.4.5   ATR

Immediately after it is powered up, a smart card sends out an *answer to reset (ATR)* message to the host. This conveys to the host the parameters required by the card for establishing a data communication pathway. The ATR is up to 33 bytes. It contains transmission parameters, such as the transport protocol supported by the card (usually the T=0 or the T=1); the data transmission rate; card hardware parameters, such as the chip serial number and the mask version number; and other information that the host needs to know about the card.

2.5   Smart Card Operating Systems

The smart card operating systems have little resemblance to desktop operating systems, such as UNIX, Microsoft Windows, or even DOS. Rather, smart card operating systems support a collection of instructions on which user applications can be built. ISO 7816-4 standardizes a wide range of instructions in the format of APDUs. A smart card operating system may support some or all of these APDUs as well as the manufacturer's additions and extensions.

Most smart card operating systems support a modest file system based on ISO 7816-4. ISO 7816-4 APDUs are largely file system–oriented commands, such as file selection and file access commands. In this case, a user application often is a data file that stores application-specific information. The semantics and instructions to access the application data file are implemented by the operating system. Therefore, the separation between the operating system and the applications is not very well defined.

These file system–centric operating systems are well established in smart cards that are available today. However, newer operating systems, which support a better system-layer separation and downloading of custom application code, are becoming more and more popular. Java Card technology is one technology in this new trend.[1]

2.5.1   Smart Card File Systems

Smart cards defined in ISO 7816-4 can have a hierarchical file system structure, as shown in Figure 2.5. The ISO 7816-4 file system supports three types of files: master file (MF), dedicated file (DF), and elementary file (EF). Each file is specified by either a 2-byte identifier or a symbolic name up to 16 bytes.

Before any other operations on a file can be performed, the file must be selected. (This is equivalent to opening a file in a modern operating system.) Some cards automatically select the master file when the card is powered on. Access to files is controlled by access conditions, which can be specified differently for read and for write access.

---

[1] Java Card technology does not provide core APIs for the ISO file system. Most of the common-use cases of the ISO file system in applications could be achieved in the Java programming language by encapsulating files as arrays or objects. The Java Card 2.1 API reference implementation sample application `JavaPurse` (which can be downloaded at `http://java.sun.com/ products/javacard/`) shows an example of implementing ISO 7816–compliant files and supporting ISO 7816-4 file system–oriented APDUs.

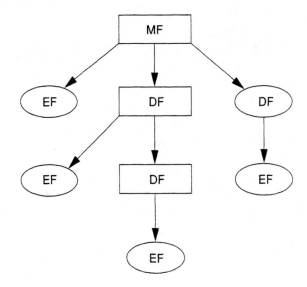

Figure 2.5   ISO 7816-4 file system structure

2.5.2   Master File

The master file (MF) is the root of the file system. The MF can contain dedicated files and elementary files. There is only one MF in a smart card.

2.5.3   Dedicated File

A DF is a smart card directory file that holds other dedicated files and elementary files. A master file is a special type of DF.

2.5.4   Elementary File

An elementary file is a data file; it cannot contain other files. Based on the file structure, there are four types of elementary files (Figure 2.6). A transparent file is structured as a sequence of data bytes, whereas the other three EF types are structured as a sequence of individually identifiable records. A linear fixed file has records of fixed size; a linear variable file has records of variable size; and a cyclic file has fixed records organized as a ring.

In a cyclic file, records are in the reverse order to the order in which they were inserted into the file—the last inserted record is identified as record 1. Once the file is full, the next write instruction overwrites the oldest record in the file, and it becomes the new record 1.

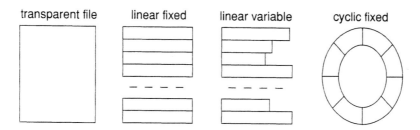

Figure 2.6 Elementary file structures

2.6 Smart Card Systems

Smart card systems are distributed systems that consist of two parts: the *host system* residing in the computer connected to the reader or in the terminal and the *card system* inside a smart card.

Most smart card software, including system software and user application software, runs on the host side. The system software recognizes a specific smart card and handles communication between the user application and the card. The system software also provides support to the smart card infrastructure, such as card management (issuance and operations), security, and key management. User applications implement functions that work with a specific card or an application on the card. A simple user application is the one that supports and handles a set of APDUs exchanged with the card, but many user applications have a rich function set. For example, an ATM application provides user authentication, transaction processing, and a friendly user interface for easy access. Host software is usually written in high-level programming languages, such as Java, C, C++, and so on.

Card software is the software that runs on the smart card itself. It too includes system software and user application software. The system software typically includes the operating system and utilities that control memory management, handle I/O communication with the host, ensure data integrity and security, support the ISO file system (if implemented), and provide system utilities to the card applications. Card applications contain data and support functions that operate on data. For example, a purse application contains a balance and implements functions to update the balance. However, in traditional smart cards, instructions supported in the system are often sufficient for applications. In this case, the special application software is not required. Card software can be implemented either in the assembly language of the card microprocessor or in a high-level programming language that can be interpreted by the microprocessor.

Smart card systems are developed by implementing and integrating card software and host software. This involves cooperations between providers of card operating systems, vendors of card terminals, application developers (both card side and host side), and card issuers. These parties are often not from the same companies. To ensure interoperability, industry initiatives, such as the Open Platform and the OpenCard Framework, offer an integrated environment for the development and operation of smart card systems so that software components from various vendors can work together.

Java Card technology provides a ubiquitous platform in which card-side applications can be written in Java and can run on any smart card that supports the Java Card runtime environment.

2.7   Smart Card Standards and Specifications

During the past 15 years, a number of smart card standards and specifications have been defined to ensure that smart cards, card acceptance devices, and applications developed and manufactured by different vendors can work together. This section lists some well-known standards and specifications for developing smart card systems.

2.7.1   ISO 7816 Standards

ISO 7816 "Identification cards—Integrated circuit cards with contacts," published by the International Organization for Standardization (ISO), is the most important standard defining the characteristics of chip cards that have electrical contacts[6]. ISO 7816 covers various aspects of smart cards:

- Part 1—physical characteristics
- Part 2—dimensions and location of the contacts
- Part 3—electronic signals and transmission protocols
- Part 4—interindustry commands for interchange
- Part 5—application identifiers
- Part 6—interindustry data elements
- Part 7—interindustry commands for SCQL

2.7.2   GSM

The European Telecommunications Standards Institute (ETSI) has published a set of standards that cover smart cards for use in public and cellular telephone systems[8]. The Global System for Mobile Communications (GSM) defined by ETSI is a specification for an international terrestrial mobile telephone system. Originally intended to cover a few countries in central Europe, it is increasingly developing into an international standard for mobile telephones. There are several GSM standards, in particular:

- GSM 11.11—specification of the SIM–mobile equipment interface.

- GSM 11.14—specification of the SIM application toolkit for the SIM–mobile equipment interface.

- GSM 03.48—security mechanisms for the SIM application toolkit.

- GSM 03.19—SIM API (Application Programming Interface) for the Java Card platform. This standard, based on GSM 11.11 and GSM 11.14, defines Java API for developing GSM applications that run on the Java Card platform. The API is an extension to the Java Card 2.1 API.

2.7.3   EMV

The EMV specification, defined by Europay, MasterCard, and Visa, is based on the ISO 7816 series of standards with additional proprietary features to meet the specific needs of the financial industry. The latest version of the specifications, EMV 96 version 3.1.1, was published in May 1998 and comes in three parts:

- EMV '96 Integrated Circuit Card Specification

- EMV '96 Integrated Circuit Card Terminal Specification

- EMV '96 Integrated Circuit Card Application Specification

2.7.4   Open Platform

The Open Platform (OP) defines an integrated environment for the development and operation of multiple-application smart card systems[9]. The Open Platform consists of a card specification and a terminal specification. The card specification defines the cross-industry, nonproduct-specific requirements to implement an Open

Platform card. It defines the off-card communication with the terminal and the on-card application management. The terminal specification defines the part of the application architecture within the terminal. It further defines the terminal to be ISO and EMV compatible.

The Open Platform specifications were initially developed by Visa and now have been transferred to GlobalPlatform, an organization to promote a global infrastructure for smart card implementation across multiple industries.

2.7.5   OpenCard Framework

The OpenCard Framework (OCF) was initially produced by IBM and is currently owned and developed by the OpenCard consortium, which includes major players in the smart card industry[5]. OCF is the host-side application framework providing a standard interface for interacting with card readers and applications in the card. The architecture of OCF is a structured model that divides functions among card terminal vendors, card operating system providers, and card issuers. The goal is to reduce dependence on each of these parties as well as dependence on the platform providers.

OCF is designed with the use of a smart card in a network computer in mind, and thus is implemented in the Java programming language.

2.7.6   PC/SC

PC/SC specifications (Interoperability Specification for ICCs and Personal Computer Systems) are owned and defined by the PC/SC Workgroup, an industry consortium with major players in the smart card industry[7]. PC/SC defines a general-purpose architecture for using smart cards on personal computer systems.

In the PC/SC architecture, host-side smart card applications are built on top of one or more service providers and a resource manager. A service provider encapsulates functionality exposed by a specific smart card and makes it accessible through high-level programming interfaces. A resource manager manages the smart card–relevant resources within the system for accessing to card acceptance devices and, through them, individual smart cards.

PC/SC and OCF have many similar concepts. When running on a Windows platform, OCF can access card acceptance devices through the installed PC/SC resource manager.

PART 2

Java Card Technology

CHAPTER 3

Java Card Technology Overview

Java Card technology enables programs written in the Java programming language to run on smart cards and other resource-constrained devices. This chapter gives an overview of Java Card technology—the system architecture and its components.

3.1 Architecture Overview

Smart cards represent one of the smallest computing platforms in use today. The memory configuration of a smart card might have on the order of 1K of RAM, 16K of EEPROM, and 24K of ROM. The greatest challenge of Java Card technology design is to fit Java system software in a smart card while conserving enough space for applications. The solution is to support only a subset of the features of the Java language and to apply a split model to implement the Java virtual machine.

The Java Card virtual machine is split into two part: one that runs off-card and the other that runs on-card. Many processing tasks that are not constrained to execute at runtime, such as class loading, bytecode verification, resolution and linking, and optimization, are dedicated to the virtual machine that is running off-card where resources are usually not a concern.

Smart cards differ from desktop computers in several ways. In addition to providing Java language support, Java Card technology defines a runtime environment that supports the smart card memory, communication, security, and application execution model. The Java Card runtime environment conforms to the smart card international standard ISO 7816.

The most significant feature of the Java Card runtime environment is that it provides a clear separation between the smart card system and the applications. The runtime environment encapsulates the underlying complexity and details of the smart card system. Applications request system services and resources through a well-defined high-level programming interface.

Therefore, Java Card technology essentially defines a platform on which applications written in the Java programming language can run in smart cards and other memory-constrained devices. (Applications written for the Java Card platform are referred to as *applets*.) Because of the split virtual machine architecture, this platform is distributed between the smart card and desktop environment in both space and time. It consists of three parts, each defined in a specification.

- The Java Card 2.1 Virtual Machine (JCVM) Specification defines a subset of the Java programming language and virtual machine definition suitable for smart card applications.

- The Java Card 2.1 Runtime Environment (JCRE) Specification precisely describes Java Card runtime behavior, including memory management, applet management, and other runtime features.

- The Java Card 2.1 Application Programming Interface (API) Specification describes the set of core and extension Java packages and classes for programming smart card applications.

3.2   Java Card Language Subset

Because of its small memory footprint, the Java Card platform supports only a carefully chosen, customized subset of the features of the Java language. This subset includes features that are well suited for writing programs for smart cards and other small devices while preserving the object-oriented capabilities of the Java programming language. Table 3.1 highlights some notable supported and unsupported Java language features.

It's no surprise that keywords of the unsupported features are also omitted from the language. Many advanced Java smart cards provide a garbage collection mechanism to enable object deletion.

Appendix A provides a comprehensive annotation of the Java Card language subset. For Java Card applets that require storing and manipulating big numbers, Chapter 14 provides programming tips for dealing with larger numbers without using large primitive data types.

Table 3.1 Supported and unsupported Java features

Supported Java Features	Unsupported Java Features
• Small primitive data types: `boolean`, `byte`, `short` • One-dimensional arrays • Java packages, classes, interfaces, and exceptions • Java object-oriented features: inheritance, virtual methods, overloading and dynamic object creation, access scope, and binding rules • The `int` keyword and 32-bit integer data type support are optional.	• Large primitive data types: `long`, `double`, `float` • Characters and strings • Multidimensional arrays • Dynamic class loading • Security manager • Garbage collection and finalization • Threads • Object serialization • Object cloning

3.3   Java Card Virtual Machine

A primary difference between the Java Card virtual machine (JCVM) and the Java virtual machine (JVM) is that the JCVM is implemented as two separate pieces, as depicted in Figure 3.1. The on-card portion of the Java Card virtual machine includes the Java Card bytecode *interpreter*. The Java Card *converter* runs on a PC or a workstation. The converter is the off-card piece of the virtual machine. Taken

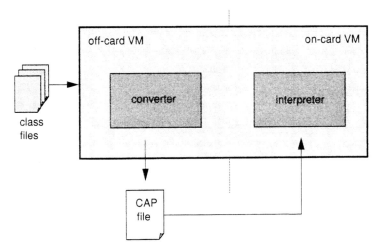

Figure 3.1   Java Card virtual machine

together, they implement all the virtual machine functions—loading Java class files and executing them with a particular set of semantics. The converter loads and pre-processes the class files that make up a Java package and outputs a CAP (converted applet) file. The CAP file is then loaded on a Java smart card and executed by the interpreter. In addition to creating a CAP file, the converter generates an export file representing the public APIs of the package being converted.

Java Card technology supports only a subset of the Java language. Correspondingly, the Java Card virtual machine supports only the features that are required by the language subset. Any unsupported language features used in an applet are detected by the converter.

3.3.1   CAP File and Export File

Java Card technology introduces two new binary file formats that enable platform-independent development, distribution, and execution of Java Card software. A CAP file contains an executable binary representation of the classes in a Java package. The JAR file format is used as the container format for CAP files. A CAP file is a JAR file that contains a set of components, each stored as an individual file in the JAR file. Each component describes an aspect of the CAP file contents, such as class information, executable bytecodes, linking information, verification information, and so forth. The CAP file format is optimized for a small footprint by using compact data structures and limited indirection. It defines a bytecode instruction set that is based on and optimized from the Java bytecode instruction set.

The "write once, run anywhere" quality of Java programs is perhaps the most significant feature of the Java platform. In Java technology, the class file is the central piece of the Java architecture. It defines the standard for the binary compatibility of the Java platform. Because of the distributed characteristic of the Java Card system architecture, the CAP file sets the standard file format for binary compatibility on the Java Card platform. The CAP file format is the form in which software is loaded onto Java smart cards. For example, CAP files enable dynamic loading of applet classes after the card has been made. That is how it gets the name converted applet (CAP) file.

Export files are not loaded onto smart cards and thus are not directly used by the interpreter. Rather, they are produced and consumed by the converter for verification and linking purposes. Export files can be thought of as the header files in the C programming language. An export file contains public API information for an entire package of classes. It defines the access scope and name of a class and the access scope and signatures of the methods and fields of the class. An export file also contains linking information used for resolving interpackage references on the card.

The export file does not contain any implementation; that is, it does not contain bytecodes. So an export file can be freely distributed by an applet developer to the potential users of the applet without revealing the internal implementation details.

3.3.2   Java Card Converter

Unlike the Java virtual machine, which processes one class at a time, the conversion unit of the converter is a package. Class files are produced by a Java compiler from source code. Then, the converter preprocesses all the class files that make up a Java package and converts the package to a CAP file.

During the conversion, the converter performs tasks that a Java virtual machine in a desktop environment would perform at class-loading time:

- Verifies that the load images of the Java classes are well formed

- Checks for Java Card language subset violations

- Performs static variables initialization

- Resolves symbolic references to classes, methods, and fields into a more compact form that can be handled more efficiently on the card

- Optimizes bytecode by taking advantage of information obtained at class-loading and linking time

- Allocates storage and creates virtual machine data structures to represent classes

The converter takes as input not only the class files to be converted but also one or more export files. Besides producing a CAP file, the converter generates an export file for the converted package. Figure 3.2 demonstrates how a package is converted. The converter loads all the classes in a Java package. If the package imports classes from other packages, the converter also loads the export files of those packages. The outputs of the converter are a CAP file and an export file for the package being converted.

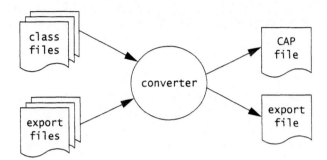

Figure 3.2   Converting a package

3.3.3   Java Card Interpreter

The Java Card interpreter provides runtime support of the Java language model and thus allows hardware independence of applet code. The interpreter performs the following tasks:

- Executes bytecode instructions and ultimately executes applets

- Controls memory allocation and object creation

- Plays a crucial role in ensuring runtime security

So far, the Java Card virtual machine has been described as comprising the converter and the interpreter. Informally, however, the Java Card virtual machine is defined as the on-card piece of the virtual machine—the interpreter, in our current definition. This convention has been applied in many early Java Card publications. Hence, for the remainder of this book, the terms Java Card interpreter and Java Card virtual machine are used synonymously unless otherwise stated. But readers should be aware that, when comparing the Java Card platform to the Java platform, the functions of executing Java class files are accomplished by the converter and the interpreter together.

3.4   Java Card Installer and Off-Card Installation Program

The Java Card interpreter does not itself load CAP files. It only executes the code found in the CAP file. In Java Card technology, the mechanisms to download and install a CAP file are embodied in a unit called the installer.

The Java Card installer resides within the card. It cooperates with an off-card installation program. The off-card installation program transmits the executable binary in a CAP file to the installer running on the card via a card acceptance device (CAD). The installer writes the binary into the smart card memory, links it with the other classes that have already been placed on the card, and creates and initializes any data structures that are used internally by the Java Card runtime environment. The installer and the installation program and how they relate to the rest of the Java Card platform are illustrated in Figure 3.3.

The division of functionality between the interpreter and the CAP file installer keeps the interpreter small and provides flexibility for installer implementations. More explanation of the installer is given in the coverage of the applet installation later in this chapter

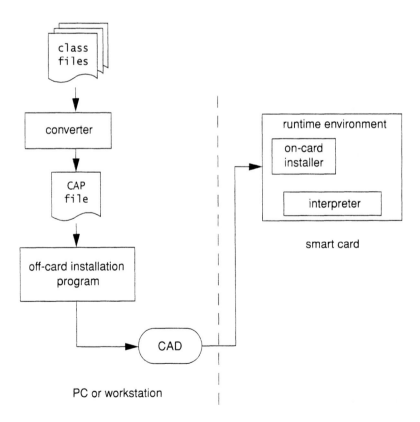

Figure 3.3   Java Card installer and off-card installation program

3.5   Java Card Runtime Environment

The Java Card runtime environment (JCRE) consists of Java Card system components that run inside a smart card. The JCRE is responsible for card resource management, network communications, applet execution, and on-card system and applet security. Thus, it essentially serves as the smart card's operating system.

As illustrated in Figure 3.4, the JCRE sits on top of the smart card hardware and native system. The JCRE consists of the Java Card virtual machine (the bytecode interpreter), the Java Card application framework classes (APIs), industry-specific extensions, and the JCRE system classes. The JCRE nicely separates applets from the proprietary technologies of smart card vendors and provides standard system and API interfaces for applets. As a result, applets are easier to write and are portable on various smart card architectures.

The bottom layer of the JCRE contains the Java Card virtual machine (JCVM) and native methods. The JCVM executes bytecodes, controls memory allocation, manages objects, and enforces the runtime security, as explained previously. The native methods provide support to the JCVM and the next-layer system classes. They are responsible for handling the low-level communication protocols, memory management, cryptographic support, and so forth.

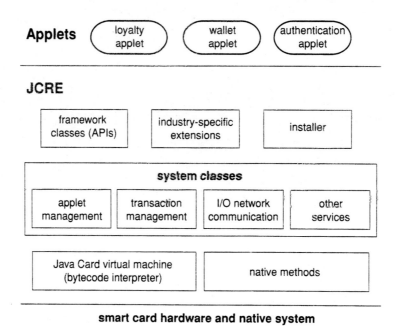

Figure 3.4   On-card system architecture

The system classes act as the JCRE executive. They are analogues to an operating system core. The system classes are in charge of managing transactions, managing communication between the host applications[1] and Java Card applets, and controlling applet creation, selection, and deselection. To complete tasks, the system classes typically invoke native methods.

The Java Card application framework defines the application programming interfaces. The framework consists of four core and extension API packages. The API classes are compact and customized for developing smart card applets. The major advantage of this framework is that it makes it relatively easy to create an applet. The applet developers can concentrate most of their effort on the details of the applets rather than on the details of the smart card system infrastructure. Applets access the JCRE services through API classes.

A specific industry or business can supply add-on libraries to provide additional services or to refine the security and system model. For example, the Open Platform extends the JCRE services to meet financial industries' specific security needs. Among many add-on features, it enforces issuers' control of the cards and specifies a standard set of commands for card personalization.

The installer enables the secure downloading of software and applets onto the card after the card is made and issued to the card holder. The installer cooperates with the off-card installation program. Together they accomplish the task of loading the binary contents of CAP files. The installer is an optional JCRE component. Without the installer, all card software, including applets, must be written into card's memory during the card manufacturing process.

Java Card applets are user applications on the Java Card platform. Applets are of course written in the subset of the Java programming language and controlled and managed by the JCRE. Applets are downloadable. Applets can be added to a Java smart card after it has been manufactured.

3.5.1   JCRE Lifetime

In a PC or a workstation, the Java virtual machine runs as an operating system process. Data and objects are created in RAM. When the OS process is terminated, the Java applications and their objects are automatically destroyed.

In a Java smart card, the Java Card virtual machine runs within the Java Card runtime environment. The JCRE is initialized at card initialization time. The JCRE initialization is performed only once during the card lifetime. During this process, the JCRE initializes the virtual machine and creates objects for providing

---

[1] Host applications are the applications running at the terminal side with which applets communicate.

the JCRE services and managing applets. As applets are installed, the JCRE creates applet instances, and applets create objects to store data.

Most of the information on a card must be preserved even when power is removed from the card. Persistent memory technology (such as EEPROM) is used to achieve this preservation. Data and objects are created in persistent memory. The lifetime of the JCRE is equivalent to the complete lifetime of the card. When power is removed, the virtual machine is only suspended. The state of the JCRE and the objects created on the card are preserved.

The next time the card is energized, the JCRE restarts virtual machine execution by loading data from persistent memory.[2] A subtle notion here is that the JCRE does not resume the virtual machine operation at the exact point where it lost power. The virtual machine is reset and executes from the beginning of the main loop. The JCRE reset differs from initialization, as it preserves applets and objects created on the card. During the reset, if a transaction was not previously completed, the JCRE performs any necessary cleanup to bring the JCRE into a consistent state.

3.5.2   How Does the JCRE Operate during a CAD Session?

The period from the time the card is inserted into the card acceptance device (CAD) and is powered up until the time the card is removed from the CAD is called a CAD session. During a CAD session, the JCRE operates like a typical smart card—it supports APDU I/O communication with a host application (Figure 3.5). APDUs

Figure 3.5   APDU I/O communication

---

[2] The JCRE also returns the answer to reset (ATR) to the host, indicating the card communication capabilities.

(application protocol data units) are data packets exchanged between applets and the host application. Each APDU contains either a command from the host to the applet or the response from the applet to the host

After a JCRE reset, the JCRE enters into a loop, waiting for APDU commands from the host. The host sends APDU commands to the Java Card platform, using the serial communication interface via the card input/output contact point.

When a command arrives, the JCRE either selects an applet to run as instructed in the command or forwards the command to the currently selected applet. The selected applet then takes control and processes the APDU command. When finished, the applet sends a response to the host application and surrenders control to the JCRE. This process repeats when the next command arrives. How applets process APDUs is explained further in Chapters 7 and 8.

3.5.3   Java Card Runtime Features

Besides supporting the Java language runtime model, the JCRE supports three additional runtime features:

- *Persistent and transient objects*—By default, Java Card objects are persistent and are created in persistent memory. The space and data of such objects span CAD sessions. For security and performance reasons, applets can create objects in RAM. Such objects are called transient objects. Transients objects contain temporary data that are not persistent across CAD sessions.

- *Atomic operations and transactions*—The Java Card virtual machine ensures that each write operation to a single field in an object or in a class is atomic. The updated field either gets the new value or is restored to the previous value. In addition, the JCRE provides transaction APIs. An applet can include several write operations in a transaction. Either all updates in a transaction are complete, or (if a failure occurs in the middle of the transaction) none of them proceeds.

- *Applet firewall and the sharing mechanisms*—The applet firewall isolates applets. Each applet runs within a designated space. The existence and operation of one applet has no effect on the other applets on the card. The applet firewall is enforced by the Java Card virtual machine as it executes bytecodes. In situations where applets need to share data or access JCRE services, the virtual machine permits such functions through secure sharing mechanisms.

3.6   Java Card APIs

The Java Card APIs consist of a set of customized classes for programming smart card applications according to the ISO 7816 model. The APIs contain three core packages and one extension package. The three core packages are java.lang, javacard.framework, and javacard.security. The extension package is javacardx.crypto.

Developers who are familiar with the Java platform will notice that many Java platform classes are not supported in the Java Card APIs. For example, the Java platform classes for GUI interfaces, network I/O, and desktop file system I/O are not supported. The reason is that smart cards do not have a display, and they use a different network protocol and file system structure. Also, many Java platform utility classes are not supported, to meet the strict memory requirements.

The classes in the Java Card APIs are compact and succinct. They include classes adapted from the Java platform for providing Java language support and cryptographic services. They also contain classes created especially for supporting the smart card ISO 7816 standard.

3.6.1   java.lang Package

The Java Card java.lang package is a strict subset of its counterpart java.lang package on the Java platform. The supported classes are Object, Throwable, and some virtual machine–related exception classes, as shown in Table 3.2. For the supported classes, many of the Java methods are not available. For example, the Java Card Object class defines only a default constructor and the equals method.

The java.lang package provides fundamental Java language support. The class Object defines a root for the Java Card class hierarchy, and the class Throwable provides a common ancestor for all exceptions. The supported exception classes ensure consistent semantics when an error occurs due to a Java language violation. For example, both the Java virtual machine and the Java Card virtual machine throw a NullPointerException when a null reference is accessed.

Table 3.2   Java Card java.lang package

Object	Throwable	Exception
RuntimeException	ArithmeticException	ArrayIndexOutOfBoundsException
ArrayStoreException	ClassCastException	IndexOutOfBoundsException
NullPointerException	SecurityException	NegativeArraySizeException

3.6.2 javacard.framework Package

The javacard.framework is an essential package. It provides framework classes and interfaces for the core functionality of a Java Card applet. Most important, it defines a base Applet class, which provides a framework for applet execution and interaction with the JCRE during the applet lifetime. Its role with respect to the JCRE is similar to that of the Java Applet class to a hosting browser. A user applet class must extend from the base Applet class and override methods in the Applet class to implement the applet's functionality.

Another important class in the javacard.framework package is the APDU class. APDUs are carried by the transmission protocol. The two standardized transmission protocols are T=0 and T=1. The APDU class is designed to be transmission protocol independent. In other words, it is carefully designed so that the intricacies of and differences between the T=0 and T=1 protocols are hidden from applet developers. Applet developers can handle APDU commands much more easily using the methods provided in the APDU class. Applets work correctly regardless of the underlying transmission protocol the platform supports. How to use the APDU class is explained in Chapter 8.

The Java platform class java.lang.System is not supported. The Java Card platform supplies the class javacard.framework.JCSystem, which provides an interface to system behavior. The JCSystem class includes a collection of methods to control applet execution, resource management, transaction management, and inter-applet object sharing on the Java Card platform.

Other classes supported in the javacard.framework package are PIN, utility, and exceptions. PIN is short for personal identification number. It is the most common form of password used in smart cards for authenticating card holders

3.6.3 javacard.security Package

The javacard.security package provides a framework for the cryptographic functions supported on the Java Card platform. Its design is based on the java.security package.

The javacard.security package defines a key factory class keyBuilder and various interfaces that represent cryptographic keys used in symmetric (DES) or asymmetric (DSA and RSA) algorithms. In addition, it supports the abstract base classes RandomData, Signature, and MessageDigest, which are used to generate random data and to compute message digests and signatures.

3.6.4   `javacardx.crypto` Package

The `javacardx.crypto` package is an extension package. It contains cryptographic classes and interfaces that are subject to United States export regulatory requirements. The `javacardx.crypto` package defines the abstract base class `Cipher` for supporting encryption and decryption functions.

The packages `javacard.security` and `javacardx.crypto` define API interfaces that applets call to request cryptographic services. However, they do not provide any implementation. A JCRE provider needs to supply classes that implement key interfaces and extend from the abstract classes `RandomData`, `Signature`, `MessageDigest`, and `Cipher`. Usually a separate coprocessor exists on smart cards to perform cryptographic computations. Chapter 10 explains how to support cryptographic functions in applets by using the classes in the `javacard.security` and `javacardx.crypto` packages.

3.7   Java Card Applets

Java Card applets should not be confused with Java applets just because they are all named applets. A Java Card applet is a Java program that adheres to a set of conventions that allow it to run within the Java Card runtime environment. A Java Card applet is not intended to run within a browser environment. The reason the name applet was chosen for Java Card applications is that Java Card applets can be loaded into the Java Card runtime environment after the card has been manufactured. That is, unlike applications in many embedded systems, applets do not need to be burned into the ROM during manufacture. Rather, they can be dynamically downloaded onto the card at a later time.

An applet class must extend from the `javacard.framework.Applet` class. The base `Applet` class is the superclass for all applets residing on a Java Card. The applet class is a blueprint that defines the variables and methods of an applet. A running applet on the card is an applet instance—an object of the applet class. As with any persistent objects, once created, an applet lives on the card forever.

The Java Card runtime environment supports a multiapplication environment. Multiple applets can coexist on a single Java smart card, and an applet can have multiple instances. For example, one wallet applet instance can be created for supporting the U.S. dollar, and another can be created for the British pound.

3.8 Package and Applet Naming Convention

Packages and programs that you are familiar with in the Java platform are uniquely identified using Unicode strings and a naming scheme based on Internet domain names. In the Java Card platform, however, each applet instance is uniquely identified and selected by an application identifier (AID). Also, each Java package is assigned an AID. When loaded on a card, a package is then linked with other packages on the card via their AIDs.

ISO 7816 specifies AIDs to be used for unique identification of card applications and certain kinds of files in card file systems. An AID is an array of bytes that can be interpreted as two distinct pieces, as shown in Figure 3.6. The first piece is a 5-byte value known as a RID (resource identifier). The second piece is a variable-length value known as a PIX (proprietary identifier extension). A PIX can be from 0 to 11 bytes in length. Thus an AID can range from 5 to 16 bytes in total length.

RID (5 bytes)	PIX (0-11 bytes)

Figure 3.6   Application identifier (AID)

ISO controls the assignment of RIDs to companies; each company has a unique RID. Companies manage assignment of PIXs in AIDs. This section provides the brief description of AIDs. For complete details, refer to ISO 7816-5, AID Registration Category D format.

In the Java Card platform, the AID for a package is constructed by concatenating the company's RID and a PIX for that package. An applet AID is constructed similarly to a package AID. It is a concatenation of the applet provider's RID and the PIX for that applet. An applet AID must not have the same value as the AID of any package or the AID of any other applet. However, since the RID in an AID identifies an applet provider, the package AID and the AID(s) of applet(s) defined in the package must share the same RID.

The package AID and the default applet AID for each applet defined in the package are specified in the CAP file. They are supplied to the converter when the CAP file is generated.

3.9   Applet Development Process

Development of a Java Card applet begins as with any other Java program: a developer writes one or more Java classes and compiles the source code with a Java compiler, producing one or more class files. Figure 3.7 demonstrates the applet development process.

Next, the applet is run, tested, and debugged in a simulation environment. The simulator simulates the Java Card runtime environment on a PC or a workstation. In the simulation environment, the applet runs on a *Java virtual machine*, and thus the class files of the applet are executed. In this way the simulator can utilize

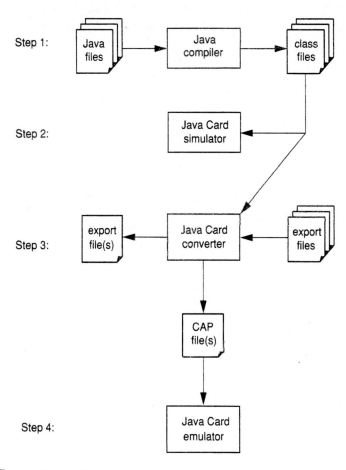

Figure 3.7   Applet development process

many Java development tools (the virtual machine, debugger, and other tools) and allow the developer to test the applet's behavior and quickly see the applet's results without going through the conversion process. During this step, the overall functional aspects of the applet are tested. However, some of the Java Card virtual machine runtime features, such as the applet firewall and the transient and persistent behavior of objects, cannot be examined.

Then the class files of the applet that make up a Java package are converted to a CAP file by using the Java Card converter. The Java Card converter takes as input not only the class files to be converted but also one or more export files. When the applet package is converted, the converter can also produce an export file for that package. A CAP file or an export file represents one Java package. If an applet comprises several packages, a CAP file and an export file are created for each package.

In the next step, the CAP file(s) that represent the applet are loaded and tested in an emulation environment. The emulator also simulates the Java Card runtime environment on a PC or a workstation. However, the emulator is a more sophisticated testing tool. It encompasses a *Java Card virtual machine* implementation. The behavior of the applet executing in the emulator should be the same as its behavior running in a real card. In this development phase, not only is the applet further tested, but also the runtime behavior of the applet is measured.

Most Java Card simulators and emulators come with a debugger. The debugger allows the developer to set breakpoints or single-step the program, watching the execution state of the applet change in the simulated or emulated Java Card runtime environment.

Finally, when the applet is tested and ready to be downloaded into a real card, the applet, represented by one or several CAP files, is loaded and installed in the Java smart card.

3.10 Applet Installation

When a Java smart card is manufactured, the smart card proprietary system and the Java Card runtime environment—including native methods, the Java Card virtual machine, API classes, and libraries—are burned into ROM. This process of writing the permanent components into the nonmutable memory of a chip is called *masking*. The technology for performing masking is a proprietary technology of a smart card vendor and is not discussed further in this book.

3.10.1   ROM Applets

Java Card applet classes can be masked in ROM together with the JCRE and other system components during the process of card manufacturing. Applet instances are instantiated in EEPROM by the JCRE during JCRE initialization or at a later stage. Such applets are called ROM applets.

The ROM applets are default applets that come with the card and are provided by card issuers. Because ROM applet contents are controlled by issuers, Java Card technology allows ROM applets to declare native methods whose implementations are written in another programming language, such as C or assembly code. Native methods are not subject to security checks enforced by the Java Card virtual machine.

3.10.2   Preissuance or Postissuance Applets

Alternatively, Java Card applet classes and associated class libraries can be downloaded and written into the mutable memory (such as EEPROM) of a Java smart card after the card is manufactured. Such applets can be further categorized as preissuance or postissuance applets. The terms preissuance and postissuance derive from the fact that applets are downloaded before or after the card has been issued. Preissuance applets are treated the same way as the ROM applets; both are controlled by the issuer.

Unlike ROM applets or preissuance applets, postissuance applets are not allowed to declare native methods. The reason is that the JCRE has no way to control the applet contents. Allowing downloaded applets to contain native code could compromise Java Card security.

The following subsections focus on postissuance applet installation. Usually preissuance applets are loaded using the same mechanism as postissuance applets, but Java Card technology leaves the decision to the card issuers.

3.10.3   Postissuance Applet Installation

Applet installation refers to the process of loading applet classes in a CAP file, combining them with the execution state of the Java Card runtime environment, and creating an applet instance to bring the applet into a selectable and execution state.

On the Java Card platform, the loading and installable unit is a CAP file. A CAP file consists of classes that make up a Java package. A minimal applet is a Java package with a single class derived from the class javacard.framework.Applet. A more complex applet with a number of classes can be organized into one Java package or a set of Java packages.

To load an applet, the off-card installer takes the CAP file and transforms it into a sequence of APDU commands, which carry the CAP file content. By exchanging the APDU commands with the off-card installation program, the on-card installer writes the CAP file content into the card's persistent memory and links the classes in the CAP file with other classes that reside on the card. The installer also creates and initializes any data that are used internally by the JCRE to support the applet. If the applet requires several packages to run, each CAP file is loaded on the card.

As the last step during applet installation, the installer creates an applet instance and registers the instance with the JCRE.[3] To do so, the installer invokes the `install` method:

```
public static void install(byte[] bArray, short offset, byte length)
```

The `install` method is an applet entry point method, similar to the `main` method in a Java application. An applet must implement the `install` method. In the `install` method, it calls the applet's constructor to create and initialize an applet instance. The parameter `bArray` of the `install` method supplies installation parameters for applet initialization. The installation parameters are sent to the card along with the CAP file. The applet developer defines the format and content of the installation parameters.

After the applet is initialized and registered with the JCRE, it can be selected and run. The JCRE identifies a running applet (an applet instance), using an AID. The applet can register itself with the JCRE by using the default AID found in the CAP file, or it can choose a different one. The installation parameters can be used to supply an alternative AID.

The `install` method can be called more than once to create multiple applet instances. Each applet instance is identified by a unique AID.

In the Java Card environment, an applet can be written and executed without knowing how its classes are loaded. An applet's sole responsibility during installation is to implement the `install` method.

3.10.4 Error Recovery during Applet Installation

The installation process is transactional. In case of an error, such as programmatic failure, running out of memory, card tear, or other errors, the installer discards the

---

[3] In a JCRE implementation, the operation for creating an applet instance can be performed at a later stage after applet installation.

CAP file and any applets it had created during installation and recovers the space and the previous state of the JCRE.

3.10.5 Installation Constraints

Readers should be aware that applet installation is different from dynamic class loading at runtime, which is supported on a Java virtual machine on the desktop environment. Java Card applet installation simply means to download classes through an installation process after the card has been made.

Therefore, Java Card applet installation has two finer points. First, applets executing on the card may refer only to classes that already exist on the card, since there is no way to download classes during the normal execution of applet code.

Second, the order of loading must guarantee that each newly loaded package references only packages that are already on the card. For example, to install an applet, the `javacard.framework` package must be present in the card, because all applet classes must extend from the class `javacard.framework.Applet`. An installation would fail if there were circularity such that package A and package B reference each other.

CHAPTER 4

Java Card Objects

In Java Card technology, the JCRE and applets create objects to represent, store, and manipulate data. Applets are written by using the Java programming language. Runnable applets on the card are objects of applet classes.

Objects in the Java Card platform are subject to the Java programming rules:

- All the objects on the Java Card platform are instances of classes or array types, which have the same root class `java.lang.Object`.

- Fields in a new object or components in a new array are set to their default values (`zero`, `null`, or `false`) unless they are initialized to some other values in the constructor.

Java Card technology supports both persistent and transient objects. However, the concepts of persistent and transient objects and the mechanisms to support them in the Java Card platform are not the same as in the Java platform (see the sidebar on page 50).

4.1 Java Card Memory Model

A smart card has three kinds of memory: ROM, RAM, and EEPROM. ROM is read-only memory but is the least expensive of the three. Programs and data are burned into ROM during card manufacture. Both RAM and EEPROM can be read and written, but they differ in many electrical characteristics. In case of a power loss, RAM loses its contents, but the contents of EEPROM are preserved. Write operations to EEPROM are typically 1,000 times slower than write operations to RAM, and the possible number of writes to EEPROM over the lifetime of a card is physically limited. In addition, a RAM cell tends to be approximately four times larger than an

EEPROM cell. Current smart cards typically offer about 16K of EEPROM and 1K of RAM.

The Java Card memory model is motivated by the kind of memory in smart cards and their physical characteristics. A typical Java Card system places the JCRE code (virtual machine, API classes, and other software) in ROM. Applet code can also be stored in ROM. RAM is used for temporary storage. The Java Card runtime stack is allocated in RAM. Intermediate results, method parameters, and local variables are put on the stack. Native methods, such as those performing cryptographic computations, also save intermediate results in RAM. Longer-lived data are stored in EEPROM, as are downloaded applet classes.

Most JCRE and applet objects represent information that needs to be preserved when power is removed. The RAM/EEPROM size ratio in a smart card also makes it natural to designate object space in EEPROM. Therefore, using the new operator automatically instantiates a persistent object in EEPROM.

However, some objects are accessed frequently, and their data (the contents of their fields) need not be persistent. Java Card technology also supports transient objects in RAM. Transient objects are created by invoking Java Card APIs.

Persistent and Transient Objects in the Java Platform

In the Java platform, objects are created in RAM. Objects are automatically destroyed when the Java virtual machine exits, or when they are collected by the garbage collector. The properties, fields, and state information of some objects can be preserved by using the object serialization and deserialization mechanism. Object serialization records the current state and properties of an object in a stream of bytes. The stream is later deserialized to restore the object with the same state and properties. The Java language also supports the transient keyword. Fields are marked as transient to indicate that they are not part of the persistent state of an object. Transient fields are not saved during object serialization.

Java Card technology does not support object serialization or the transient keyword.

4.2   Persistent Objects

The memory and data of persistent objects are preserved across CAD sessions. A persistent object has the following properties:

- A persistent object is created by the new operator.

- A persistent object holds states and values across CAD sessions.

- Any update to a single field in a persistent object is atomic. That is, if the card loses power or a failure occurs during the update, the field is restored to its previous value.

- A persistent object can be referenced by a field in a transient object.

- A field in a persistent object can reference a transient object.

- If a persistent object is not referenced by other objects, it becomes unreachable or can be garbage collected.

When an applet instance is created, like any other persistent object, the applet's space and data persist indefinitely from one CAD session to the next.

4.3   Transient Objects

The term transient object is somewhat of a misnomer. It can be incorrectly interpreted to mean that the object itself is temporary: when power is removed, the transient object is destroyed. In fact, the term transient object means that the contents of the fields of the object have a temporary nature. As with persistent objects, the space allocated for transient objects is reserved and cannot be reclaimed unless a garbage collector is implemented.

An applet should create a transient object only once during its lifetime and should save the object reference in a persistent field, as shown in Figure 4.1. The next time the card is powered on, the applet uses the same object reference to access the transient object, even though the object data from the previous session are lost.

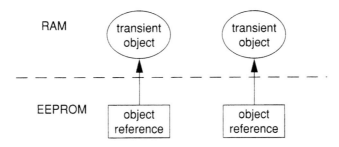

Figure 4.1   Transient objects

4.3.1   Properties of Transient Objects

In Java Card 2.1, only arrays with primitive types or arrays with references to `Object` can be declared transient. The primitive types in the Java Card platform are `byte`, `short`, `int`, and `boolean`. Throughout this book, the terms transient objects and transient arrays are used interchangeably. A transient object within the Java Card platform has the following properties:

- A transient object is created by invoking the Java Card APIs.

- A transient object does not hold states and values across CAD sessions. The fields of a transient object are cleared to their default value (`zero`, `false`, or `null`) at the occurrence of certain events.

- Any update to a single field in a transient object is not atomic. That is, if the card loses power or a failure occurs during an update, the field is not restored to its previous value. If writes to the fields of a transient object are included in a transaction (see Chapter 5), an abort transaction will never cause a field in the transient object to be restored to a previous value.

- A transient object can be referenced by a field in a persistent object.

- A field in a transient object can reference a persistent object.

- If a transient object is not referenced by other objects, it becomes unreachable or can be garbage collected.

- Writes to the fields of a transient object do not have a performance penalty, because RAM has a much faster write cycle time than EEPROM.

The properties of transient objects make them ideal for *small amounts* of temporary applet data that are frequently modified but that need not be preserved across CAD sessions. The applet developer should ensure that such temporary data are stored in transient arrays. This reduces potential wear on persistent memory, guarantees better write performance, and adds additional security to protect sensitive data. As a rule of thumb, if temporary data are being updated multiple times for every APDU processed, the applet developer should move them into a transient array.

4.3.2   Transient Object Types

There are two types of transient objects, namely, `CLEAR_ON_RESET` and `CLEAR_ON_DESELECT`. Either type of transient object is associated with an event, which, when it occurs, causes the JCRE to clear the fields of the objects.

CLEAR_ON_RESET transient objects are used for maintaining data that need to be preserved across applet selections but not across card resets. For example, a card master session key should be declared as CLEAR_ON_RESET type so that the same session key can be shared among applets that are selected during one CAD session. When a card is reset, the fields of CLEAR_ON_RESET transient objects are cleared. A card reset can be caused by a reset signal sent to the card circuitry (warm reset) or by switching the power supply off and on again.

CLEAR_ON_DESELECT transient objects are used for maintaining data that must be preserved as long as an applet is selected but not across applet selections or card resets. For example, an applet-owned session key needs to be declared as CLEAR_ON_DESELECT type so that when the applet is deselected, the session key is automatically cleared by the JCRE. This is a security precaution so that another applet cannot discover the session key data and pretend to be the previously selected applet that owns the key object.

Because a card reset implicitly deselects the currently selected applet, the fields of CLEAR_ON_DESELECT objects are also cleared by the same events specified for CLEAR_ON_RESET. In other words, CLEAR_ON_DESELECT objects are also CLEAR_ON_RESET objects. In addition, CLEAR_ON_DESELECT transient objects have additional properties because of the applet firewall. (See Chapter 9 for details.)

4.3.3 Creating Transient Objects

In Java Card technology, transient objects are created by using one of the factory methods in the JCSystem class, as shown in Table 4.1.

Table 4.1 Methods for creating transient arrays in the class JCSystem

Methods	Result of the method call

`public static boolean[]`
`makeTransientBooleanArray(short length,`
`                          byte event)`
	Create a transient boolean array

`public static byte[]`
`makeTransientByteArray(short length,`
`                       byte event)`
	Create a transient byte array

`public static short[]`
`makeTransientShortArray(short length,`
`                        byte event)`
	Create a transient short array

`public static Object[]`
`makeTransientObjectArray(short length,`
`                         byte event)`
	Create a transient Object array

The first parameter, length, in each method call specifies the requested transient array length. The second parameter, event, indicates which kind of event clears the object. Thus, it specifies the type of transient array, either CLEAR_ON_RESET or CLEAR_ON_DESELECT. Two constants in the class JCSystem are used to denote the transient array type:

```
// CLEAR_ON_RESET type of transient array
public static final byte CLEAR_ON_RESET

// CLEAR_ON_DESELECT type of transient array
public static final byte CLEAR_ON_DESELECT
```

The following code fragment creates a CLEAR_ON_DESELECT array:

```
byte[] buffer =
    JCSystem.makeTransientByteArray (BUFFER_LENGTH,
                                 JCSystem.CLEAR_ON_DESELECT);
```

4.3.4   Querying Transient Objects

An applet may need to access an object that is created by a different applet. The class JCSystem provides a convenient query method for an applet to determine whether an object being accessed is transient:

```
public static byte isTransient(Object theObject)
```

The method isTransient returns a transient type constant (either CLEAR_ON_RESET or CLEAR_ON_DESELECT) or the constant JCSystem.NOT_A_TRANSIENT_OBJECT to indicate that the object is null or is a persistent object.

4.4   A Few Words about Object Creation and Deletion

Because memory in a smart card is very scarce, neither persistent nor transient objects should be created willy-nilly. If there isn't sufficient nonvolatile space available when an applet tries to create a persistent object using the new operator, the JCRE will throw a SystemException with the reason code[1] JCSystem.NO_RESOURCE.

---

[1] A reason code is similar to the detailed message contained in a Java exception object. It encapsulates the exception cause identifier in a Java Card exception object. Chapter 6 shows how to specify and retrieve the reason code from an exception object.

When an applet calls one of the make-transient-object methods and there is insufficient RAM space available, the JCRE throws a `SystemException` with the reason code `JCSystem.NO_TRANSIENT_SPACE`.

Once created, both persistent and transient objects are reachable as long as they are referenced from the stack, from class static fields, from fields in other existing objects, or from the JCRE. When all the references to an object are dropped, the object becomes unreachable. Whether the space the object occupies can be reclaimed depends on whether a garbage collector is implemented in the virtual machine. Java Card technology does not require a JCRE implementation to include a garbage collector, because it is not feasible to do so in low-end smart cards. Chapter 13 provides programming tips on how to reuse objects in applets when a garbage collector is not supported.

CHAPTER 5

Atomicity and Transactions

Smart cards are emerging as a preferred device in such applications as storing personal confidential data and providing authentication services in a mobile and distributed environment. However, with smart cards, there is a risk of failure at any time during applet execution. Failure can happen due to a computational error, or, more often, a user of the smart card may accidentally remove the card from the CAD, cutting off the power supply to the card CPU and terminating execution of any applets. Such premature removal of the smart card from the CAD is called *tearing, or card tear*. The risk of incomplete execution presents a challenge for preserving the integrity of operations on sensitive data in a smart card.

The JCRE provides a robust mechanism to ensure atomic operations. This mechanism is supported at two levels. First, the Java Card platform guarantees that any update to a single field in a persistent object or a single class field is atomic. Second, the Java Card platform supports a transactional model, in which an applet can group a set of updates into a transaction. In this model, the atomicity of all the updates is ensured.

This chapter explains what atomicity means in the Java Card platform and how applet developers can program an applet by using transactions to protect data integrity.

5.1 Atomicity

On the Java Card platform, atomicity means that any update to a single persistent object field (including an array element) or to a class field is guaranteed to either complete successfully or else be restored to its original value if an error occurs during the update. For example, a field in an object currently contains a value 1, and it is being updated with a value 2. The card is accidentally torn from the CAD at the critical moment when the card is overwriting the field. When power comes back, the field is not left with a random value but is restored to its previous value, 1.

The concept of atomicity applies to the contents of persistent storage. It defines how the JCRE handles a single data element in the case of a power loss or other error during an update to that element. The JCRE atomicity feature does not apply to transient arrays. Updating an element of a transient array does not preserve the element's previous value in case of power loss. The next time the card is inserted into a CAD, elements of a transient array are set to their default values (zero, false, or null).

5.2   Block Data Updates in an Array

The class javacard.framework.Util provides a method arrayCopy that guarantees atomicity for block updates of multiple data elements in an array:

```
public static short arrayCopy
(byte[] src, short srcOff, byte[] dest, short desOff, short length)
```

The Util.arrayCopy method guarantees that either all bytes are correctly copied or the destination array is restored to its previous byte values. If the destination array is transient, the atomic feature does not hold.

However, arrayCopy requires extra EEPROM writes to support atomicity, and thus it is slow. An applet might not require atomicity for array updates. The Util.arrayCopyNonAtomic method is provided for this purpose:

```
public static short arrayCopyNonAtomic
(byte[] src, short srcOff, byte[] dest, short desOff, short length)
```

The method arrayCopyNonAtomic does not use the transaction facility during the copy operation even if a transaction is in progress. So this method should be used only if the contents of the destination array can be left in a partially modified state in the event of power loss in the middle of the copy operation. A similar method, Util.arrayFillNonAtomic, nonatomically fills the elements of a byte array with a specified value:

```
public static short arrayFillNonAtomic
(byte[] bArray, short bOff, short bLen, byte bValue)
```

5.3 Transactions

Atomicity guarantees atomic modification of a single data element. However, an applet may need to atomically update several different fields in several different objects. For example, a credit or debit transaction might require a purse applet to increment the transaction number, update the purse balance, and write a transaction log all as an atomic unit of work.

Readers may be familiar with the use of the database transaction notions of begin, commit, and rollback to ensure that updates to multiple values are either completed in their entirety or not at all. Java Card technology supports a similar transactional model, with commit and rollback capability to guarantee that complex operations can be accomplished atomically; either they successfully complete or their partial results are not put into effect. The transaction mechanism protects against such events as power loss in the middle of a transaction and against program errors that might cause data corruption should all steps of a transaction not complete normally.

5.3.1 Commit Transaction

A transaction is started by invoking the method JCSystem.beginTransaction and ended by calling the method JCSystem.commitTransaction:

```
// begin a transaction
JCSystem.beginTransaction();

// all modifications in a set of updates of persistent data
// are temporary until the transaction is committed
...

// commit a transaction
JCSystem.commitTransaction();
```

The changes within a transaction are conditional—the fields or array elements appear to be updated. Reading the fields or array elements back yields their latest conditional values, but the updates are not committed until the JCSystem.commit-Transaction method is called.

5.3.2 Abort Transaction

Transactions can be aborted either by an applet or by the JCRE. If an applet encounters an internal problem, it can expressly cancel the transaction by calling the

JCSystem.abortTransaction method. Aborting a transaction causes the JCRE to throw away any changes made during the transaction and to restore conditionally updated fields or array elements to their previous values. A transaction must be in progress when the abortTransaction method is invoked; otherwise, the JCRE throws a TransactionException.

When the JCRE regains programmatic control on return from an applet with a transaction still in progress—that is, when the applet did not explicitly commit or abort an ongoing transaction—the JCRE automatically calls the abortTransaction method. Similarly, the JCRE aborts a transaction if an exception is thrown within the transaction and the exception is not handled by the applet.

If power is lost or an error occurs during a transaction, the JCRE invokes a JCRE internal rollback facility the next time the card is powered on to restore the data involved in the transaction to their pretransaction values.

In any case, both transient and persistent objects created during a transaction that fails (due to power loss, card reset, computational error, or a program abort action) are deleted and their memory is freed by the JCRE.

5.3.3   Nested Transaction

Unlike most database transactions, transactions in the Java Card platform cannot be nested. There can be only one transaction in progress at a time. This requirement is due to the limited computing resources of smart cards.

If JCSystem.beginTransaction is called while a transaction is already in progress, the JCRE throws a TransactionException. An applet can discover whether a transaction is in progress by invoking the method JCSystem.transactionDepth. The method returns 1 if a transaction is in progress, 0 otherwise.

5.3.4   Commit Capacity

To support the rollback of uncommitted transactions, the JCRE maintains a *commit buffer* where the original contents of the updated fields are stored until the transaction is committed. Should a failure occur before a transaction is completed, the participating fields in the transaction are restored to their original contents from the commit buffer. The more operations inside a transaction block, the larger the commit buffer needs to be to accommodate them.

The size of the commit buffer varies from one implementation to another, depending on the available card memory. In general, the commit buffer allocated in a JCRE implementation is large enough to accommodate most applets' needs—an applet typically accumulates tens of bytes during a transaction. However, because smart card resources are limited, it is important that only the updates in a logical unit of operations are included in a transaction. Putting too many things in a transaction may not be possible.

Before attempting a transaction, an applet can check the size of the available commit buffer against the size of the data requiring an atomic update. The class JCSystem provides two methods to help applets determine how much commit capacity is available on a Java Card platform implementation.

- JCSystem.getMaxCommitCapacity() returns the total number of bytes in the commit buffer.

- JCSystem.getUnusedCommitCapacity() returns the number of unused bytes left in the commit buffer.

In addition to storing the contents of fields modified during a transaction, the commit buffer holds additional bytes of overhead data, such as the locations of the fields. The amount of overhead data depends on the number of fields being modified and on the transaction system implementation. The commit capacity returned by the two methods is the total number of bytes of persistent data—including overhead—that can be modified during a transaction.

If the commit capacity is exceeded during a transaction, the JCRE throws a TransactionException. Even so, the transaction is still in progress unless it is explicitly aborted by the applet or by the JCRE.

5.3.5   TransactionException

The JCRE throws a TransactionException if certain kinds of problems, such as a nested transaction or a commit buffer overflow, are detected within a transaction.

TransactionException is a subclass of RuntimeException. It provides a reason code to indicate the cause of the exception. Java Card exceptions and reason codes are explained in Chapter 6. Following are the reason codes defined in the class TransactionException:

- IN_PROGRESS—beginTransaction was called while a transaction was already in progress.

- NOT_IN_PROGRESS—commitTransaction or abortTransaction was called while a transaction was not in progress.

- BUFFER_FULL—During a transaction, an update to persistent memory was attempted that would have caused the commit buffer to overflow.

- INTERNAL_FAILURE—An internal fatal problem occurred within the transaction system.

If a `TransactionException` is not caught by the applet, it will be caught by the JCRE. In the latter case, the JCRE automatically aborts the transaction.

5.3.6   Local Variables and Transient Objects during a Transaction

Readers should be aware that only updates to persistent objects participate in a transaction. Updates to transient objects and local variables (including method parameters) are never undone regardless of whether or not they were "inside" a transaction. Local variables are created on the Java Card stack, which resides in RAM.

The following code fragment demonstrates three copy operations involving a transient array `key_buffer`. When the transaction aborts, neither of the array copy operations nor any single update of the `key_buffer` element in the `for` loop are protected by the transaction. Similarly, the local variable a_local retains the new value 1.

```
byte[] key_buffer = JCSystem.makeTransientByteArray
                    (KEY_LENGTH, JCSytem.CLEAR_ON_RESET);

JCSystem.beginTransaction();

Util.arrayCopy(src, src_off, key_buffer, 0, KEY_LENGTH);
Util.arrayCopyNonAtomic(src, src_off, key_buffer, 0, KEY_LENGTH);

for (byte i = 0; i < KEY_LENGTH; i++)
    key_buffer[i] = 0;

byte a_local = 1;

JCSystem.abortTransaction();
```

Because local variables or transient array elements do not participate in a transaction, creating an object and assigning the object to a local variable or a transient array element need to be considered carefully. Here is a code example:

```
JCSystem.beginTransaction();

// ref_1 is an instance (object) field
ref_1 = JCSystem.makeTransientObjectArray
        (LENGTH, JCSystem.CLEAR_ON_DESELECT);
```

```
// ref_2 is a local variable
ref_2 = new SomeClass();

// check status
if (!condition)
    JCSystem.abortTransaction();
else
    JCSystem.commitTransaction();

return ref_2;
```

In the example, the instance field `ref_1` stores a reference to a transient object, and the local variable `ref_2` stores a reference to a persistent object. As described previously, if a transaction aborts, persistent and transient objects created during a transaction are automatically destroyed. This has no side effect on the instance field `ref_1`, because its content is restored to the original value if the transaction does not complete normally. However, a potential problem occurs in the next line, when a newly created object is assigned to a local variable. On transaction failure, the JCRE deletes the object; however, `ref_2` still points to the location where no object exists anymore. The situation gets worse if `ref_2` is later used as a return value. In this case, the caller receives a dangling pointer.

To avoid generating a dangling pointer, which compromises the Java language type security, the JCRE ensures that references to objects created during an aborted transaction are set to `null`. In the example, if the `abortTransaction` method is invoked, the local variable `ref_2` is set to `null`. This solution may not be ideal, but it avoids security violation while minimizing system overhead.

This example is not applicable to most applets, because casually creating objects within a method is strongly discouraged. When possible, an applet should allocate all the objects it needs during applet initialization (see Chapter 7). However, an implementor of a Java Card installer might need to deal with considerable object creation within a transaction and should avoid the scenario described in the code.

CHAPTER 6

Java Card Exceptions and Exception Handling

An *exception* is an event that disrupts the normal flow of instructions during the execution of a program. Exceptions are important in the Java language because they provide an elegant way of handling errors in a program.

The Java Card platform supports all the Java programming language constructs for exceptions. A Java Card applet can use keywords `throw`, `try`, `catch`, or `finally`, and they work the same as in the Java platform.

Exceptions are thrown by the JCRE classes and the Java Card virtual machine when internal runtime problems are detected or are thrown programmatically by applets. Although the Java Card platform has full support for Java-style exceptions, there are differences in usage, due to the restrictive environment of smart cards. This chapter introduces the exceptions in the Java Card platform and discusses how applets throw and handle exceptions.

6.1 Exceptions in the `java.lang` Package

In general, the Java Card platform does not support all the exception types found in the Java technology core packages, because many of them are not applicable in a smart card context. For example, threads are not supported in the Java Card platform, and as a result, none of the thread-related exceptions are supported.

However, the Java Card `java.lang` package does support some exception classes from the Java version of the package. In all supported exception classes, only the `equals` method, inherited from the root class `Object`, and a constructor with no parameters are provided. Table 6.1 lists all the exception classes in the `java.lang` package on the Java Card platform.

Table 6.1   Exception classes in the `java.lang` package

Throwable	Exception	RuntimeException
ArithmeticException	ArrayStoreException	ArrayIndexOutOfBoundsException
ClassCastException	NullPointerException	IndexOutOfBoundsException
SecurityException	NegativeArraySizeException	

The class `Throwable` defines a common ancestor for all the exception classes in the Java Card platform. This class also ensures that the Java Card exceptions have the same semantics as their counterparts in the Java platform. For example, applets can throw and catch only objects that derive from the `Throwable` class.

The class `Exception` extends from the `Throwable` class. As in the Java platform, it is the root class in the Java Card platform for all checked exceptions. The class `RuntimeException` derives from the `Exception` class, and it is the root class for all unchecked exceptions in the Java Card platform. The concepts of checked and unchecked exceptions are defined in the Java language specification. Their definitions are given in the next section.

The rest of the classes in Table 6.1 are unchecked exceptions. The exception classes in the `java.lang` package provide the fundamental language support for the Java exception framework. They are thrown by the Java Card virtual machine when an error occurs because of a Java language violation.

6.2   Java Card Exceptions

The Java Card platform provides a class inheritance hierarchy for both checked and unchecked exceptions, as shown in Figure 6.1.

Checked exceptions are subclasses of the `Exception` class and must either be caught in the throwing method or be declared in a `throws` clause of the method header. This requirement is enforced by the Java compiler. All Java Card checked exception classes extend from the class `CardException`, which derives from the class `Exception`.

For two reasons, all checked exceptions must eventually be caught by the applet. First, checked exceptions indicate a programming error in an applet and thus should be corrected by the applet. Second, checked exceptions are an important part of the interface to a method. Because no applet API methods specify a checked exception in the `throws` clause, the Java compiler issues an error if an applet does not catch a checked exception.

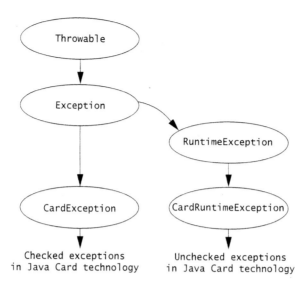

Figure 6.1   The Java Card exception hierarchy

Unchecked exceptions, often called *runtime exceptions*, are subclasses of the class RuntimeException and need neither be caught in a program nor declared in a throws clause. Unchecked exceptions typically indicate unexpected runtime problems, programming errors, or erroneous APDU processing states. Such exceptions are caught by the outmost levels of the JCRE. All unchecked exceptions in the Java Card platform should extend from the class CardRuntimeException, which derives from the class RuntimeException.

Why do we need the classes CardException and CardRuntimeException? Because they enable a resource-saving mechanism so that an exception object can be reused multiple times, as explained in Sections 6.2.1 and 6.2.2.

6.2.1   Java Card Exception Reason Code

The Java exception classes supply a "message" string that indicates a specific error. The String class is not supported in the Java Card platform, so string messages cannot be provided in exceptions. As an alternative way to attach extra information to the exception, the Java Card exception classes supply a numerical reason code. The reason code is used to describe optional details related to the throwing of the exception. The type of the reason code is short.

The reason code is defined as a field in classes CardException and CardRuntimeException and thus is inherited by their subclasses. In addition, both classes define two public accessor methods—getReason and setReason—to retrieve and set a reason code.

6.2.2   Throwing an Exception in the Java Card Platform

To throw an exception in the Java system, an applet creates an instance of an exception class, and the code is written as follows:

```
throw new MyException("a specific error message");
```

Of course, you could create a new exception object every time an exception is thrown in the Java Card platform. However, space economy is always a concern in a smart card. If an applet creates an object every time an exception is thrown, the applet will over time accumulate many unused exception instances in precious EEPROM memory.

To optimize memory usage, all exception objects should be precreated at initialization time and their references saved permanently. When an exception event occurs, rather than creating a new exception object, an applet can do the following:

1. Retrieve and reuse the reference for the desired exception object

2. Fill in the reason code in the object

3. Throw the object

To support reusable exception objects, the JCRE precreates an instance of each exception type in the Java Card APIs. The classes CardException and CardRuntimeException and each of their subclasses provide a static method throwIt for applets to reuse the exception instance:

```
public static void throwIt (short reason)
```

The throwIt method throws the JCRE-created exception instance every time it is invoked. An applet specifies a reason code to the throwIt method. For example, to reject an APDU command, an applet can throw an ISOException and indicate the reason code as "command not allowed":

```
ISOException.throwIt(ISO7816.SW_COMMAND_NOT_ALLOWED);
```

An applet can create its own exception objects. During initialization, the applet instantiates such an exception object and saves the reference in a persistent field. Later, the applet reuses the instance whenever it needs to throw that exception.

6.2.3 ISOException

ISOException is a special unchecked exception in the Java Card APIs. It is raised during runtime to indicate a warning or error-processing state in the card. ISOException encapsulates an ISO 7816 response status word (SW) in its reason code.

ISOException allows an applet to deal with errors efficiently. When a command is processed successfully, a method returns normally. But if an error occurs, the method simply throws an ISOException with the appropriate status word.

Typically, an applet does not handle an ISOException. The JCRE eventually catches an ISOException and returns the reason code it contains as an ISO status word to a host application. That's why the exception class carries ISO in its name.

The ISO status word is part of the APDU protocol. It is used as a way for a smart card application to return the status of processing an APDU command to the host application. The Java Card platform provides an interface javacard.framework.ISO7816 that defines the most commonly used status word constants related to ISO 7816-3 and ISO 7816-4. An applet can define its own status words and can use an ISOException to communicate them to the host application.

6.2.4 UserException

When an applet encounters a programmatic error that needs to be corrected by the applet, it throws a UserException. Unlike an ISOException, a UserException is a checked exception derived from CardException and hence must be handled by the applet. If an applet needs to create additional exception types, it can create classes deriving from UserException.

CHAPTER 7

Java Card Applets

Applications running on Java smart cards are called applets. This chapter introduces the framework for writing applets. It is organized into seven sections. The first section provides an overall picture of how applets work within the JCRE. The remaining sections discuss the techniques of applet writing.

Applet features are described in more detail throughout the book. Chapters 8 and 9, for example, discuss APDU command handling and object sharing among applets.

7.1 Applet Overview

A Java Card applet is a smart card application written in the Java programming language and conforming to a set of conventions so that it can run within the Java Card runtime environment (JCRE). A running applet in the JCRE is an instance of the applet class that extends from `javacard.framework.Applet`. As with other persistent objects, an applet created on the card lives on through the entire lifetime of the card.[1] The Java Card platform supports a multiapplication environment. Each applet instance is uniquely identified by an AID (see Chapter 3 for more details on AIDs).

7.1.1 Applet Installation and Execution

After the package(s) defining an applet have been properly loaded on a Java smart card and linked with other packages on the card, an applet's life starts when an instance of the applet is created and registered with the JCRE. The JCRE is a single-thread environment. This means that only one applet is running at a time. When

---

[1] Some Java smart cards also support applet deletion.

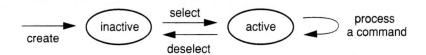

Figure 7.1   Applet execution states

an applet is first installed, it is in an inactive state. The applet becomes active when it is explicitly selected by a host application.

Applets, like any smart card applications, are reactive applications. Once selected, a typical applet waits for an application running on the host side to send a command. The applet then executes the command and returns a response to the host.

This command-and-response dialogue continues until a new applet is selected or the card is removed from the card acceptance device. The applet remains inactive until the next time it is selected. Applet execution states are illustrated in Figure 7.1.

7.1.2   Applet Communication

The communication between an applet and a host application is achieved through exchanging APDUs, as illustrated in Figure 7.2. An APDU contains either a command or a response message. A host application sends a command to an applet and the applet returns a response. (See chapter 2 for more information on APDUs.)

When the host application wants to select an applet to run, it sends an APDU that specifies the SELECT command and the AID of the requested applet. The JCRE searches its internal table for an applet whose AID matches the one specified in the command. If a match is found, the JCRE selects that applet to run. All subsequent APDUs (including the SELECT APDU) are forwarded to the current applet until a new applet is selected.

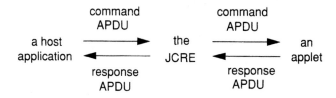

Figure 7.2   Applet communication

7.2   Class `javacard.framework.Applet`

Every applet is implemented by creating a subclass of the class javacard.framework.Applet. The JCRE invokes the methods install, select, process, or deselect, which are defined in the base Applet class, when it wants to install, select, or deselect the applet or to ask the applet to process an APDU command.

Methods in Table 7.1 are listed in the order in which they are invoked by the JCRE during applet creation and execution. The JCRE calls the install method to

Table 7.1   Methods in the class `javacard.framework.Applet`

`public static void`	`install (byte[] bArray, short bOffset, byte bLength)` The JCRE calls this static method to create an instance of the Applet subclass.
`protected final void`	`register()` This method is used by the applet to register this applet instance with the JCRE and to assign the default AID in the CAP file to the applet instance.
`protected final void`	`register (byte[] bArray, short bOffset, byte bLength)` This method is used by the applet to register this applet instance with the JCRE and to assign to the applet instance the AID specified in the array bArray.
`public boolean`	`select ()` The JCRE calls this method to inform the applet that it has been selected.
`public abstract void`	`process (APDU apdu)` This JCRE calls this method to instruct the applet to process an incoming APDU command.
`public void`	`deselect ()` The JCRE calls this method to inform the currently selected applet that another (or the same) applet will be selected.

create an applet instance. The applet instance is registered with the JCRE, using one of the two register methods.

When receiving a SELECT APDU, the JCRE first checks whether an applet is already selected. If so, the JCRE deselects the current applet by invoking the deselect method. In the deselect method, the applet performs any cleanup or bookkeeping work before it becomes inactive. Then the JCRE selects the new applet by invoking the select method. The applet performs any initialization necessary in the select method.

After successful selection, each APDU (including the SELECT APDU) is delivered to the active applet via a call to its process method. The process method is an essential method in the applet class. It processes APDU commands and thus provides an applet's functions.

The methods install, select, deselect, and process are applet entry point methods. They are invoked by the JCRE at the appropriate state of applet creation and execution. The base Applet class provides only the default behavior for these methods. An applet needs to override some or all of these methods to implement its functions. The details of each of these methods are specified in the remainder of this chapter.

7.3   install Method

The install method is typically called by the JCRE as the last step during applet installation to create an applet instance—a runnable applet (applet installation is discussed in chapter 3). The install method is similar to the main method in a Java application. The arguments to the install method carry the applet installation parameters. They are analogous to command-line arguments supplied to the main method.

The install method creates an applet instance by using the new operator followed by a call to the applet's constructor. In the constructor, an applet typically performs the following tasks:

- Creates objects that the applet needs during its lifetime

- Initializes objects and the applet's internal variables

- Registeres the applet instance with the JCRE by calling one of the two register methods defined in the base Applet class

Applet registration marks the beginning of the applet's lifetime. An applet must register with the JCRE so that it can be selected and set to run by the JCRE.

The following code shows an example of creating a wallet applet by using the default constructor.

```
public class WalletApp extends Applet{

    private Log transaction_log;
    private byte[] wallet_id;
    private byte wallet_balance;

    public static void install
            (byte[] bArray, short bOffset, byte bLength) {

        new WalletApp();
    }

    private WalletApp() {

        // create a transaction log with the specified number
        // of transaction records
        transaction_log = new Log(TRAN_RECORD_NUM);

        // create a byte array to store the wallet ID
        wallet_id = new byte[ID_LENGTH];

        // initialize the wallet balance
        wallet_balance = INITIAL_BALANCE;

        // register the applet instance with the JCRE
        register();
    }
}
```

Alternatively, an applet can define a constructor that takes the installation parameters.

```
public walletApp(byte[] bArray, short bOffset, byte bLength) {...}
```

The installation parameters provide additional data for initializing and personalizing the applet. Processing the installation parameters is explained in Section 7.3.3.

On successful return from the install method, the applet is ready to be selected and to process the upcoming APDU commands. Only one instance of an applet can be successfully created and registered from one invocation of the `install` method. If the JCRE wants to create multiple instances of the same applet, each instance is created with a separate invocation of the `install` method.

If a failure occurs during the `install` method and *prior* to the successful invocation of the `register` method, the JCRE will perform necessary cleanup to reclaim the card resources when it gets back control. The JCRE deletes the applet instance as well as the other objects created during the `install` method and recovers the previous JCRE state. It is not necessary to set up a transaction in the `install` method, since the JCRE ensures that the `install` method is transactional. Applet registration signals the successful end of the transaction. Therefore, it is important to register the applet as the last step during applet creation. If any error occurs after the `register` method, the applet will remain registered but might be left in a crippled state.

Notice that the `install` method in the base `Applet` class is simply a prototype. An applet must define an `install` method of the same prototype.

7.3.1   Creating Objects in the Applet's Constructor

Although objects and arrays can be created at any point in the execution of an applet, it is recommended that, when possible, such allocations occur only during the initialization of the applet. Any objects that might be required during execution of an applet should be preallocated in the constructor, to ensure that the applet will never fail due to lack of memory.

The constructor is invoked inside the `install` method. Thus, if the JCRE detects resource shortage and is unable to allocate memory space for the applet during object creation or during some other resource allocation processing, the JCRE will delete the applet and reclaim all memory space. In this way, no partially created applet will be left behind in an unrunnable state.

However, an applet should not create more objects than it needs, since the memory occupied by unused objects cannot be reused or shared by other applets or the JCRE.

7.3.2   Registering the Applet Instance with the JCRE

To register an applet with the JCRE, you use one of the two `register` methods provided in the base `Applet` class.

```
protected final void register()
```

or

```
protected final void register
        (byte[] bArray, short bOffset, byte bLength)
```

The register method has two functions. First, it stores a reference to the applet instance with the JCRE. Second, it assigns an AID to the applet instance. Recall from Chapter 3 that each applet instance on the card is uniquely identified by an AID. The CAP file that defines the applet classes contains a default AID. However, an applet may choose to have an AID different from the default one. The default AID can be supplied in the installation parameters.

The first register method (the one with no arguments) registers the applet with the JCRE using the default AID from the CAP file. The second register method (with arguments) registers the applet instance with the JCRE using the AID specified in the argument bArray. The argument bOffset specifies the starting offset in bArray, and bLength specifies the AID length in bytes.

7.3.3   Processing the Installation Parameters

Typically, during applet installation, the installation parameters are sent to the card along with the CAP files that define an applet. The JCRE then provides the installation parameters to the applet via the arguments to the install method. The install method accepts three arguments:

- byte[] bArray—Array containing installation parameters
- short bOffset—Starting offset in bArray
- byte bLength—Length in bytes of the parameter data in bArray

The content and format of the installation parameters are defined by the applet designers or the card issuers. Often, they contain applet configuration parameters and applet initialization values. Configuration parameters can be used to specify the size of an internal file, an array, and so on. In this way, the applet can allocate adequate memory to support anticipated processing while avoiding memory waste. Applet initialization values, for example, can specify the initial balance, the card holder's ID, and the account number in an electronic wallet. Another common use of the installation parameters is to supply an AID other than the default one in the CAP file. For example, suppose that two wallet applet instances are needed: one for personal use and the other for business. In such a case, the JCRE must invoke the applet's install method twice. Each time, a wallet applet instance is created with a unique AID.

Suppose that the designer of the wallet applet specifies that the installation parameter byte array consist of the following fields:

1. A 1-byte binary value specifying the number of records in the transaction log.

2. A fixed-size array of 4 bytes specifying the wallet ID.

3. One byte containing the initial wallet balance.

4. One byte specifying the size of the next subarray.

5. A variable-size array of bytes specifying the AID for this applet instance. If this array is empty, the applet uses the default AID from the CAP file.

To create a wallet applet for personal use with the default AID, the installation parameters might be the bytes [0x10, 0x1, 0x2, 0x3, 0x4, 0x32, 0], which would be interpreted by the applet as

- number of transactions in the transaction log = 0x10 = 16
- wallet ID = [0x1, 0x2, 0x3, 0x4]
- initial balance = 0x32 = 50
- AID = the default AID from the CAP file

To create a wallet instance to handle business expense with an AID other than the default one, the installation parameters might be the bytes [0x10, 0x4, 0x3, 0x2, 0x1, 0x64, 0xF, 'B', 'A', 'N', 'K', '_', 'w', 'a', 'l', 'l', 'e', 't', '_', 'B', 'T', 'S'], which would be interpreted by the applet as

- number of transactions in the transaction log = 0x10 = 16
- wallet ID = [0x4, 0x3, 0x2, 0x1]
- initial balance = 0x64 = 100
- AID = ['B', 'A', 'N', 'K', '_', 'w', 'a', 'l', 'l', 'e', 't', '_', 'B', 'T', 'S']

The following code demonstrates how the wallet applet processes the installation parameters in the constructor:

```
private WalletApp(byte[] bArray, short bOffset, byte bLength) {

    // create a transaction log and specify the maximum number
    // of log records
    // max_record_num = bArray[bOffset]
    transaction_log = new Log(bArray[bOffset++]);

    // set the wallet ID
    wallet_id = new byte[ID_LENGTH];
    Util.arrayCopy(bArray, bOffset, wallet_id, (byte)0, ID_LENGTH]);
```

```
    // advance bOffset by ID_LENGTH of bytes
    bOffset += ID_LENGTH;

    // initialize the wallet balance
    wallet_balance = bArray[bOffset++];

    // check the AID
    byte AID_len = bArray[bOffset++];
    if (AID_len == 0) {
        // register the applet instance with the JCRE
        // using the default AID
        this.register();
    } else {
        // register the applet instance with the JCRE
        // using the AID specified in the installation parameters.
        // AID bytes in the bArray start from the index bOffset
        // and consist of the AID_len number of bytes
        this.register(bArray, bOffset, AID_len);
    }
}
```

The content of bArray does not belong to the applet. For security reasons, the JCRE clears the array on return from the install method. If the applet desires to preserve any of these data, it should copy the data into its own object. In the example, the wallet ID bytes in bArray are copied into the field wallet_id.

The Java Card platform supports installation parameters of up to 32 bytes. Thus, the maximum value of bLength is 32. In chapter 8 you will see that the JCRE employs a buffer to transmit APDUs. The minimum size of the APDU buffer is 37, including 5 bytes of header and 32 bytes of data. The number 32 is chosen as the maximum size of the installation parameters so that they can be transported in the buffer with one APDU I/O.

7.3.4   Further Applet Initialization

After a successful return from the install method, simple applets might be fully ready to function in their normal role. More complex applets might need further personalization information before they are ready to execute normally. Such information might not all be available at applet creation time or might exceed the capacity of the installation parameters (32 bytes). In this case, a separate scheme (specified by applet designers or issuers) might be required to allow an applet to complete personalization in the `process` method. In such a scheme, the applet needs to set internal state variables and is responsible for keeping track of these state transitions. To receive personalization information, the applet exchanges APDUs with the host.

7.4   `select` Method

An applet remains in a suspended state until it is explicitly selected. Applet selection occurs when the JCRE receives a SELECT APDU whose data match the AID of the applet. The JCRE informs the applet of its selection by invoking its `select` method.

In the `select` method, the applet can check whether its conditions for selection have been met, and if so, it can set internal variables and states necessary to handle subsequent APDUs. The applet returns `true` from the call to the `select` method if it is ready to accept incoming APDUs via its `process` method, or it can decline to be selected by returning `false` or by throwing an exception.

If the selection fails, the JCRE returns the status word 0x6999 to the host. If the `select` method returns `true`, the SELECT APDU command is then supplied to the applet in the subsequent call to its `process` method so that the applet can respond to the host with applet-related information. For example, the wallet applet might return the wallet issuer's identification number, currency conversion information, or other parameters. The host might need this information to start DEBIT or CREDIT transactions. Applet designers or issuers are free to define the content and the format of the response data.

The `select` method in the base `Applet` class simply returns `true`. An applet can override this method and define the actions required during selection.

7.4.1   SELECT APDU Format and Processing

The SELECT APDU command is the only APDU command that is standardized on the Java Card platform. It ensures interoperable applet selection on various Java Card platform implementations. The APDU format is depicted in Table 7.2. The data portion of the SELECT APDU contains an applet AID, which is between 5 and 16 bytes in length. For an applet to be selected, the entire data field of the APDU must match the AID of the applet.

On receiving an APDU, the JCRE decodes its header (CLA, INS, P1, and P2) to determine whether it is an applet selection command, and if so, whether the AID in the APDU data matches that of an applet on the card. A successful applet

Table 7.2   Applet SELECT command

CLA	INS	P1	P2	Lc	Data Field
0x0	0xA4	0x4	0x0	Length of AID	AID bytes

selection involves deselecting the current applet, selecting the new applet, and sending the SELECT APDU to the new applet's process method. If the APDU is not for applet selection, the JCRE delivers it to the current applet for processing. In any case, if an error occurs during selection, the JCRE flags the error by returning the status word 0x6999 to the host, and no applet becomes selected on the card. Processing the SELECT APDU is illustrated in Figure 7.3.

7.4.2   Default Applet

Normally, applets become selected only via a successful SELECT command. However, some smart card systems require a default applet that is implicitly selected after every card reset.

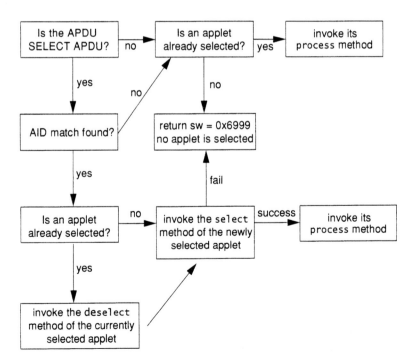

Figure 7.3   APDU command processing

To select a default applet, the JCRE calls the default applet's `select` method and marks it as the currently selected applet. Because no SELECT APDU is required, the applet's `process` method is not called subsequently during selection. If the default applet's `select` method throws an exception or returns `false`, no applet is selected until the next SELECT APDU is processed.

Default applet selection is an optional JCRE feature. When supported, a JCRE implementation should devise a mechanism for specifying the default applet.

7.5   deselect Method

Before a new applet is selected, the JCRE deactivates the current applet by calling its `deselect` method. It is possible that the newly selected applet is the same as the current applet. In this case, the JCRE deselects it anyway and then reselects it.

The `deselect` method allows the applet to perform any cleanup operations to prepare itself to go "off stage" and to enable another applet to execute. The default implementation in the class `Applet` is an empty method. An applet should override this method for any required cleanup operations. For example, the wallet might need to reset the security condition or the transaction state, which is valid only during one selection period.

The `deselect` method might fail. Even so, the current applet is deselected and a new applet is selected despite the result of executing the `deselect` method. The JCRE also ignores any exceptions thrown from the `deselect` method.

Furthermore, on reset or power loss, the applet is automatically deselected by the JCRE without its `deselect` method being called. Therefore, an applet cannot always rely on the cleanup operations in the `deselect` method.

7.6   process Method

When receiving an APDU command, the JCRE calls the current applet's `process` method. In the `process` method, an applet is expected to perform a function requested in the APDU. The `process` method in the base `Applet` class is an abstract method. An applet must directly or indirectly override this method. Usually the `process` method is implemented as a dispatcher. On receiving an APDU command, the method decodes the APDU header and calls a service method to execute the requested function.

The JCRE encapsulates the APDU in the argument to the `process` method, `apdu` (an instance of the class APDU). The applet invokes methods on the `apdu` object to receive and to return the APDU data. Handling APDU commands in an applet is covered thoroughly in Chapter 8.

7.7 Other Methods in the Class `javacard.framework.Applet`

There are two other methods in the `Applet` class: `selectingApplet` and `get-`
`ShareableInterfaceObject`.

The traditional smart card system is file system oriented. Application data are
stored in files. A file must be selected before any action is performed on the data
in the file. Readers who are familiar with ISO 7816 commands will recognize that
the SELECT APDU in Table 7.2 is the ISO command select DF (dedicated file)
by name. The JCRE can determine whether the command is for applet selection
by matching the data in the command with the AID of any applet on the card (see
Figure 7.3).[2] Because all APDUs are forwarded to the currently selected applet's
`process` method, the applet calls the `selectingApplet` method to distinguish
whether the SELECT APDU command is used to select this applet itself or
whether it is attempting to select a DF of this applet. The `selectingApplet`
method returns `true` if the APDU selects this applet. Otherwise, it returns `false`.

The `getShareableInterfaceObject` method is intended for object sharing
among applets. It is invoked by the JCRE when another applet requests a shareable interface object from this applet. This method is further described in chapter
9 in the coverage of the applet firewall and object sharing.

---

[2] It is possible that the JCRE might mistakenly select an applet if the encoding of a DF name is
identical to the AID of an applet on the card.

CHAPTER 8

Working with APDUs

This chapter describes the techniques of handling *application protocol data units* (APDUs) in an applet. APDUs are data packets; they are the application-level communication protocol between the application software on the card and the application software on the host side of the link. Readers who are not familiar with APDUs or need a refresher on the subject should read Chapter 2 before exploring this chapter.

In Java Card applets, the mechanism of communicating with the host is different from the networking techniques in Java applications. Much of the difference is due to the nature the APDU protocol. Java Card technology provides the class `javacard.framework.APDU`, which defines a powerful yet simple interface to help applets handle APDUs easily.

This chapter starts with an overview of the `APDU` class, which explains how an APDU is encapsulated by an `APDU` object and delivered to an applet by the JCRE. Next, the focus is on processing APDUs in an applet using the `APDU` class—how to receive a command APDU, how to interpret and execute the command in the APDU, and how to return data to the host. At the end of the chapter is a summary discussion of how each of four APDU cases is handled using the `APDU` class.

8.1 APDU Class

The `APDU` class in the Java Card APIs provides a powerful and flexible interface for handling APDUs whose command and response structures conform to the ISO 7816-4 specification. APDUs are transmitted between the host and the card by the lower-level transport protocol. Two transport protocols are in primary use with smart card systems today: the T=0 protocol and the T=1 protocol.

In most legacy smart card systems, there is no clear separation between the smart card operating system and applications. Applications must be aware of the transport protocol employed by the underlying system. In the Java Card platform, the class APDU is carefully designed so that the intricacies of and differences between the T=0 and T=1 protocols are hidden from applet developers. In other words, using the APDU class, applets can be written so that they will work correctly regardless of whether the platform is using the T=0 or the T=1 protocol.

The APDU class also provides an object-oriented way of handling APDUs. Applets receive and send APDUs by invoking methods defined in the APDU class. Therefore, applet developers can concentrate their efforts on processing the contents of APDU messages rather than on the details of how APDUs are constructed and transmitted.

8.1.1   APDU Object

As discussed in the previous chapter, applets do not communicate with the applications on the host side directly. They interact with the JCRE, which in turn uses serial I/O to communicate with the host. The JCRE creates an APDU object—an instance of the APDU class—that encapsulates APDU messages in an internal byte array, called the *APDU buffer.*

In the Java Card environment, the APDU object can be viewed as a communication object. When receiving an APDU from the host, the JCRE writes the APDU header in the APDU buffer. It then invokes the process method of the currently selected applet and delivers the APDU object to the applet as a method parameter. Inside the process method, if the incoming APDU has data, the applet can call methods on the APDU object to receive data. After processing the command, if the applet wants to send data to the host, it again calls methods on the APDU object to do so. The response data are also written into the APDU buffer. The JCRE then sends the response data to the host.

8.1.2   APDU Buffer Size

To achieve interoperability among the Java Card platform implementations, the APDU buffer is required to be at least 37 bytes—5 bytes of header plus the default *information field size on card* (IFSC). A smart card with more memory can allocate a bigger APDU buffer.

IFSC is defined in ISO 7816-3 for the T=1 protocol. Why the minimum APDU buffer size is determined by the default size of the IFSC is explained in the discussion of protocol-specific APDU processing in Section 8.4.

8.2   Interface ISO7816

To facilitate APDU command handling, the interface ISO7816 in the Java Card APIs defines a set of common constants related to ISO 7816-3 and ISO 7816-4. Constants defined in the interface ISO7816 can be divided into three groups:

1. *Constants that are used to index into the APDU buffer*—These constants start with OFFSET prefixes. They declare the offset of each APDU header byte in the APDU buffer. For example, OFFSET_CLA represents the offset of the CLA byte in the APDU buffer. An applet uses these constants to access the APDU header.

2. *ISO 7816-4-defined response status words*—These constants start with SW prefixes. They are the most commonly used ISO 7816-4-defined response status words. The status word is a mandatory field in a response APDU. All status word constants are type short, which comprises two bytes.

3. *CLA and INS constants*—The interface ISO7816 also defines the CLA and the INS byte encoding for the SELECT and the EXTERNAL AUTHENTICATE APDU commands as specified in ISO 7816-4.

8.3   Working with APDUs in Applets

Applets handle APDU commands in the process method, described in the following steps. Along with the discussion of each step, methods in the APDU class and their use are explained.

8.3.1   Retrieve the APDU Buffer

To process an APDU, an applet first retrieves a reference to the APDU buffer by invoking the getBuffer method. The APDU buffer is a byte array whose length can be determined by using apdu_buffer.length.

```
public void process(APDU apdu) {

    // retrieve the APDU buffer
    byte[] apdu_buffer = apdu.getBuffer();
}
```

Note that the JCRE requires that the reference to the APDU object or the reference to the APDU buffer *cannot* be stored in class variables, instance variables, or array components. Instead, an applet should store the references only in local variables and method parameters, which are temporary data within the scope of a method. This requirement is due to the security concerns that an applet might improperly retain a reference to APDU data owned by another applet. For more information, see the description of global arrays and temporary JCRE entry point objects in Chapter 9.

8.3.2   Examine the Command APDU Header

When an applet's process method is invoked, only the first 5 bytes are available in the APDU buffer—the first 4 bytes are the APDU header [CLA, INS, P1, P2] and the fifth byte (P3) is an additional length field. The meaning of P3 is implicit, determined by the case of the command:

- For case 1, P3 = 0.

- For case 2, P3 = Le, the length of outgoing response data.

- For cases 3 and 4, P3 = Lc, the length of incoming command data.

The remaining bytes in the buffer are undefined and should not be read or written by the applet.

When an applet obtains the APDU buffer, it should first examine the APDU header to determine whether the command is well formatted and whether the command can be executed:

- The command is well formatted—the header bytes are encoded correctly.

- The command can be executed—the command is supported by the applet and the internal and security conditions are met for the command.

If the check fails, the applet should terminate the operation by throwing an ISOException.

The constants defined in the interface ISO7816 should be used as indexes into the APDU buffer for accessing the header bytes (see Table 8.1). For example, the following code fragment examines the CLA byte:

```
if (apdu_buffer[ISO7816.OFFSET_CLA] != EXPECTED_VALUE) {
    ISOException.throwIt(ISO7816.SW_CLA_NOT_SUPPORTED);
}
```

Using the constant definition makes the applet code more readable.

Table 8.1 APDU header offset defined in the interface ISO7816

Constant Name	Meaning	Value
OFFSET_CLA	offset to the CLA field in the APDU buffer	OFFSET_CLA = 0
OFFSET_INS	offset to the INS field in the APDU buffer	OFFSET_INS = 1
OFFSET_P1	offset to the P1 field in the APDU buffer	OFFSET_P1 = 2
OFFSET_P2	offset to the P2 field in the APDU buffer	OFFSET_P2 = 3

8.3.3 Receive APDU Command Data

In addition to specifying an instruction for the applet to perform, the APDU header [CLA, INS, P1, P2] conveys the structure (case) of the APDU—whether it has incoming data and whether the outgoing data are expected in the response. If it is the case 3 or the case 4 type, the command APDU has incoming data as part of the instruction. The applet can find out the number of data bytes from the Lc field (the fifth byte in the APDU buffer).

```
short data_length = (short)(apdu_buffer[ISO7816.OFFSET_LC] & 0xFF);
```

The integer data types in the Java programming language are signed; that is, the most significant bit determines whether it is a positive or negative number. However, the Lc field should be interpreted as an unsigned value, because it does not make sense to have a negative length. In the code fragment, the Lc byte is bit-wise anded with the constant 0xFF to convert a signed byte to an unsigned value.

To read data into the APDU buffer, the applet invokes the setIncomingAndReceive method in the APDU class:

```
public short setIncomingAndReceive() throws APDUException
```

As the name implies, the setIncomingAndReceive method accomplishes two tasks. First, it sets the JCRE into the data-receiving mode. The communication pathway to and from a smart card is *half-duplex*; that is, data are either sent from the host to the card or from the card to the host but not both at the same time. This step instructs the JCRE to treat the fifth byte in the APDU buffer as the Lc field and prepares the JCRE to accept the incoming data. Next, it requests the JCRE to receive the incoming command data bytes, starting at offset ISO7816.OFFSET_DATA (=5) in the APDU buffer following the header, as shown in Figure 8.1.

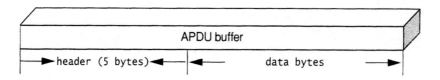

Figure 8.1   The APDU buffer after invoking the method setIncomingAndReceive

The setIncomingAndReceive method returns the number of bytes it reads in. It returns 0 if no data are available. If the setIncomingAndReceive method is called when the JCRE is already in the receive mode from a previous call to the same method, an APDUException occurs with the reason code APDUException. ILLEGAL_USE.

8.3.3.1 Receiving Long Command Data

In most cases, the setIncomingAndReceive method is sufficient to read the number of data bytes into the APDU buffer as specified in the Lc field. However, for a command APDU that has more data than can fit into the APDU buffer, the setIncomingAndReceive method must be followed by one or more calls to the receiveBytes method:

```
public short receiveBytes(short bOff) throws APDUException
```

For long command APDU data, the applet can process the data piecemeal and then call the receiveBytes method to read additional data into the APDU buffer. With the receiveBytes method, the offset into the APDU buffer where the data are received can be specified. This allows the applet to control how the APDU buffer is used in the processing of incoming data. For example, as shown in Figure 8.2, the applet may have processed the data from the previous call to the setIncomingAndReceive method or the receiveBytes method—except for a few bytes.

The applet can move these bytes to the beginning of the buffer and then receive the next group so that it is appended to the bytes still in the buffer. This feature is important in instances where data are read across method invocations that need to be processed as a whole.

Like the setIncomingAndReceive method, the receiveBytes method is guaranteed to return synchronously, retrieving as many bytes as possible. However, depending on how many bytes the host will send as one batch and depending on the JCRE implementation, both methods may read in fewer bytes than the available space in the APDU buffer.

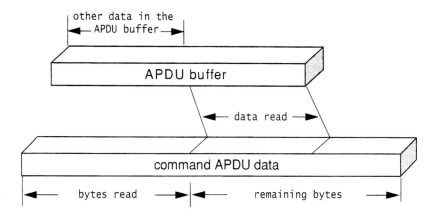

Figure 8.2 Invoking the receiveBytes method

As a general rule, both the setIncomingAndReceive and the receiveBytes method are optimized. If the entire command data fit in the APDU buffer starting at the offset ISO7816.OFFSET_CDATA (=5), one invocation of the setIncomingAnd-Receive method should be sufficient for getting all the data. No call to the receiveBytes method is necessary. Most APDU commands fall into this category.

When more data are available than can fit in the APDU buffer, an applet must call the receiveBytes method. If the remaining bytes fit into the available space at the specified offset in the APDU buffer, the receiveBytes method is guaranteed to return with all the remaining data. Otherwise, the method reads as many bytes as will fit in the buffer, and possibly less. The applet should call receive-Bytes repeatedly, processing or moving the bytes in the APDU data buffer with each call, until all available data are read. The following example includes the receiveBytes method inside a while loop:

```
public void process(APDU apdu) {

    byte[] apdu_buffer = apdu.getBuffer();
    short total_bytes = (short)(apdu_buffer[ISO7816.OFFSET_LC] &
                                0xFF);

    // read data into the APDU buffer
    short read_count = apdu.setIncomingAndReceive();

    // get the number of remaining bytes
    short bytes_left = (short) (total_bytes - read_count);
```

```
while (true) {

    // process data in the APDU buffer or copy
    // data to an internal buffer
    // ...

    // check if there are still remaining data
    // if not, jump out of the loop
    if (bytes_left <= 0) break;

    // if there are remaining data, read more data
    read_count = apdu.receiveBytes((short)0);

    bytes_left -= read_count;
}

// execute other tasks and respond to the host
// ...
}
```

8.3.4   Process the APDU Command and Generate the Response Data

The APDU header [CLA, INS, P1, P2] identifies an instruction that the applet should perform. When executing the instruction, the applet should process the command data in the APDU buffer if the command is the case 3 or the case 4 type, and it generates response data if the command is the case 2 or the case 4 type. To reduce memory usage, the applet often uses the APDU buffer as a scratch pad for holding the intermediate result or the response data.

8.3.5   Return APDU Response Data

After completing the instruction specified in the command APDU, the applet can return data to the host. Since the underlying communication pathway is half-duplexed, to send data, the applet must first call the setOutgoing method to indicate that now it wishes to send out response data.

```
public short setOutgoing() throws APDUException
```

The setOutgoing method sets the JCRE to the data-send mode by resetting the data transfer direction to outbound. Unlike the corresponding setIncoming-

AndReceive method for reading data, the setOutgoing method does not send any bytes; it just sets the data transfer mode. Once the setOutgoing method is called, any remaining incoming data will be discarded, and the applet cannot continue to receive bytes.

The setOutgoing method returns the number of response data bytes (Le) expected by the host for the command APDU to which the applet is responding. In case 4 of the T=0 protocol, because the actual Le field cannot be determined, the maximum value allowed for the Le field, 255 bytes, is assumed. For the other cases, the actual Le field in the command APDU is returned. However, it is not necessary for the applet to know which transport protocol is being used.

Even though the host application requests the Le bytes of data to be returned, the applet may send more or less than that number. After invoking the setOutgoing method, the applet must call the setOutgoingLength method to indicate to the host how many total response data bytes (not including SW) it will actually send:

```
public void setOutgoingLength(short length) throws APDUException
```

The host assumes that the default length of the response data is 0, so this method need not be called if the applet will not be sending any data. The applet cannot send more than 256 bytes to the host, or invoking the setOutgoingLength method will result in an APDUException with the reason code APDUException.BAD_LENGTH.

Next, to actually send out the response data, the applet calls the sendBytes method:

```
public void sendBytes(short bOff, short len) throws APDUException
```

The sendBytes method sends the len bytes of data from the APDU buffer at the specified offset bOff. Therefore, the applet must generate or copy the response to the APDU buffer prior to invoking this method.

The methods setOutgoing, setOutgoingLength, and sendBytes must be invoked in the correct order; otherwise, the JCRE will throw an APDUException. The following code fragment demonstrates their usages in an applet:

```
public void process(APDU apdu) {

    // receive and process the command APDU
    // ...

    // now ready to send the response data.
    // first set the JCRE to data-send mode and obtain the
```

```
    // expected length of response (Le)
    short le = apdu.setOutgoing();

    // next inform the host that the applet will actually
    // send 10 bytes
    apdu.setOutgoingLength((short)10);

    // prepare the data in the APDU buffer starting at offset 0
    // ...

    // at the end, send data
    apdu.sendBytes((short)0, (short)10);
}
```

If the applet needs to send more data, it can update the APDU buffer with the new data and call sendBytes method repeatedly until all bytes are sent.

To reduce overhead, the APDU class provides the convenient method setOutgoingAndSend for sending the outgoing data:

```
public void setOutgoingAndSend (short bOff, short len)
                                    throws APDUException
```

The setOutgoingAndSend method combines the methods setOutgoing, setOutgoingLength, and sendBytes into one call and implements the following tasks:

- Sets the transfer mode to send.

- Sets the response data length to len.

- Sends the response data bytes from the APDU buffer at the offset bOff.

The setOutgoingAndSend method is analogous to the method setIncomingAndReceive. Both methods set the transfer mode and send or receive data in one call. However, there is a catch using the setOutgoingAndSend method: the data must fit completely in the APDU buffer. In other words, unlike the setIncomingAndReceive method, no more data can be sent; nor can the APDU buffer be altered after the applet calls the setOutgoingAndSend method. Because most response APDUs of an applet encompass a data field that contains no more than a few bytes and fits well into the APDU buffer, the method setOutgoingAndSend provides the most efficient way to send a short response, the way that requires the least protocol overhead.

8.3.5.1 *Sending Data from Other Locations*

The methods sendBytes and setOutgoingAndSend both send data from the APDU buffer. This is convenient if the response data are already in the APDU buffer. If the data are stored in the applet's local buffer or in a file, the applet needs to copy the data into the APDU buffer. To reduce the overhead of moving data, the applet can call the method sendBytesLong:

```
public void sendBytesLong(byte[] outData, short bOff, short len)
                                             throws APDUException
```

The sendBytesLong method sends the len bytes of data at the offset bOff from the byte array outData. Similar to the sendBytes method, the sendBytesLong method can be called repeatedly, but it can be called only if the setOutgoing and setOutgoingLength methods have been invoked first.

8.3.5.2 *Sending a Long Response*

To send a long response, the applet can repeatedly call the sendBytes method or the sendBytesLong method. In fact, both methods can be called in turn to send data from various locations. The following code demonstrates how an applet sends a long response.

```
// the Get_Account_Info command APDU requires the applet to
// send the account holder's name, the account number, and
// the expiration date
// in addition, the applet is required to send the hash value
// computed from the name, the account number, and the
// expiration date to ensure that data are transmitted correctly
//
// the applet stores the account holder's name, the account
// number, and the expiration date in separate byte arrays

private byte[] name;// 20 bytes
private byte[] account_number;  // 9 bytes
private byte[] expiration_date;  // 4 bytes

// after processing the command APDU, the applet now is ready to
// send the response data
// the number of bytes in the response data
// total_bytes = 20 (name) + 9 (account_number) +
//     4 (expiration_date) + 8 (hash value) = 41 bytes
```

```
    short total_bytes = (short)41;

    // step 1:
    // set the data transfer direction to outbound
    short le = apdu.setOutgoing();

    // step 2:
    // inform the host of the actual number of bytes in the response
    apdu.setOutgoingLength(total_bytes);

    // step 3:
    // send the name
    apdu.sendBytesLong(name, (short)0, (short) name.length);

    // send the account number
    apdu.sendBytesLong(account_number, (short)0,
                        (short)account_number.length);

    // send the expiration date
    apdu.sendBytesLong(expiration_date, (short)0,
                        (short)expiration_date.length);

    // now compute the hash value in the APDU buffer.
    // assume the hash value is generated at the offset 0
    // ...

    // send the hash value
    apdu.sendBytes((short)0, HASH_VALUE_LENGTH);

    // now return
    return;
}
```

A response APDU consists of the optional data field followed by the mandatory two-byte status word. The JCRE determines the appropriate status word after
the applet returns from the process method (see Section 8.3.6). To reduce the protocol overhead, the JCRE sends the last part of the response data along with the
status bytes. Normally, the sendBytes method or the sendBytesLong method sends
out data and returns synchronously, so the applet can immediately update the
APDU buffer. However, the applet should not alter the APDU buffer after the last
invocation to such a method. In the preceding code example, the JCRE does not

send the hash value immediately after the last invocation to the sendBytes method. If the applet needs to perform other tasks before returning from the process method, it should leave the APDU buffer intact, or the last portion of data may be corrupted when it is sent out.

8.3.6 Return the Status Word

One invocation to an applet's process method involves exchanging a command APDU and a response APDU between the host and applet. In the process method, the applet first reads the command APDU received, then writes the response data to be sent out. The "end" state is reached by setting the response APDU status word. The status word informs the host of the state of processing the instruction in the command APDU. One of three results may occur at this step.

1. On normal return from the process method, the JCRE automatically sends the normal completion status bytes (0x9000) to the host. For a case 2 or case 4 type command, the JCRE appends the status word to the applet's response data.

2. At any point during the command processing, if an error occurs, the applet terminates the operation and throws an ISOException by invoking the static method ISOException.throwIt(reason). The applet assigns the status word to the parameter reason. If the ISOException is not handled by the applet, it is caught by the JCRE. The JCRE retrieves the reason code and sends it as the status word the same way it sends the normal completion status word 0x9000. The applet can also use the status word to issue a warning that it has completed the command, but a potential problem exists.

   The interface ISO7816 includes most commonly used ISO 7816-4-defined response status words. For example, the constant SW_CLA_NOT_SUPPORTED indicates that the CLA byte in the command APDU is not supported by the applet. The status word constants in the interface ISO7816 provide a convenient way for an applet to specify status words that are compliant with ISO 7816-4 and make the applet code more readable and maintainable.

   Before an exception is thrown, the JCRE may have already been set to the send mode, and data bytes may have been transmitted. To finish the response, the JCRE appends the status word to the data that have been already sent from the applet.

3. If an error is detected by the underlying Java Card system, the behavior of the JCRE is undefined. For example, the JCRE may throw an exception, such as an APDUException or a TransactionException. The JCRE may not implement a handler for each type of exception, or it may not find the reason

code in an exception object it catches. In either case, the JCRE returns
ISO7816.SW_UNKNOWN (0x6F00) without specifying a precise diagnosis. If the
error is more severe, the JCRE may decide to mute the card, block the
applet for execution, or perform any necessary operations to ensure the
security and integrity of the applet and the card.

8.4   Protocol-Specific APDU Processing

In the Java Card platform, applet developers program at the application layer—handling APDUs using the APDU class. The APDU class provides a simplified and common interface to applets regardless of the underlying transport protocol (T=0 or T=1) used. However, some legacy smart card systems were designed employing a specific transport protocol. To be compatible with such systems, applets must use protocol-specific attributes so they can communicate with a large base of installed card acceptance devices. Therefore, the APDU class also defines methods that an applet can use to discover the underlying protocol, to schedule space for receiving and sending data, and to request additional processing time.

This section explains why these methods are defined and how to use them. However, all the methods defined in the APDU class can be used in a protocol-independent way. In other words, knowledge of the transport protocol details is not necessary for using the methods.

Most applet developers can skim through this section or use it as a reference when a special case in programming an applet arises.

8.4.1   Method `getProtocol`

```
public static byte getProtocol()
```

The method `getProtocol` returns the ISO 7816 transport protocol type supported on the Java Card platform. The result can be either `APDU.PROTOCOL_T0` for the T=0 protocol or `APDU.PROTOCOL_T1` for the T=1 protocol.

8.4.2   Method `getInBlockSize`

```
public static short getInBlockSize()
```

The method `getInBlockSize` returns the configured incoming block size. The T=1 protocol is a block-oriented protocol. An APDU command is transmitted in one block or in a few blocks if the chaining mechanism is supported. The chaining mechanism allows a long APDU command to be transmitted in consecutive blocks.

Each block consists of three fields: prologue field, information field, and epilogue field. The prologue field and the epilogue field describe the block, and the information field carries the APDU.

In the T=1 protocol, the block size returned by this method corresponds to the IFSC (information field size on card) parameter. The IFSC specifies the maximum length of the information field in a block that can be accepted by the card. The IFSC value varies from card to card. The default value of IFSC is 32 bytes. This is why the minimum APDU buffer size is set to 37 bytes (5-byte header plus the default IFSC value of 32 bytes). Typically, the APDU buffer is somewhat larger, which allows an applet to reserve a few bytes of data in the APDU buffer and still receive subsequent command data bytes without the risk of overflow.

The T=0 protocol is a byte-oriented protocol. It has no such maximum length requirement and needs to receive only 1 byte at a time. Thus, the `getInBlockSize` method returns 1 for the T=0 protocol.

An applet can use the `getInBlockSize` method in a protocol-independent way to indicate the maximum number of bytes that can be received in the APDU buffer in a single underlying I/O operation. The `receiveBytes` and `setIncomingAndReceive` methods consist of one or more such I/O operations.

In addition, an applet can check `InBlockSize` to ensure that there is enough space remaining in the APDU buffer when the `receiveBytes` method is invoked. For example, to optimize the space usage, an applet may conserve the beginning n bytes in the APDU buffer for storing intermediate data without using a separate buffer. To do so, the applet needs to find out whether the remaining bytes in the APDU buffer are enough to hold at least one block of the data that can be sent by the host.

8.4.3   Method `getOutBlockSize`

```
public static short getOutBlockSize()
```

The `getOutBlockSize` method is analogous to the `getInBlockSize` method. It returns the configured outgoing block size. In the T=1 protocol, this size corresponds to IFSD (information field size for interface device)—the maximum length of the information field in a block that can be accepted by the host. The initial value defined in ISO 7816-3 is 32 bytes. In the T=0 protocol, this method returns 258, accounting for 2 status bytes. Thus the maximum data bytes that can be sent from the applet to the host is 256.

The IFSD specifies the attribute at the host side. Unlike `InBlockSize`, an applet normally does not check `OutBlockSize`. For the T=1 protocol, if the JCRE cannot send all the data in one block—the total number of response data reaches the limit of IFSD—the JCRE can divide the data into blocks and send the blocks by using the chaining mechanism. However, if the underlying T=1 protocol does not support chaining, when the JCRE cannot respond to the host with a large piece of data, it throws an APDUException. The following code sample demonstrates how an applet can work around this limitation when block chaining is not allowed.

```
// a wallet applet stores transaction logs for
// the last three transactions
//
// for simplicity, each log record is stored in a byte array
// and the total log record size is less than 256 bytes
//
// to respond to a READ_TRANSACTION_LOG APDU command, the
// wallet applet sends each transaction log record to the host
//

// check the protocol
if (apdu.getProtocol() == APDU.PROTOCOL_T0) {
    // no problem, the transaction logs can be all sent once
    // ...
} else {
    // get out block size
    short out_block_size = apdu.getOutBlockSize();

    // check if the total log record size is smaller than
    // the out block size
    if (TOTAL_LOG_RECORD_SIZE <= out_block_size) {
        // no problem, send all log records
        apdu.setOutgoingLength(TOTAL_LOG_RECORD_SIZE);
        apdu.sendBytesLong(log_record_1, (short)0,
                        (short)log_record_1.length);
        apdu.sendBytesLong(log_record_2, (short)0,
                        (short)log_record_2.length);
        apdu.sendBytesLong(log_record_3, (short)0,
                        (short)log_record_3.length);
        return;
    } else {
        // send one record, but inform the host that there are
        // more records
        apdu.setOutgoingLength((short)log_record_1.length);
        apdu.sendBytesLong(log_record_1, (short)0,
                        (short)log_record_1.length);
```

```
                // tell the host there are two more log records
                // the host can issue another APDU command
                // to retrieve the remaining records
                ISOException.throwIt(SW_2_MORE_RECORDS);
        }
    }
```

8.4.4   Method `setOutgoingNoChaining`

```
    public short setOutgoingNoChaining() throws APDUException
```

This method is used to set the data transfer direction to outbound without using block chaining and to obtain the expected length of data (the Le field) in the response APDU. Applets should use this method in place of the `setOutgoing` method to be compatible with the EMV specification.

The `setOutgoingNoChaining` method can be used in the same way as the `setOutgoing` method. Once it is invoked, any remaining incoming data are discarded. The applet must invoke the `setOutgoingLength` method to inform the host of the actual number of bytes it will send.

8.4.5   Method `getNAD`

```
    public byte getNAD()
```

In the T=1 protocol, this method returns the node address byte (NAD). The NAD field is the first byte in the prologue field of a T=1 block. The NAD field specifies both the source node address (SAD) and the destination node address (DAD). A smart card system may use NAD to maintain multiple logical connections between the host and the card.

In the T=0 protocol, the `getNAD` method returns 0.

8.4.6   Method `waitExtension`

```
    public byte waitExtension()
```

When the host does not receive any response for an ISO 7816-3-specified maximum time, it considers the card to be unresponsive and times out. An applet calls the `waitExtension` method to request additional processing time from the host so that it does not time out while the applet is performing a long operation (a significant number of EEPROM writes or complex cryptographic operations).

An applet can call the waitExtension method at any time during processing an APDU command. It does not need to call this method if the card has a hardware timer that automatically sends waitExtension to the host.

8.5   Summary

This chapter shows how to process APDUs in applets. The discussion centers on using the methods in the APDU class to examine the APDU header, read command data, and send response data.

Following is a summary of steps that an applet should follow to handle each case of APDU commands. In all cases, the applet can throw an ISOException with the appropriate reason code to flag errors.

Case 1—No command data, no response data

1. The applet's process method is called. The applet examines the first 4 bytes of the APDU buffer and determines that this is a case 1 command. The field P3 (the fifth byte in the APDU buffer) is 0.

2. The applet performs the request specified by the APDU header.

3. The applet returns from the process method.

Case 2—No command data, send response data

1. The applet's process method is called. The applet examines the first 4 bytes of the APDU buffer and determines that this is a case 2 command. The field P3 is interpreted as the Le field.

2. The applet performs the request specified by the APDU header.

3. The applet sends response data. The response can be short or long and is handled differently, based on the data size.

    Short response (the response data fit in the APDU buffer):

    1. The applet calls the setOutgoingAndSend method and specifies the actual response data length.

    2. The applet returns from the process method.

Long response (the response data do not fit in the APDU buffer):

1. The applet calls the setOutgoing method and obtains the Le field.

2. The applet calls the setOutgoingLength method to inform the host of the actual length of the response data.

3. The applet calls the methods sendBytes or sendBytesLong (repeatedly if necessary) to send groups of response bytes.

4. The applet returns from the process method.

Case 3—Receive command data, no response data

1. The applet's process method is called. The applet examines the first 4 bytes of the APDU buffer and determines that this is a case 3 command. The field P3 is interpreted as the Lc field.

2. The applet calls the setIncomingAndReceive method and repeats the call to the receiveBytes method if necessary to receive bytes. Each group of command data bytes is processed or copied to an internal buffer as it is received.

3. The applet returns from the process method.

Case 4—Receive command data, send response data

Case 4 is a combination of cases 3 and 2. First, the applet receives the command data as described for case 3. Next, the applet sends the response data as described for case 2. At the end, the applet returns from the process method.

CHAPTER 9

Applet Firewall
and Object Sharing

The Java Card platform is a multiapplication environment. Multiple applets from different vendors can coexist in a single card, and additional applets can be downloaded after card manufacture. An applet often stores highly sensitive information, such as electronic money, fingerprints, private cryptographic keys, and so on. Sharing such sensitive data among applets must be carefully limited.

In the Java Card platform, applet isolation is achieved through the *applet firewall* mechanism. The applet firewall confines an applet to its own designated area. An applet is prevented from accessing the contents or behaviors of objects owned by other applets.

To support cooperative applications on a single card—for instance, providing wallet, authentication, loyalty, and phone card functions—Java Card technology provides well-defined and secure object sharing mechanisms.

The applet firewall and the sharing mechanisms affect the way you write applets. This chapter explains the behavior of objects, exceptions, and applets in the presence of the firewall and discusses how applets can safely share data by using the Java Card APIs. JCRE implementation details that are not exposed to applets are intentionally ignored.

9.1 Applet Firewall

With applet isolation, the applet firewall provides protection against the most frequently anticipated security concern: developer mistakes and design oversights that might allow sensitive data to be leaked to another applet. It also provides protection against hacking. An applet might be able to obtain an object reference from a publicly accessible location, but if the object is owned by another applet in a different package, the firewall prevents access to the object. Thus, a malfunctioning applet, or even a "hostile" applet, cannot affect the operations of other applets or the JCRE.

9.1.1   Contexts

The applet firewall partitions the Java Card object system into separate protected object spaces called *contexts*. The firewall is the boundary between one context and another. When an applet instance is created, the JCRE assigns it a context. This context is essentially a *group context*. All applet instances of a single Java package share the same group context. There is no firewall between two applet instances in a group context. Object access between applets in the same group context is allowed. However, accessing an object in a different group context is denied by the firewall.

In addition, the JCRE maintains its own *JCRE context*. The JCRE context is a dedicated system context that has special privileges: access from the JCRE context to any applet's context is allowed, but the converse, access from an applet's context to the JCRE context, is prohibited by the firewall. The Java Card object system partitions are illustrated in Figure 9.1.

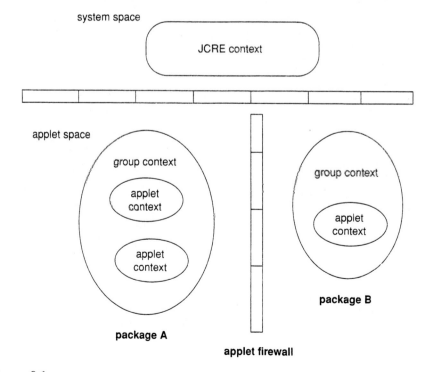

Figure 9.1   The object system partitions on the Java Card platform

9.1.2   Object Ownership

At any time, there is only one *active context* within the virtual machine: either the JCRE context or an applet's group context. When a new object is created, it is assigned an owning context—the currently active context. The object can be accessed from within that context, that is, by all applet instances in its owning context. Also, we say that the object is owned by the active applet in the current context when the object is instantiated. If the JCRE context is the currently active context, the object is owned by the JCRE.

Primitive type static arrays in applets can be initialized when they are declared. Such static arrays are created and initialized by the converter. Because they are statically created before any applet instance is instantiated on the card, the ownership of these arrays can be assigned to any applet instance in their defining package. Any applet within this package can access these arrays. In other words, the owning context of these arrays is the group context of the package.

9.1.3   Object Access

When an object is accessed, the Java language access controls are enforced. For example, a private instance method cannot be invoked from outside the object. In addition, the object's owning context is compared to the currently active context. If the contexts do not match, the access is denied, and the comparison results in a `SecurityException`. For instance, in the examples that follow, assume that object b owned is by context A. The following operations accessing object b from context A' cause the Java Card virtual machine to throw a `SecurityException`:

- Get and set fields:

```
short a = b.field_a;// get object b's field
b.field_a = 5;// set object b's field
```

- Invoke a public instance method:

```
b.virtual_method_a();
```

- Invoke an interface method:

```
b.interface_method_a(); // if b is an interface type
```

- Throw it as an exception:

```
throw b;
```

- Cast it to a given type:

```
(givenType)b;
```

- Determine whether it is of a given type:

```
if (b instanceof givenType)
```

- Access an array element:

```
short a = b[0];// if object b is an array type
b[0] = 5;
```

- Obtain the array length

```
int a = b.length;// if b is an array type
```

9.1.4   Transient Array and Context

Like a persistent object, a transient array of CLEAR_ON_RESET type can be accessed only when the currently active context is the array's owning context.

Transient arrays of CLEAR_ON_DESELECT type are applet-specific resources. They can be created only when the currently active context is the context of the currently selected applet. Because applets from the same package share a group context, a transient array of CLEAR_ON_DESELECT type can also be accessed by all applets in its owning context. However, such access is granted only if one of these applets is the currently selected applet.

9.1.5   Static Fields and Methods

Only instances of classes—objects—are owned by contexts; classes themselves are not. No runtime context check is performed when a static field is accessed or when a static method is invoked. In other words, static fields and methods are accessible from any context. For example, any applet can invoke the static method throwIt in the class ISOException:

```
If (apdu_buffer[ISO7816.OFFSET_CLA] != EXPECTED_VALUE)
    ISOException.throwIt(ISO7816.SW_CLA_NOT_SUPPORTED);
```

Of course, the Java access rules still apply to static fields and methods. For example, static fields and methods with the *private* modifier are visible only to their defining classes.

When a static method is invoked, it executes in the caller's context. This suggests that objects created inside a static method are assigned with the caller's context (the currently active context).

Static fields are accessible from any context. However, objects (including arrays) referenced in static fields are like regular objects. Such objects are owned by the applet (or the JCRE) that created them, and standard firewall access rules apply.

9.2   Object Sharing across Contexts

The applet firewall confines an applet's actions to its designated context. The applet cannot reach beyond its context to access objects owned by the JCRE or by another applet in a different context. But in situations where applets need to execute cooperatively, Java Card technology provides well-defined and secure sharing mechanisms that are accomplished by the following means:

- JCRE privileges
- JCRE entry point objects
- Global arrays
- Shareable interfaces

The sharing mechanisms essentially enable one context to access objects belonging to another context under specific conditions.

9.2.1   Context Switch

Recall that there is only one active context at any time within the execution of the Java Card virtual machine. All object accesses are checked by the virtual machine to determine whether the access is allowed. Normally, such access is denied if the owning context of the object being accessed is not the same as the currently active context. When a sharing mechanism is applied, the Java Card virtual machine enables access by performing a *context switch*.

Members in an object consist of instance methods and fields. Accessing instance fields of an object in a different context does not cause a context switch. Only the JCRE can access instance fields of an object in a different context. Context switches occur only during invocation of and return from instance methods of an object owned by a different context, as well as during exception exits from those methods.

During a context-switching method invocation, the current context is saved, and the new context becomes the currently active context. The invoked method is now executing in the new context and has the access rights of the current context. When the method exits from a normal return or an exception, the original context (the caller's context) is restored as the currently active context. For example, if an applet invokes a method of a JCRE entry point object, a context switch occurs from the applet's context to the JCRE context. Any objects created by the invoked method are associated with the JCRE context.

Because method invocations can be nested, context switches can also be nested in the Java Card virtual machine. When the virtual machine begins running after a card reset, the JCRE context is always the currently active context.

The following sections explore each sharing mechanism and discuss when and how context switch occurs in each access scenario.

9.2.2   JCRE Privileges

In the Java Card platform, the JCRE acts as the card executive. Because it is the "system" context, the JCRE context has special privileges. It can invoke a method on any object or access an instance field of any object on the card. Such system privileges enable the JCRE to control system resources and manage applets. For example, when the JCRE receives an APDU command, it invokes the currently selected applet's `select`, `deselect`, or `process` method.

When the JCRE invokes an applet's method, the JCRE context is switched to the applet's context. The applet now takes control and loses the JCRE privileges. Any objects created after the context switch are owned by the applet and associated with the current applet's context. On return from the applet's method, the JCRE context is restored.

9.2.3   JCRE Entry Point Objects

The JCRE can access any applet contexts, but applets are not allowed to access the JCRE context. A secure computer system must have a way for nonprivileged users (those restricted to a subset of resources) to request system services that are performed by privileged system routines. In the Java Card platform, this requirement is accomplished by using *JCRE entry point objects*.

JCRE entry point objects are normal objects owned by the JCRE context, but they have been flagged as containing entry point methods. Normally, the firewall would completely protect such objects from access by any applets. The entry point designation allows the public methods of such objects to be invoked from any context. When that occurs, a context switch to the JCRE context is performed. Thus, these methods are the gateways through which applets request privileged JCRE services. Notice that only the public methods of JCRE entry point objects are accessible through the firewall. The fields of these objects are still protected by the firewall.

The APDU object is perhaps the most frequently used JCRE entry point object. Chapter 8 explains how applets instruct the JCRE to read or send APDU data by invoking methods on the APDU object.

There are two categories of JCRE entry point objects:

- *Temporary JCRE entry point objects*—Like all JCRE entry point objects, methods of temporary JCRE entry point objects can be invoked from any context. However, references to these objects cannot be stored in class variables, instance variables, or array fields (including transient arrays) of an applet. The JCRE detects and restricts attempts to store references to these objects as part of the firewall functions of preventing unauthorized reuse. The APDU object and all JCRE-owned exception objects are examples of temporary JCRE entry point objects.

- *Permanent JCRE entry point objects*—Like all JCRE entry point objects, methods of permanent JCRE entry point objects can be invoked from any context. Additionally, references to these objects can be stored and freely reused. The JCRE-owned AID instances are examples of permanent JCRE entry point objects. The JCRE creates an AID instance to encapsulate an applet's AID when the applet instance is created.

Only the JCRE itself can designate entry point objects and whether they are temporary or permanent. JCRE implementors are responsible for implementing the JCRE, including the mechanism by which JCRE entry point objects are designated and how they become temporary or permanent.

9.2.4   Global Arrays

JCRE entry point objects allow applets to access particular JCRE services by invoking their respective entry point methods. The data encapsulated in the JCRE entry point objects are not directly accessible by applets. But in the Java Card platform, the global nature of some data requires that they be accessible from any applet and the JCRE context.

To access global data in a flexible way, the firewall allows the JCRE to designate primitive arrays as *global*. Global arrays essentially provide a shared memory buffer whose data can be accessed by any applets and by the JCRE. Because there is only one context executing at any time, access synchronization is not an issue.

Global arrays are a special type of JCRE entry point object. The applet firewall enables public fields (array components and array length) of such arrays to be accessed from any context. Public methods of global arrays are treated the same way as methods of other JCRE entry point objects. The only method in the array class is the `equals` method, which is inherited from the root class `Object`. As does invoking any method of a JCRE entry point object, invoking the `equals` method of a global array causes the current context to be switched to the JCRE context.

Only primitive arrays can be designated as global, and only the JCRE itself can designate global arrays. All global arrays must be temporary JCRE entry point objects. Therefore, references to these arrays cannot be stored in class variables, instance variables, or array components (including transient arrays).

The only global arrays required in the Java Card APIs are the APDU buffer and the byte array parameter in an applet's `install` method. Typically, a JCRE implementation passes the APDU buffer as the byte array parameter to the `install` method. Because global arrays can be viewed and accessed by anyone, the JCRE clears the APDU buffer whenever an applet is selected or before the JCRE accepts a new APDU command, to prevent an applet's sensitive data from being potentially "leaked" to another applet via the global APDU buffer.

9.2.5   Object Shareable Interface Mechanism

To reiterate the sharing mechanisms between the JCRE and applets:

- The JCRE can access any object due to its privileged nature.
- An applet gains access to system services via JCRE entry point objects.
- The JCRE and applets share primitive data by using designated global arrays.

Java Card technology also enables object sharing between applets through the *shareable interface* mechanism.

9.2.5.1 Shareable Interface

A shareable interface is simply an interface that extends, either directly or indirectly, the tagging interface `javacard.framework.Shareable`.

```
public interface Shareable {}
```

This interface is similar in concept to the `Remote` interface used by the RMI facility. Neither interface defines any methods or fields. Their sole purpose is to be extended by other interfaces and to tag those interfaces as having special properties.

A shareable interface defines a set of methods that are available to other applets. A class can implement any number of shareable interfaces and can extend other classes that implement shareable interfaces.

9.2.5.2 Shareable Interface Object

An object of a class that implements a shareable interface is called a *shareable interface object* (SIO). To the owning context, an SIO is a normal object whose fields and methods can be accessed. To any other context, the SIO is an instance of the shareable interface type, and only the methods defined in the shareable interface are accessible. All fields and other methods of the SIO are protected by the firewall.

9.2.5.3 Thoughts behind the Shareable Interface Mechanism

Applets store data in objects. Data sharing between applets means that an applet makes an object it owns available to other applets, thus sharing the data encapsulated in the object.

In the object-oriented world, an object's behavior (aside from direct variable access) is expressed through its methods. Message passing, or method invocation, supports interactions and communications between objects. The shareable interface mechanism enables applets sending messages to bypass the surveillance of the firewall. An owning applet creates a shareable interface object and implements methods defined in the shareable interface. These methods represent the public interface of the owning applet, through which another applet can send messages and consequently access services provided by this applet.

The sharing scenario illustrated in Figure 9.2 can be described as a client/server relationship. Applet A (providing SIOs) is a server, and applets B and C (using the SIOs of applet A) are clients. An applet may be a server to some applets and yet a client of other applets.

In the Java programming language, an interface defines a reference type that contains a collection of method signatures and constants. A client applet views an SIO as having a shareable interface type. The class type of the SIO that implements the shareable interface is not exposed. In other words, only methods defined in the shareable interface are presented to the client applet; instance fields and other methods are not disclosed. In this way, a server applet can provide controlled access to data it wants to share.

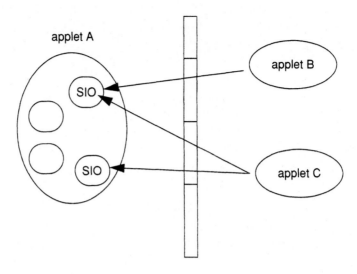

Figure 9.2   Shareable interface object mechanism

When interacting with a different client applet, a server applet could wear a different hat. This would require the server applet to customize its services with respect to the client applet without having the door wide open. A server applet can do so by defining multiple interfaces, each interface declaring methods that are suitable for a group of client applets. If methods in interfaces are distinct, a server applet may choose to create classes, each of which implements an interface. But often services overlap; a server applet can define a class that implements multiple interfaces. Therefore, an SIO of that class can play multiple roles.

9.2.5.4 An Example of Object Sharing between Applets

This section uses a wallet applet and an air-miles applet to provide an example of object sharing between applets. The wallet applet stores electronic cash. The money can be spent to purchase goods.

The air-miles applet provides travel incentives. Similar to the wallet applet, the air-miles applet also stores values—the miles the card holder has traveled. Under a comarketing deal, for every dollar spent using the wallet applet, one air mile is credited to the air-miles applet.

Suppose that the wallet applet and the air-miles applet are in different contexts (they are defined in separate packages). Following are the steps of how they interact in the presence of the firewall.

1. The air-miles applet creates a shareable interface object (SIO).

2. The wallet applet requests the SIO from the air-miles applet.

3. The wallet applet requests miles to be credited by invoking a service method of the SIO.

In this case, the air-miles applet is a server that grants miles on request from the wallet applet (a client), as shown in Figure 9.3.

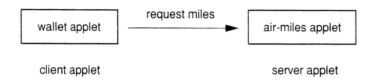

Figure 9.3   Object sharing between the wallet applet and the air-miles applet

Next, how to implement the wallet applet and the air-miles applet is discussed. The code examples are edited for brevity—methods and fields not pertinent to the discussion are omitted, and condition and boundary checks during a transaction are also ignored.

9.2.5.5 Create a Shareable Interface Object

To create an SIO, the server applet (the air-miles applet) must first define a shareable interface that extends javacard.framework.Shareable.

```
package com.fasttravel.airmiles;
import javacard.framework.Shareable;

public interface AirMilesInterface extends Shareable {

    public void grantMiles (short amount);
}
```

Next, the server applet creates a service provider class (a service provider class can be the applet class itself) that implements the shareable interface. The server applet can then create one or more objects of the service provider class and can share such objects (SIOs) with other applets in a different context.

```
package com.fasttravel.airmiles;
import javacard.framework.*;

public class AirMilesApp extends Applet
                          implements AirMilesInterface {

    private short miles;

    public void grantMiles(short amount){

        miles = (short)(miles + amount);
    }
}
```

Before a client can request an SIO, it must find a way to identify the server. In the Java Card platform, each applet instance is uniquely identified by an AID.

Recall from Chapter 7 that when an applet instance is created, it is registered with the JCRE using one of the two register methods. The method with no parameter registers the applet with the JCRE using the default AID defined in the CAP file. The other register method allows the applet to specify an AID other than the default one. The JCRE encapsulates the AID bytes in an AID object (owned by the JCRE) and associates this AID object with the applet. During object sharing, this AID object is used by a client applet to specify the server.

9.2.5.6 Request a Shareable Interface Object

Before requesting an SIO from a server applet, a client applet must first obtain the AID object associated with the server applet. To do that, the client applet calls the lookupAID method in the class JCSystem:

```
public static AID lookupAID
                 (byte[] buffer, short offset, byte length)
```

The client applet must know ahead of time the server applet's AID bytes, and it supplies the AID bytes in the parameter buffer. The lookupAID method returns the JCRE-owned AID object of the server applet or returns null if the server applet is not installed on the card. Because the AID object is a permanent JCRE entry point object, the client applet can request it once and cache it in a permanent location for later use.

Next, the client applet calls the method `JCSystem.getAppletShareableInter-faceObject`, using the AID object to identify the server:

```
public static Shareable
getAppletShareableInterfaceObject(AID server_aid, byte parameter)
```

The second parameter in the method `getAppletShareableInterfaceObject` is interpreted by the server applet. It can be used to select an SIO if the server has more than one available. Alternatively, the parameter can be used as a security token, which carries a secret shared by the server and the client.

In the `getAppletShareableInterfaceObject` method, the JCRE looks up the server applet by comparing the `server_aid` with the AIDs of applets that are registered with the JCRE. If the server applet is not found, the JCRE returns null. Otherwise, the JCRE invokes the server applet's `getShareableInterfaceObject` method.

```
public Shareable
getShareableInterfaceObject(AID client_aid, byte parameter)
```

Notice that, in the `getShareableInterfaceObject` method, the JCRE replaces the first argument with the `client_aid` object and passes along the same parameter byte supplied by the client applet. The server applet uses both parameters to determine whether to provide services to the requesting applet and if so, which SIO to export.

The method `getShareableInterfaceObject` is defined in the base applet class `javacard.framework.Applet`. The default implementation returns `null`. An applet's class must override this method if it intends to share any SIOs. Here is how the air-miles applet implements the `getShareableInterfaceObject` method. (The process to authenticate the client is described in 9.2.5.10.)

```
public class AirMilesApp extends Applet
                    implements AirMilesInterface {

    short miles;
    public Shareable getShareableInterfaceObject(AID client_aid,
                                                byte parameter) {

        // authenticate the client -- explained later
        // ...

        // return the shareable interface object
```

```
        return this;
    }

    public void grantMiles(short amount){

        miles = (short)(miles + amount);
    }
}
```

When the server applet returns the SIO, the JCRE forwards it to the requester—the client applet. The process of requesting a shareable interface object is summarized in Figure 9.4.

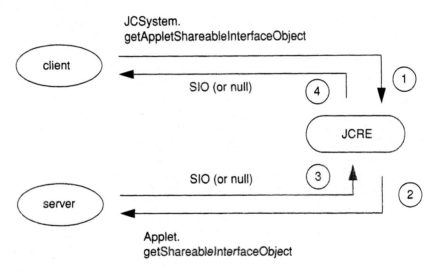

Figure 9.4   Requesting an SIO

9.2.5.7 Use a Shareable Interface Object

To enable a server to return any shareable interface type using a single interface, both methods `JCSystem.getAppletShareableInterfaceObject` and `Applet.getShareableInterfaceObject` have the return type `Shareable`—the base type of all shareable interface objects. A client applet must cast the SIO returned to the appropriate subinterface type and store it in an object reference of that type. For example, the wallet applet casts the SIO to `AirMilesInterface`:

```
AirMilesInterface sio = (AirMilesInterface)
JCSystem.getAppletShareableInterfaceObject(server_aid, parameter);
```

After the client applet receives the SIO, it invokes the shareable interface methods to access services from the server. However, only the methods defined in the shareable interface are visible to the client applet.

For instance, in the preceding code snippet, even though the sio actually points to the air-miles applet (its applet class implements the interface AirMiles-Interface), all instance fields and nonshareable interface methods (such as methods process, select, and deselect) are protected by the firewall.

Following is an example of how the wallet applet requests air miles in a debit transaction.

```
package com.smartbank.wallet;

import javacard.framework.*;
import com.fasttravel.airmiles.AirMilesInterface;

public class WalletApp extends Applet {

    private short balance;
    // hardcoded in the applet or assigned at
    // applet personalization
    private byte[] air_miles_aid_bytes = SERVER_AID_BYTES;


    // called by the process method on receiving
    // a DEBIT APDU command
    private void debit(short amount) {

        if ( balance < amount)
            ISOException.throwIt(SW_EXCEED_BALANCE);

        // update the balance
        balance = (short)(balance - amount);

        // ask the server to grant miles
        requestMiles(amount);
    }


    private void requestMiles(short amount) {

        // obtain the server AID object
```

```
        AID air_miles_aid =
            JCSystem.lookupAID(air_miles_aid_bytes,
                                (short)0,
                                (byte)air_miles_aid_bytes.length);

        if (air_miles_aid == null)
            ISOException.throwIt(SW_AIR_MILES_APP_NOT_EXIST);

        // request the sio from the server
        AirMilesInterface sio = (AirMilesInterface)
        (JCSystem.getAppletShareableInterfaceObject(air_miles_aid,
                                                SECRET));

        if ( sio == null )
            ISOException.throwIt(SW_FAILED_TO_OBTAIN_SIO);

        // ask the server to grant miles
        sio.grantMiles(amount);
    }
}
```

When an error occurs, an applet can throw an `ISOException` by invoking the static method `throwIt` (see the example in the `requestMiles` method). The `throwIt` method throws the JCRE-owned `ISOException` object. Such an object is a JCRE entry point object and can be accessed from any applet's context.

9.2.5.8 Context Switches during Object Sharing

The JCRE, the client applet, and the server applet reside in separate contexts. Context switches must occur to enable object sharing. The client applet calls the `JCSystem.getAppletShareableInterfaceObject` method to request an SIO. An internal mechanism in the method switches the client applet's context to the JCRE context. Then, the JCRE invokes the server applet's `getShareableInterface-Object` method. Such invocation results in another context switch so that the server applet's context becomes current. On return from both methods, the client applet's context is restored.

Next, the client applet can request service from the server applet by invoking one of the shareable interface methods of the received SIO. During the invocation, the Java Card virtual machine performs a context switch. The server applet's context becomes the currently active context.

Because execution is now in the server applet's context, the code gains access to the protected resources of the server applet—instance fields, other methods, and even objects owned by the server applet's context. When the service method completes, the client applet's context is restored. Context switching during object sharing is illustrated in Figure 9.5.

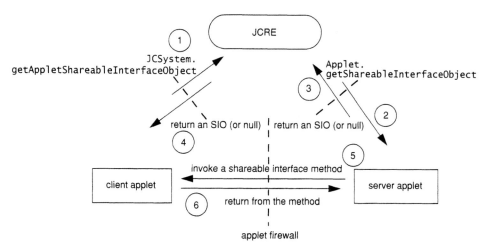

Figure 9.5 Context switch during object sharing

9.2.5.9 Parameter Types and Return Types in Shareable Interface Methods

In the Java programming language, method parameters and return values can be any primitive or reference types. But in the Java Card platform, passing objects (including arrays) as parameters or return values in a shareable interface method is allowed in a limited fashion. For example, if the wallet applet passes one of its own objects as a parameter in the grantMiles method, the firewall prevents the air-miles applet from accessing this object. Likewise, if the air-miles applet returns one of its own objects as a return value, the firewall prevents the wallet applet from accessing this object. Although this may seem annoying, it is actually the applet firewall doing its job.

To avoid this problem, the following types of values can be passed in shareable interface methods as parameters and return values:

- *Primitive values*—These are easily passed on the stack. The primitive types supported in the Java Card platform are boolean, byte, short, and (optionally) int.

- *Static fields*—Public static fields are accessible from any context. However, objects referenced by such static fields are protected by the firewall.

- *JCRE entry point objects*—Public methods of these objects can be accessed from any context.

- *Global arrays*—These can be accessed from any context. For example, the APDU buffer can be used for this purpose.

- *SIOs*—Sharable interface methods of these objects can be accessed from any context. An SIO returned from a client allows the server context to call back into the client context to obtain some service or data. However, the developer should be careful to avoid excessive context switching (which might reduce performance) and deep nesting of context switches (which might use up extra stack space).

The code in the next section provides an example of passing objects and arrays across the firewall.

9.2.5.10 Authenticate a Client Applet

To prevent an unauthorized client from gaining access to protected data, the server applet should authenticate the client applet before granting an SIO and before executing a service method on the SIO.

To determine whether to grant an SIO, a server can check the AID of the requester (the client applet). For instance, the air-miles applet can enforce the following checks in the getShareableInterfaceObject method.

```
public class AirMilesApp extends Applet
                        implements AirMilesInterface {

    public Shareable getShareableInterfaceObject(AID client_aid,
                                        byte parameter) {

        // assume the wallet AID bytes are preknown
        if (client_aid.equals(wallet_app_aid_bytes, (short)0,
            (byte)(wallet_app_aid_bytes.length)) == false)
            return null;

        // examine the secret to further authenticate the
        // wallet applet
        if (parameter != SECRET)
            return null;

        // grant the SIO
        return (this);
    }
}
```

When a shareable interface method is next invoked, the server should verify the client applet again. This precaution is necessary because the client applet that originally requests the SIO could break the contract and share the SIO with a third party without getting the proper permission. The server applet must exclude this scenario to protect sensitive data from an untrusted client. To find out the AID of the actual caller, the server applet can invoke the JCSystem.getPreviousContext-AID method (explained in 9.2.5.11). The code to detect the caller's identity is added to the grantMiles method as follows:

```
public void grantMiles (short amount) {

    // get the caller's AID
    AID client_aid = JCSystem.getPreviousContextAID();

    // check if this method is indeed invoked
    // by the wallet applet
    if (client_aid.equals(wallet_app_aid_bytes, (short)0,
        (byte)(wallet_app_aid_bytes.length)) == false)
        ISOException.throwIt(SW_UNAUTHORIZED_CLIENT);

    // grant miles
    miles = (short)(miles + amount);
}
```

The security of the authentication scheme in the preceding code requires that applet loading be controlled under restricted security measures to avoid applet AID impersonation. Such a scheme may not be sufficient for an applet that requires a higher degree of security. In this case, additional authentication methods must be defined, such as cryptographic exchange.

The following code implements an authentication scheme called challenge-response in the wallet and air-miles applet example. When the service method grantMiles is invoked, the air-miles applet generates a random challenge phrase and sends the challenge to the wallet applet. The wallet applet encrypts the challenge and returns a response to the air-miles applet. By verifying the response, the air-miles applet authenticates the wallet applet and adds requested miles to its balance.

To support this scheme, first, the grantMiles method is updated to take two additional parameters—an authentication object and a buffer.

```
public interface AirMilesInterface extends Shareable {

    public void grantMiles(AuthenticationInterface authObject,
                           byte[] buffer, short amount);
}
```

The air-miles applet authenticates the wallet applet by invoking the challenge method of the authentication object. The buffer is used to pass challenge and response data.

```
public class AirMilesApp extends Applet
                    implements AirMilesInterface {


    public void grantMiles(AuthenticationInterface authObject,
                           byte[] buffer, short amount) {

        // generate a random challenge phrase in the buffer
        generateChallenge(buffer);

        // challenge the client applet
        // the response is returned in the buffer
        authObject.challenge(buffer);

        // check the response
        if (checkResponse(buffer) == false)
            ISOException.throwIt(SW_UNAUTHORIZED_CLIENT);

        miles = (short)(miles + amount);
    }
}
```

Notice that the authentication object is created and owned by the caller—the wallet applet. The applet firewall requires such an object to be an SIO:

```
public interface AuthenticationInterface extends Shareable {

    public void challenge(byte[] buffer);
}

public class WalletApp extends Applet
                    implements AuthenticationInterface {
```

```
public void challenge(byte[] buffer) {

    // get response.
    // both challenge and response data are carried
    // in the buffer
    getResponse(buffer);
}

public void process(APDU apdu) {

    if (getCommand(apdu) == DEBIT)
        debit(apdu);
}

private void debit(APDU apdu) {

    short amount = getDebitAmount(apdu);

    // update the balance
    balance = (short)(balance - amount);

    // ask the air-miles applet to grant miles
    requestMiles(apdu.getBuffer(), amount);
}

private void requestMiles(byte[] buffer, short amount) {

    // obtain the AID object
    AID air_miles_aid =
        JCSystem.lookupAID(air_miles_aid_bytes,
                        (short)0,
                        (byte)air_miles_aid_bytes.length);

    // request the SIO from the air-miles applet
    AirMilesInterface sio = (AirMilesInterface)
    (JCSystem.getAppletShareableInterfaceObject(air_miles_aid,
                                        SECRET));

    // ask the air-miles applet to grant miles
    sio.grantMiles(this, buffer, amount);
}
}
```

In this code example, the buffer used for passing the challenge and response data is the APDU buffer. The APDU buffer is a global array that can be accessed from any context.[1]

9.2.5.11 getPreviousContextAID *Method*

During object sharing, a server can find out the AID of the caller applet by invoking the JCSystem.getPreviousContextAID method:

```
public AID getPreviousContextAID()
```

This method returns the JCRE-owned AID object associated with the applet instance that was active at the time of the last context switch. In the code example on page 123, when the wallet applet calls the shareable interface method grant-Miles, a context switch occurs. The getPreviousContextAID method returns the AID of the wallet applet that was active before the context switch.

Now consider a more complex scenario, as shown in Figure 9.6. Suppose that two applet instances A and B share a group context. No group context switch occurs if applet A calls a method of object b (owned by applet B). This action is allowed regardless of whether object b is an SIO.

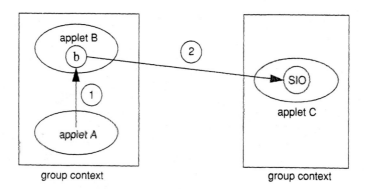

Figure 9.6   Object sharing between applets A, B, and C

Now when object b accesses an SIO of applet C, execution moves into a new context. The active applet at the last context switch was applet B, and thus, the getPreviousContextAID method returns the AID of applet B.

---

[1] Even so, there are still limitations in using the APDU buffet to pass structured data. For example, data being passed may not be of the appropriate length or type for the APDU buffer. Both the server and the client may need to put considerable effort to manipulate the APDU buffer.

9.2.5.12 Summary

To conclude, the process of sharing objects between a server applet and a client applet is summarized.

1. If a server applet A wants to share an object with another applet, it first defines a shareable interface SI. A shareable interface extends the interface javacard. framework.Shareable. The methods defined in the shareable interface SI represent services that applet A wishes to make accessible to other applets.

2. Applet A then defines a service provider class C that implements the shareable interface SI. C provides actual implementations for the methods defined in SI. C may also define other methods and fields, but these are protected by the applet firewall. Only the methods defined in SI are accessible to other applets.

3. Applet A creates an object instance O of class C. O belongs to applet A, and the firewall allows A to access the fields and methods of O.

4. If a client applet B wants to access applet A's object O, it invokes the JCSystem.getAppletShareableInterface method to request a shareable interface object from applet A.

5. The JCRE searches its internal applet table for applet A. When found, it invokes applet A's getShareableInterfaceObject method.

6. Applet A receives the request and determines whether it wants to share object O with applet B. If applet A agrees to share with applet B, A responds to the request with a reference to O.

7. Applet B receives the object reference from applet A, casts it to type SI, and stores it in object reference SIO. Even though SIO actually refers to A's object O, SIO is of type SI. Only the shareable interface methods defined in SI are visible to B. The firewall prevents the other fields and methods of O from being accessed by B. Applet B can request service from applet A by invoking one of the shareable interface methods of SIO.

8. Before performing the service, the shareable interface method can authenticate the client (B) to determine whether to grant the service.

CHAPTER **10**

Programming Cryptography

In addition to their uses as secure data storage and data processing devices, smart cards can act as proof of authorization and as encryption modules. For such applications, the cryptographic functions in smart cards become of central importance.

This chapter discusses programming cryptography in Java Card applets. It is organized in four sections. First, a quick tour of cryptography introduces many important cryptographic concepts and algorithms. Second, the use of cryptography in smart card applications is discussed and analyzed. Third, the cryptographic APIs in the Java Card platform are covered. Finally, code examples demonstrate how to use Java Card cryptographic APIs for generating a random number, for computing and verifying a message digest or a signature, and for encrypting and decrypting data in applets.

10.1 Quick Tour of Cryptography

Cryptography is the art and science of secret writing to keep messages secure. It concerns the encoding and decoding of information. *Cryptoanalysis* is the reverse of cryptography. It is the art and science of breaking secretly encoded information. The term *cryptology* (or *crypto*, for short) refers to a branch of mathematics that encompasses both cryptography and cryptoanalysis.

Although cryptography by itself does not guarantee security, systems and programs often can benefit from the use of cryptography. When applied correctly, cryptography provides the following security objectives:

- *Confidentiality* ensures privacy. It prevents unauthorized people from viewing the secret data.

- *Integrity* ensures correctness. It means that the original data cannot be changed or substituted without your knowledge.

- *Authentication* ensures true identity. It ascertains that people with whom you electronically communicate are really who they claim they are.

This section explains the basic cryptographic concepts that are necessary to understand how to use the Java Card cryptography APIs. For readers who want a deep understanding of cryptographic theories, a good reference is *Applied Cryptography* by Bruce Schneier.[12]

10.1.1 Encryption and Decryption

A common method to protect secret information is to encrypt it at the sending end and decrypt it at the receiving end. A message is plaintext (sometimes called cleartext). Encryption is the process of disguising a message to hide its substance [12]. The encrypted message is called ciphertext. Decryption is the reverse process of encryption. It takes the ciphertext and translates it back into the original plaintext. The encryption and decryption process is illustrated in Figure 10.1. The mathematical algorithm that is applied to perform the transformation is called a cipher. Generally, there are two related algorithms: one for encryption and one for decryption.

Useful ciphers apply keys to encrypt or decrypt data. Conceptually, you can think of a key as a secret value, like a password or a bank card PIN. In practice, a key is just a sequence of numbers. A key is a parameter to the mathematical formula of the cipher, so that if you encrypt the same plaintext using different keys, you will get different ciphertext. Conversely, the plaintext can be recovered from the ciphertext by using the proper key. Using keys in a cipher allows you to publish the cryptographic algorithm without losing security. The secrecy of encoded data is achieved through holding a secret key.

There are two general types of key-based ciphers: symmetric and asymmetric ciphers. *Symmetric ciphers* are algorithms of which the encryption key can be calculated from the decryption key and vice versa. In most cases, the encryption key is the decryption key, so you can apply the same key to encode and decode data.

The most commonly used symmetric ciphers are DES and DESede. DES stands for Data Encryption Standard, a worldwide standard for 20 years. DES

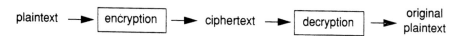

Figure 10.1 Encryption and decryption

keys are 56 bits in size (stored in 8 bytes). Both encryption and decryption are performed using the same key.

DESede is better known as triple DES. It results from three cipher operations connected in a chain with alternating encryption and decryption, as shown in Figure 10.2.

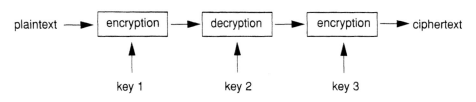

Figure 10.2 DESede encryption process

Decryption of DESede ciphertext is accomplished by reversing the order of operation, that is, decryption-encryption-decryption (Figure 10.3).

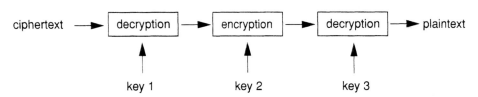

Figure 10.3 DESede decryption process

Instead of using one 8-byte key as in a DES cipher, DESede applies three keys. So it is considerably more secure than DES. DESede comes in several variations, according to the choices of keys. One version uses three distinct DES keys. Another version uses a double-size key, where key 1 and key 3 in the DESede algorithm are identical. If all three keys are equal, the security of DESede is identical to DES.

Symmetric ciphers require all the participants to store and distribute the only secret key properly. If the key is discovered by others, the entire system can easily be broken.

Asymmetric ciphers are designed to address the deficiencies of symmetric ciphers. These ciphers employ two different keys: a public key, which can be publicly distributed, and a private key, which is held secretly.

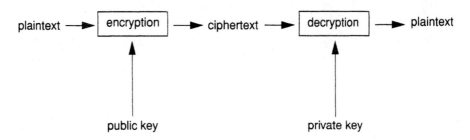

Figure 10.4 Asymmetric cipher encryption and decryption

As shown in Figure 10.4, a complete stranger can use the public key, which is available to anyone, to encrypt a message, but only authorized people with the matching private key can decrypt the message. In many asymmetric cipher algorithms, the reverse process also works. That is, a message can be encrypted by using a private key and decrypted by anyone using a public key.

The RSA algorithm—named after its three inventors, Ronald Rivest, Adi Shamir, and Leonard Adleman—is the best known and most versatile asymmetric algorithm currently in use.

Of course, there is never a free lunch. Computationally speaking, asymmetric ciphers are much more processor intensive than symmetric ciphers, so typically they are not used to encrypt long messages. Many security protocols combine symmetric and asymmetric ciphers. An example of this is the SSL (Secure Socket Layer) protocol, which is supported in most Web browsers. At the beginning of an SSL conversation, all the participants exchange data to agree on a session key. The data exchanged initially are encrypted using an asymmetric cipher and are typically not voluminous. Next, the session key is used in a symmetric cipher for encrypting and decrypting the remaining conversation. As its name implies, the useful lifetime of a session key is only one session. The session key is no longer valid when the conversation is over. To start a new conversation, all the participants need to agree on a new session key.

Encryption technology (using either symmetric or asymmetric ciphers) scrambles data into a secret format. Only authorized people with computational assistance can decode the data. When used correctly, encryption ensures confidentiality. Encryption can also be used in conjunction with message digests to ensure integrity and to establish authentication.

10.1.2 Message Digest

Message digests are secure one-way hash functions that take arbitrary-size data and output a fixed-length hash value, as shown in Figure 10.5. A hash function is designed so that it is easy to compute a hash value but difficult to reverse the computation. Also, the function is designed so that it is rare to compute the same hash from two different streams of input data.

Based on these properties, the message digest is an important mechanism to help achieve data integrity. Typically, the sender sends a message digest along with the data. The receiver computes a message digest from the data received and compares it to the digest received. Any discrepancy would indicate either a man-in-the-middle attack or a data transmission error.

Two popular hash functions in use today are MD5 and SHA-1. MD5 was published by Ronald Rivest in 1990/1991. It is based on an earlier algorithm, MD4. Both MD4 and MD5 generate a 128-bit hash value. SHA, standing for secure hash algorithm, produces a message digest that is 160 bits long. It was first published by NIST in 1992. After the discovery of certain weaknesses, an improved algorithm was developed, known as SHA-1. Today, the terms SHA and SHA-1 are used to mean the same algorithm.

A message digest can be used to verify the integrity of the data. However, if the hash function is known in advance, anyone could compute the hash value from the data. This puts message digest in a position vulnerable to a man-in-the-middle attack. An intruder can intercept the data and the message digest and replace them with new data and the computed message digest of the new data. If that occurs, the receiver has no way of detecting that the data have been changed.

A variant of the one-way hash function has been developed that requires a key. It produces a hash value based on both its input data and the key. This scheme is referred to as message authentication code, or MAC for short. Typically, a MAC is computed by encrypting the data using a symmetric cipher with a given key. A MAC can be verified if the key is known to both the sender and the receiver.

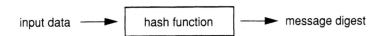

Figure 10.5 Compute a message digest

10.1.3   Digital Signature

A digital signature is computed by encrypting a message digest using an asymmetric cipher. It can help to verify the identity of the person who sends the data as well as the integrity of the data.

The sender computes the message digest from the data she prepares to send and signs it by encrypting the message digest with her own private key. The encrypted message digest is called a signature. Figure 10.6 illustrates the signing process.

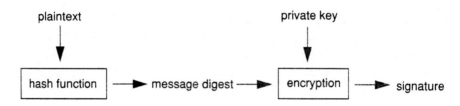

Figure 10.6   Generate a signature

The sender then sends both the actual data and the signature to the recipient. The receiver verifies the signature by first decrypting it with the sender's public key. This leaves her with the message digest. Then the receiver can compute the message digest from the data received and compare the two message digests. If both values match, the receiver can verify that the data are indeed from the sender and have not been altered during transmission. (See Figure 10.7.)

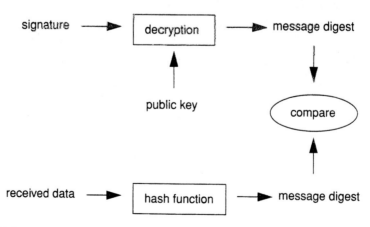

Figure 10.7   Verify a signature

10.1.4 Random Data

Random numbers are crucial in cryptography. Typically, they are added to the input data as padding to ensure the uniqueness of a session during authentication or to generate secure cryptographic keys. The security of these cryptographic procedures relies on random numbers that cannot be predicted.

A true random number should not be influenced by external conditions, such as temperature and supply voltage. Some computers use a hardware-based random number generator, which measures an unstable electronic circuit or radioactive decay or other random physical process and thus can achieve independence of external effects. Such hardware may not always be available or practical. Therefore, computers have to fall back on software algorithms. The result is pseudo-random number generators that can produce randomized output good enough for most usage. Pseudo-random number generators use deterministic algorithms. To generate random numbers, they are initialized, or "seeded," using a random number, such as the current time. If the algorithm and the initial values are known, the random numbers are predictable. That's why such random numbers are termed pseudo-random.

10.2 Cryptographic Practice in Smart Card Applications

Loosely speaking, there are two motivations for smart card applications to use cryptography:

- To ensure application security and to ensure data communication security between the card and the host

- To function as a secure token through which the security of other systems can be enhanced

10.2.1 Ensuring Application Security

Consider a wallet applet that stores electronic currency. The first challenge in building a secure applet is authentication. For example, the wallet must verify the merchant to whom it pays money. And just as important, it must confirm that money added to the wallet's balance is from a legitimate source. Often mutual authentication is required. Both the wallet in the smart card and the entity on the host side can apply cryptographic authentication mechanisms to ensure that they talk to the authorized party.

Second, confidentiality of sensitive data must be protected. For example, in a debit or a credit transaction, the data exchanged between the applet and the host might contain a sum of money in digital format, the bank account number, the password to access the account, and so forth. To ensure privacy, data can be encrypted before transmitting over the wire and decrypted at the receiving end. Sometimes it is necessary to store on-card data in encrypted format to prevent someone from breaking into the card.

Third, it is equally important to guarantee data integrity. When transferring money from a bank account to an electronic purse, you do not want someone to snoop on transmission, realize it involves money, and transfer half the amount (if you are lucky) to his own account and leave the other half for you. To help prevent this during an APDU exchange, a calculated MAC is placed after the actual data in an APDU, as shown in Figure 10.8. The MAC value is computed from the actual data. To protect privacy, the MAC can be computed after the actual data are first encrypted.

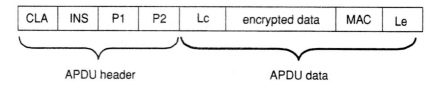

Figure 10.8   APDU command with a MAC

10.2.2   Functioning as a Secure Token

Smart cards are ideally suited to act as proof of authorization and as encryption modules when running inside host appliances, such as cell phones or set top boxes or in a network environment[1]. When used in such applications, cryptography is applied to implement functional requirements. For example, an authentication application could hold a secret (for example, a cryptographic key) shared with a network server. When the card holder requests network access, the server generates a challenge in the format of random data and sends these data in plaintext to the card. Then the application inside the card encrypts the challenge and responds to the server with the ciphertext. The server decrypts the encrypted data and compares them with the challenge that it generated earlier. If there is a match, the server grants network access to the card holder. This authentication scheme is known as challenge and response. A real implementation of a challenge and response scheme requires more robustness than the simple concept described in this section to prevent security attacks.

10.2.3 Summary

When designing a security strategy, it is important to consider the available computing resources on the card. In general, it is not feasible to deploy computationally expensive cryptographic mechanisms on voluminous data in the card. Also, it is important to realize that a cryptographically empowered applet does not guarantee a secure one. The security of an applet must be evaluated in the context of the overall security of the system infrastructure, in addition to considering the benefits of correctly applying cryptography. The system infrastructure consists of the card, the host machine, and—in a broader sense—the entire network that these machines are connected to. Therefore, when designing an applet, you must consider many factors in the entire system to decide whether cryptography is suitable for the application and if so, which cryptographic mechanisms are the most appropriate.

For further reading on use of cryptography in smart cards, such books as *Smart Card Developer's Kit* by Guthery and Jurgensen[2], *Smart Card Handbook* by Rankl and Effing[1], and *Smart Card Security and Applications* by Hendry[13] provide extensive discussion on the subject.

10.3 Java Card Cryptography APIs

Java Card cryptography APIs (called the crypto APIs for short) have been significantly revised in Java Card version 2.1 to meet United States export regulatory requirements and to supply an extensible and flexible feature set.

Java Card crypto APIs are modeled after the Java Cryptography Architecture (JCA)[11]. The goal is to be closely aligned with the Java platform.

10.3.1 Design Principles

The crypto APIs are designed around these principles:

- Implementation independence and interoperability
- Algorithm independence and extensibility

Implementation independence and algorithm independence are complementary. The aim is to let users of the APIs utilize cryptographic services, such as digital signatures and message digests, without concern for the implementations or even the algorithms being used to implement these services. Implementation interoperability allows applets written using the crypto APIs to be interoperable on all Java Card platform implementations that have the correct set of cryptography support.

Algorithm extensibility means that additional cryptographic algorithms can be added to the APIs and that the existing algorithms can easily be removed from the APIs. Such changes require only a minor version revision; thus the new API implementations will be compatible with the previous implementations.

10.3.2 Architecture

The architecture of the crypto APIs is designed to reflect the design principles through the following mechanisms:

- Separating interface and implementation
- Making extensive use of factory methods
- Standardizing names for specifying cryptographic algorithms
- Defining lightweight APIs

The Java Card crypto APIs (most are abstract classes and interfaces) define types of cryptographic services and the interface to access the services. A JCRE provider extends a base class in the APIs to provide an implementation for a particular cryptographic service or to implement an interface to provide a symmetric or an asymmetric key implementation. For example, to provide the hashing function using the MD5 algorithm, a JCRE provider can create an implementation class `MessageDigestMD5` that extends from the `MessageDigest` class in the APIs. The class `MessageDigestMD5` overrides the methods in the base class to implement the MD5 hashing algorithm.

Without knowing the actual name of an implementation class and where to locate it, applets use factory methods to request a crypto service object. For example, to request a message digest using the MD5 algorithm, you will write code like this:

```
MessageDigest md5;
md5 = MessageDigest.getInstance(MessageDigest.ALG_MD5, false);
```

The real instance returned from a factory method is typically some descendant of the class you ask for. In the example, an instance of `MessageDigestMD5` may be returned. However, in your program this does not matter. You treat it as a message digest and work with interface methods in the base class. As a result, the applet is not tied to a particular implementation.

To support factory methods, there must be a naming convention that an applet can use to specify an algorithm along with parameters of the algorithm. This naming convention is achieved through selection parameters. Selection parameters are essentially constants that specify a standard name for each cryptographic algorithm or for each cryptographic key type and key length. In the message digest example, the constant `MessageDigest.ALG_MD5` is a selection parameter that specifies the MD5 algorithm.

In addition, selection parameters provide a flexible way to extend cryptographic algorithms and services. In the future, as new cryptographic algorithms are developed and employed by applets, such algorithms can be easily supported by adding their names to the set of algorithm selection parameters. A JCRE implementation can support the newly added algorithms by providing their implementations. Because only constants are added or removed from the APIs, supporting additional algorithms requires only a minor version revision; the newer API implementations will be compatible with the previous implementations.

By separating interface from implementation, the crypto APIs are lightweight in code size while supporting an extensible set of cryptographic services. Depending on the available memory on a card, a particular JCRE implementation may choose to implement all, some, or none of the possible algorithms. However, this imposes a requirement on you, the applet developer. You do have to know the types of cryptographic services supported in the cards on which your applets will be running. The JCRE will throw a `CryptoException` if a targeted cryptographic service or an algorithm of the service is not available on a card.

10.3.3 Package Structure

The Java Card crypto APIs are structured into two packages: `javacard.security` and `javacardx.crypto`. This factoring mirrors that of the JCA and represents a separation of functionality between cryptographic mechanisms not subject to export control and those classified as allowing strong encryption.

The `javacard.security` package consists of various interfaces for implementing symmetric and asymmetric keys, the key builder class, the authentication classes (message digest and signature), and the class for generating random data. The interfaces and classes in the `javacard.security` package are shown in Table 10.1.

The package `javacardx.crypto` is an extension. It contains the `cipher` class, which allows the use of strong encryption, and the `KeyEncryption` interface for enabling a key implementation to access the encrypted key data. The classes in the `javacardx.crypto` package (see Table 10.2) are subject to export control.

Table 10.1 `javacard.security` package

Class or Interface	Description
Key	Base interface for all keys
SecretKey	Base interface for keys used in symmetric algorithms
DESKey	Represents an 8/16/24 byte key for DES or two-key triple DES or three-key triple DES
PrivateKey	Base interface for private keys used in asymmetric algorithms
PublicKey	Base interface for public keys used in asymmetric algorithms
RSAPrivateKey	Used to sign data using the RSA algorithm in the modulus/exponent form
RSAPrivateCrtKey	Used to sign data using the RSA algorithm in the Chinese Remainder Theorem form
RSAPublicKey	Used to verify signatures on signed data using the RSA algorithm
DSAKey	Base interface for the DSA algorithm private and public key implementations
DSAPrivateKey	Used to sign data using the DSA algorithm
DSAPublicKey	Used to verify signature using the DSA algorithm
KeyBuilder	Factory class to generate a key object
MessageDigest	Abstract base class for hashing algorithms
Signature	Abstract base class for signature algorithms
RandomData	Abstract base class for random data generation
CryptoException	Represents a cryptography-related exception

Table 10.2 `javacardx.crypto` package

Class or Interface	Description
Cipher	Provides the functionality of a cryptographic cipher for encryption and decryption. The class `Cipher` is an abstract base class.
KeyEncryption	Enables a key implementation to access the encrypted key data.

10.4   Code Examples

This section provides code examples to demonstrate how to generate a message digest, how to build a cryptographic key, how to compute and verify a signature, how to encrypt and decrypt data in applets, and how to use the RandomData class.

10.4.1   Compute a Message Digest

A message digest is a unique and reliable hash of the message that lets the receiver know that the message received is the exact same message that was sent.

The first step for computing a digest is to create a message digest object. To do so, you will call the factory method getInstance of the MessageDigest class.

```
public static MessageDigest
        getInstance(byte algorithm, boolean externalAccess)
```

The parameter algorithm specifies a desired algorithm using one of the algorithm selection parameters. Java Card 2.1 APIs support three possible algorithms: SHA1, MD5, and RIPE MD-160. Their corresponding selection parameters are named ALG_SHA, ALG_MD5, and ALG_RIPEMD160.

The second parameter, externalAccess, is specifically designed for the Java Card environment. As described in Chapter 9, when a message digest object is created, it can be accessed by the currently active applet and any applets from the same package. An applet defined in a different package may access the message digest object via a shareable interface method. If the externalAccess parameter is set to false (meaning that the returned message digest object is not intended for external access), the message digest object can be accessed only by applets in its owning context and when one of these applets is the currently selected applet.[1]

---

[1] For readers who want to dig into this subject further: when set to false, the externalAccess parameter essentially allows the message digest implementation to use applet-specific resources, such as CLEAR_ON_DESELECT transient arrays. A CLEAR_ON_DESELECT array is accessible only by applets in its owning context and when one of these applets is the currently selected applet. The access scope of transient arrays is discussed in (Section 9.1.4). By default, you should set the externalAccess parameter to false. This allows the message digest implementation to optimize RAM usage by using CLEAR_ON_DESELECT type RAM space.

If an applet needs to use a message digest instance across multiple CAD sessions, it should not call the getInstance method when such an object is needed. Instead, it should request a message digest instance in the applet's constructor and store it in a permanent location (such as in an instance field) so that it can be used in another session. This prevents a potential memory leak when a garbage collector is not available on the card. The following example shows how to compute a message digest using the SHA algorithm.

```
public class MyApp extends Applet {

    private MessageDigest sha;

    public MyApplet() {
        sha = MessageDigest.getInstance(MessageDigest.ALG_SHA,
false);
        ...
    }
}
```

Next, suppose that you have three byte arrays, m1, m2, and m3, which form the total input whose message digest you want to compute. You should calculate the digest via the following calls:

```
// feed the entire data in byte array m1 to message digest
    sha.update(m1, (short)0, (short)(m1.length));
    // feed 8 more bytes of data from byte array m2 starting
    // at offset 0
sha.update(m2, (short)0, (short)8);
    // send the entire data in byte array m3 as the last batch
    // and store the hash value in byte array digest starting
    // at offset 0
sha.doFinal(m3, (short)0, (short)(m3.length), digest, (short)0);
```

The method update allows you to feed the input data cumulatively to generate a digest. But when you get to the last batch of data, you should call the doFinal method. This informs the message digest that it is the end of the input data and that the system should perform final operations, such as padding. The doFinal method completes and returns the hash computation in the specified output array. In the example, it writes the hash value at the beginning of the byte array `digest`. In the `doFinal` method, the output data can overlap with the input data, so you can reuse the byte array `m3` for output.

```
sha.doFinal(m3, (short)0, (short)(m3.length), m3, (short)0);
```

After the call to the `doFinal` method is made, the message digest object is automatically reset. Thus it can be used to compute new values.

If all the input data fit in a byte array, you should skip the `update` method and call only the `doFinal` method. Because the `update` method uses temporary storage for intermediate hash results, it should be used only if all the input data required for the hash cannot be contained in a byte array.

Note: Because the `update` method may result in additional resource consumption or slow performance, use only the `doFinal` method whenever possible.

At any point during the hash computation and before the `doFinal` method is called, you can call the `reset` method to ignore the previous input and reset the initial state for a new computation.

The `MessageDigest` class also defines two query methods that an applet can invoke on the message digest instance. The method `getAlgorithm` returns the particular algorithm used in the implementation of the instance, and the method `getLength` returns the number of bytes in the hash value of that algorithm.

10.4.2 Build a Cryptographic Key

A cryptographic key is a secret value that is supplied to a cipher algorithm for data encryption and decryption. The Java Card cryptography APIs define an extensive set of interfaces for implementing both symmetric and asymmetric keys. To build a key, you will call the factory method `buildKey` of the `KeyBuilder` class:

```
public static Key buildKey
          (byte keyType, short keyLength, boolean keyEncryption);
```

The class KeyBuilder defines a set of selection parameters that you can choose to select a key type and a key length. For example, to create an RSA private key of 64 bytes in length (64 * 8 = 512 bits), you call the buildKey method like this:

```
Key rsa_private_key;
rsa_private_key = KeyBuilder.buildKey(KeyBuilder.TYPE_RSA_PRIVATE,
                                      KeyBuilder.LENGTH_RSA_512,
                                      false);
```

The method buildKey returns an object of the Key interface type. The real type of the object is a class that implements the key interface of the requested key type. In the example, the key implementation class should implement the RSAPrivateKey interface. To be able to invoke methods in the interface RSAPrivateKey, you cast the key object to RSAPrivateKey:

```
RSAPrivateKey rsa_private_key;
rsa_private_key = (RSAPrivateKey)KeyBuilder.buildKey
                            (KeyBuilder.TYPE_RSA_PRIVATE,
                             KeyBuilder.LENGTH_RSA_512,
                             false);
```

The buildKey method returns a key object with the requested key type, but the key object is not initialized.

For an RSA private key,[2] the key is initialized and ready for use when both the modulus and exponent of the key are set. To set them, you call the setModulus and setExponent methods in the RSAPrivateKey interface:

```
public void setExponent(byte[] buffer, short offset, short length)
public void setModulus(byte[] buffer, short offset, short length)
```

To initialize a DES key, for example, you call the setKey method in the DESKey interface:

```
public void setKey(byte[] keyData, short kOff)
```

The key data are specified in the array keyData starting at the offset kOff. After returning from the setKey method, an applet does not need to retain the data in the keyData array, as the data are copied into an internal buffer.

For security reasons, a key might be initialized with the encrypted key data. In such a case, the key object must be associated with a cipher object, which can then

---

[2] An RSA public key is initialized in the same way.

decrypt the key data internally. You might have noticed that the `buildKey` method takes a third parameter, `keyEncryption`, in addition to `keyType` and `keyLength`. If this parameter is set to be `true`,[3] the key implementation is required to implement the interface `javacardx.crypto.KeyEncryption`. The `KeyEncryption` interface defines the `setKeyCipher` method and the `getKeyCipher` method.

If the key object is associated with a cipher object via the method `setKeyCipher`, the input key data should be provided in ciphertext. Otherwise, if the key object does not implement the `KeyEncryption` interface or if the associated cipher object is set to `null`, the input data should be provided in plaintext.

In any case, when you want to retrieve the key data later by invoking a get method, the key data are returned in plaintext. For example, the `getKey` method in the `DESKey` interface returns a plaintext DES key.

10.4.3 Sign and Verify a Signature

A signature (digital signature) provides two security services: authentication and integrity. The class `javacard.security.Signature` is designed to be used in a style similar to that of the `MessageDigest` class. To create a `Signature` object, you call the factory method `getInstance` of the class `Signature`:

```
Signature signature;
signature = Signature.getInstance(Signature.ALG_DSA_SHA, false);
```

To specify an algorithm, one of the algorithm selection parameters defined in the `Signature` class can be used. An algorithm selection parameter specifies both the message digest and the encryption algorithm. The `Signature` class supports an extensive set of possible signature algorithms. The example signs and verifies a SHA digest, using the DSA algorithm. The second parameter, `externalAccess`, indicates whether the `Signature` object returned can be accessed externally by a context other than its owning context. (See the parameter `externalAccess` in the `buildKey` method of the `KeyBuilder` class.)

Because a signature uses a key, you need to first initialize the `Signature` object. To do so, you call one of two `init` methods.

```
public void init (Key theKey, byte theMode);
public void init (Key theKey, byte theMode,
                  byte[] bArray, short bOff, short bLen);
```

---

[3] The key implementation class may implement the `javacardx.crypto.KeyEncryption` interface even when this parameter is `false`.

In an asymmetric algorithm, signing and verification do not use the same key. Therefore, you need to specify how the key is used in the second parameter the-Mode. There are two modes, as defined in the class Signature:

- MODE_SIGN—indicate sign mode

- MODE_VERIFY—indicate verify mode

The second init method also allows you to specify the algorithm initialization data in the byte array bArray. An example of initialization data is the initial vector (IV) for DES and triple DES in the CBC mode.[4]

To compute a signature, you first feed the data using the update method. As you feed the last batch of the data, call the sign method. Here is a code example that computes a signature from data in the arrays s1, s2 and s3.

```
// feed the data in byte array s1
signature.update(s1, (short)0, (short)(s1.length));
// feed the data in byte array s3 as the last batch
// and generates the signature in array sig_buffer
// starting at offset 0
signature.sign(s2, (short)0, (short)(s2.length), sig_buffer,
               (short)0);
```

To verify a signature, you first feed the same input data using the update method. As you feed the last batch of data, call the verify method. The verify method verifies the computed signature from the input data against the one provided. If both match, it returns true. The following example shows how to verify the signature computed in the preceding example:

```
signature.update(s1, (short)0, (short)(s1.length));

// feed the last batch of data in array s3
// and verify the computed signature against the
// sig_buffer contains the given signature
```

---

[4] CBC (cipher block chaining) mode adds a feedback mechanism to a block cipher (a block of plaintext encrypts into a block of ciphertext). In CBC mode, the results of the encryption of previous blocks are fed back into the encryption of the current block. The initial vector is fed into the encryption of the first block. CBC mode should not be confused with MODE_SIGN and MODE_VERIFY parameters in the Signature class. They are used to specify whether the key is initialized for signing or for verification.

```
if (signature.verify(s2, (short)0, (short)(s2.length),
        sig_buffer, sig_offset, sig_length) != true)
{
    ISOException.throwIt(SW_WRONG_SIGNATURE);
}
```

Similar to methods in the `MessageDigest` class, the `update` method should be used only if all the input data do not fit in a byte array. After the call to the `sign` or `verify` method is made, the `Signature` object is reset to the state after it was previously initialized via a call to the `init` method. Also in the `sign` method, the input data and the output signature data can use the same array, and data may overlap. The `getAlgorithm` and `getLength` query methods are also defined in the class `Signature`.

10.4.4 Encrypt and Decrypt Data

Encryption is a tool for protecting data privacy. Encryption scrambles data that exist in plaintext and transforms them into ciphertext. Decryption recovers the original plaintext from the ciphertext.

The `javacardx.crypto.Cipher` class provides both encryption and decryption services with symmetric or asymmetric algorithms. Similarly to the classes `MessageDigest` and `Signature`, you call the factory method `getInstance` and supply two parameters to create a `Cipher` object. The first parameter specifies a cipher algorithm. The second parameter, `externalAccess`, indicates whether the `Cipher` object returned can be accessed externally by a context other than its owning context (see the `keyBuilder` class).

Then you initialize the `Cipher` object with an appropriate key and specify whether the key is used for encryption or for decryption. To do so, you call one of the two `init` methods:

```
public void init (Key theKey, byte theMode);
public void init (Key theKey, byte theMode,
                  byte[] bArray, short bOff, short bLen);
```

The following example creates a `Cipher` object with the DES algorithm in CBC mode. The input data will not be padded. The `Cipher` object is initialized with a DES key for encryption:

```
Cipher cipher;
cipher = Cipher.getInstance(Cipher.ALG_DES_CBC_NO_PAD, false);
cipher.init(des_key, Cipher.MODE_ENCRYPT);
```

You can also initialize the Cipher object for decryption by choosing the selection parameter as MODE_DECRYPT, which specifies the key supplied in the init method is for decryption,

Next, to encrypt data, use the update method and the doFinal method:

```
public short update(byte[] inBuf, short inOffset, short inLength,
                byte[] outBuff, short outOffset);

public short doFinal (byte[] inBuf, short inOffset, short inLength,
                byte[] outBuff, short outOffset);
```

Both methods take the plaintext in the input buffer and write out the computed ciphertext to the output buffer. You should call the update method to feed input data cumulatively and call the doFinal method as you feed in the last batch of data. The final version of the ciphertext is computed in the output buffer from the doFinal method. After the call to the doFinal method is made, the Cipher object is reset to the state it was in when it was previously initialized via a call to the init method. To decrypt data, also call the methods update and doFinal. But notice that for decryption, the ciphertext is fed into the input buffer and the plaintext is written into the output buffer. Again, because the update method involves overhead for storing intermediate result, you should call it only if the entire input data cannot be fit in a byte array.

10.4.5 Generate Random Data

Random numbers are routinely needed for cryptographic procedures. To create a random number generator, you call the getInstance method in the class javacard.security.RandomData and specify an algorithm. The algorithm selection parameter can be either RandomData.ALG_PSEUDO_RANDOM for the utility pseudo random number generation algorithm or RandomData.ALG_SECURE_RANDOM for the cryptographically strong secure random number generation algorithm.

Like other algorithm-based classes in the Java Card cryptography APIs, the class javacard.security.RandomData is an abstract base class. Thus it must be extended by an implementation class. The RandomData object returned from the getInstance method is an object of such an implementation class, which implements the desired algorithm.

The pseudo RandomData object's seed is initialized to an internal default value, whereas the secure RandomData object attempts to initialize the seed with a completely random value. You could seed the random number generation via a call to the setSeed method.

Finally, to get a random number, you call the `generateData` method as follows:

```
RandomData random_data =
          RandomData.getInstance(RandomData.ALG_SECURE_RANDOM);
// the seed is supplied in the byte array seed
random_data.setSeed(seed, seed_offset, seed_length);
// a random number is written into the byte array random_num
random_data.generateData(random_num, random_num_offset,
                        random_num_length);
```

CHAPTER 11

Java Card Platform Security

Secure processing is the fundamental reason for using smart cards. So security considerations are paramount for smart card developers. This chapter centers on security in the Java Card platform. It is organized in three sections. Section 11.1 describes the security features in the Java Card platform. Section 11.2 discusses how these security features are enforced through a variety of mechanisms. Section 11.3 highlights the security considerations in designing and implementing Java Card applets.

This chapter is not intended to be a security specification. Rather, it aims at helping you to understand the overall security capabilities of the Java Card platform. It also serves as a summary chapter of the topics that have been discussed in Part 2.

Security must be considered from the point of view of an overall system. The Java Card platform is built on top of the smart card platform, which consists of the smart card hardware and native operating system, and the host system with which the card communicates. Smart card platform security is not within the scope of this book. Readers can find related discussions in smart card books, such as *Smart Card Handbook* by Rankl and Effing[1], *Smart Card Developer's Kit* by Guthery and Jurgensen[2], and *Smart Card Security and Applications* by Hendry[13].

11.1 Java Card Platform Security Features

The security features of the Java Card platform are a combination of the basics of Java language security and additional security protections defined by the Java Card platform.

11.1.1 Java Language Security

The Java Card platform supports a subset of the Java programming language and virtual machine specifications appropriate for smart card applications. Therefore, the Java Card platform inherits the security features built into the supported subset of the Java language (as characterized in the following list). Java language security forms the foundation of Java Card platform security.

- The Java language is strongly typed. No illegal data conversions can be done, such as converting integers to pointers.

- The Java language enforces boundary checks on array access.

- The Java language has no pointer arithmetic. Thus, there is no way to forge pointers to allow malicious programs to snoop around inside memory.

- Variables must be initialized before they are used.

- The level of access to all classes, methods, and fields is strictly controlled. For example, a private method cannot be invoked from outside its defining class.

11.1.2 Additional Security Features of the Java Card Platform

In the very security-conscious world of smart cards, card issuers desire a secure computing platform to meet the special requirements of the smart card system. Following are additional security features defined in the Java Card platform:

- *Transient and persistent object models*—In the Java Card platform, objects are stored by default in persistent memory. For security and performance reasons, the Java Card platform allows temporary data, such as session keys, to be stored in transient objects in RAM. The lifetime of such objects can be declared to be either CLEAR_ON_RESET or CLEAR_ON_DESELECT. The contents of a transient object are set to the object's default value (zero, false, or null) either when the card is reset or when the currently selected applet is deselected.

- *Atomicity and transactions*—In the Java Card platform, data are stored in objects in persistent memory. Failure or power loss could occur during write operations on the data. To ensure data integrity, three security features are defined in Java Card technology. First, the Java Card platform guarantees that a single update to a field of a persistent object or a class will be atomic. When an error occurs during update, the platform ensures that the content of the field will be restored to its previous value. Second, the method arrayCopy in the class javacard.framework.Util guarantees atomicity for block updates of multiple data elements in an array. Here, atomicity means that either all bytes are correctly copied or the destination array is restored to its previous byte values. Third, the Java Card platform supports a transaction model in which an applet can atomically update several different fields in different persistent objects. Either all updates in the transaction must take place correctly and consistently, or all persistent fields are restored to their previous values.

- *Applet firewall*—The security and integrity of the system (the JCRE) and of each applet residing on a Java smart card are protected by the applet firewall. The applet firewall enforces applet isolation and separates the system space from the applet space. In the firewall scheme, each applet runs within a context (object space). Applets cannot access each other's objects unless they are defined in the same package (and thus share the same context) or through well-defined and secure object-sharing mechanisms supported by the platform.

- *Object sharing*—Object sharing in the Java Card system is achieved in the following ways. First, the JCRE is a privileged user that has full access to applets and to objects created by applets. Second, an applet gains access to JCRE services and resources through JCRE entry point objects. Third, applets in different contexts can share objects that are instances of a class implementing a shareable interface. Such objects are called *shareable interface objects*. Finally, applets and the JCRE can share data through global arrays.

- *Native methods in applets*—Native methods are not executed by the Java Card virtual machine and so are not subject to the security protections of the Java Card platform. Therefore, postissuance applets (applets that are downloaded to the card after the card has been issued) are prohibited from containing native methods. ROM applets and preissuance applets that are controlled by card issuers are allowed to have native methods. The interface to native code from such applets is the proprietary technology of card vendors.

11.2 Java Card Platform Security Mechanisms

Security is a chain, and a single weak link can break it. The Java Card security features are enforced through a number of mechanisms that are addressed at every level from the applet development process and the installation procedure to the runtime enforcement.

11.2.1 Compile-Time Checking[1]

An applet consists of one or more Java files. The Java code is compiled by using any standard Java development environment, such as Sun's JDK or Symantec's Café. The binary files produced by the compiler from source code are called *class files*.

The Java compiler performs extensive and stringent compile-time checking so that as many errors as possible are detected by the compiler. The Java language is strongly typed. Unlike C or C++, the type system has no loopholes. For example:

- Objects cannot be cast to a subclass without an explicit runtime check.

- All references to methods and variables are checked to make sure that the objects are of the appropriate type.

- The compiler checks that access controls (such as referencing a private variable or method from another class) are not violated.

- Integers cannot be converted into objects. Objects cannot be converted into integers.

- The compiler strictly ensures that a program does not access the value of an uninitialized local variable.

11.2.2 Class File Verification and Subset Checking

Although a trustworthy compiler can ensure that Java source code does not violate safety rules, class files could come from a network that is untrustworthy. In the Java environment, all class files loaded in are checked by a verifier—a component in the Java virtual machine—before they are executed. The class file verifier goes through class files in several passes to ensure that they have the correct format and that their bytecodes adhere to a set of structural constraints. In particular, class files are checked to ensure the following:

- There are no violations of memory management and no stack underflows or overflows.

- Access restrictions are enforced: for example, private methods and fields cannot be accessed outside their defining class.

---

[1]   From Frank Yellin's paper "Low-Level Security in Java"[15].

- Methods are called with appropriate arguments of the appropriate type.

- Fields are modified with values of the appropriate type.

- Objects are accessed as what they are. For example, an APDU object is always used as an APDU object, never as anything else.

- No pointers are forged.

- No illegal data conversions are done, such as converting integers to pointers.

- Binary compatibility rules are enforced.

Unlike the Java virtual machine, the Java Card virtual machine has a split architecture that consists of two parts: the converter running off card on a PC or a workstation and the interpreter running inside a card. The converter is the front end of the virtual machine and takes class files as input. During conversion, the class files of an applet are subject to the same level of rigorous verification as they would be by the Java virtual machine with its class file verifier at class-loading time. The converter can incorporate the verifier component of the Java virtual machine, or it can implement its own class file verifier.

Because Java Card technology defines a subset of the Java language, the converter must check class files further to ensure that only features in that subset are used. This step is called *subset checking*. During this step, the converter checks that the applet does not violate the following subset rules:

- No unsupported data types are used (for example, variables of type char, long, double, and float). Data of type int are used only if the Java Card interpreter supports them.

- No unsupported Java language features are used. For example, an applet should not have threads or multidimensional arrays.

- Usage of certain Java operations are within limited ranges. The ranges of such operations on the Java Card platform are smaller than those of the Java platform. For example, a package can have no more than 255 public classes and interfaces, and an array can hold a maximum of 32,767 fields.

- No potential overflow or underflow can occur that might cause arithmetic results to be computed differently than they would be on the Java platform (see Chapter 14).

11.2.3 CAP File and Export File Verification

The classes of an applet make up one or more packages. The converter takes all classes in a package and converts them into a CAP file. The CAP file is then loaded onto a Java smart card and executed by the interpreter. In addition to creating a CAP file, the converter generates an export file representing the public APIs of the package being converted. The export file is not used directly by the interpreter. It is used later to convert another package that imports classes from the package represented in the export file. The information in the export file is used for linking and external reference checking.

The CAP file in the Java Card platform is of equal importance to the class file in the Java platform. It is an interoperable binary format for loading a Java package onto a Java smart card.

In practice, there is no guarantee that a CAP file generated from verified class files by a trustworthy converter will immediately be loaded onto a Java smart card in a secure environment. Thus, the correctness and integrity of a CAP file cannot be taken for granted. It is the job of the CAP file verifier to ensure that the CAP file plays by the rules. Due to the limited memory space and computing power of a smart card, the CAP file verifier runs off card. The verifier performs static checks on a CAP file before it is loaded onto a Java smart card.

Because of the analogous role of class files and CAP files, the CAP file verifier has a function similar to that of the class file verifier. That is, it ensures that a CAP file has the correct format and that the bytecodes in it adhere to a set of structural constraints. In particular, it checks the CAP file to ensure the following:

- There are no violations of memory management and no stack underflows or overflows.

- Access restrictions are enforced: for example, private methods and fields cannot be accessed outside the object.

- Methods are called with appropriate arguments of the appropriate type.

- Fields are modified with values of the appropriate type.

- Objects are accessed as what they are. For example, an APDU object is always used as an APDU object, never as anything else.

- No pointers are forged.

- No illegal data conversions are done, such as converting integers to pointers.

- Binary compatibility rules are enforced.

Note that these checks are identical to those of the class file verifier. In addition, the CAP file verifier enforces rules that are special to the CAP file structure and the Java Card environment.

- The package and each applet defined in the package must have a valid AID that is between 5 and 16 bytes in length. The package AID and the applet AIDs must share the same RID number (the first 5 bytes in the AIDs).

- An applet must define an install method with the correct signature so that instances of the applet can be appropriately created on the card.

- The order of class and interface definitions in a CAP file must follow the rules that interfaces appear ahead of classes and superclasses appear ahead of sub-classes. This ensures that the CAP file-loading and linking process can be handled sequentially on the card.

- The int flag is set if the int type is used in the CAP file. This check allows a Java Card implementation that does not support the int type to reject the CAP file during loading by simply checking the int flag.

During verification (Figure 11.1), the CAP file verifier ensures that a CAP file is internally consistent, is consistent with the export files it imports, and is consistent with the export file that represents its API. The verifier also examines whether

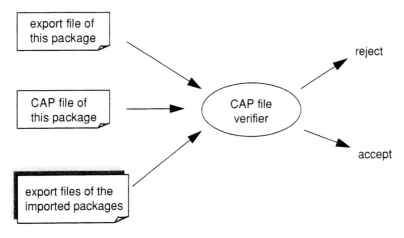

Figure 11.1 CAP file verification

the Java Card version rules, including those imposed for binary compatibility,[2] have been followed.

If export files used during verification are not trustworthy, they should also be verified. Export file verification checks an export file both internally and against its corresponding CAP file to ensure that it is wellformatted and satisfies the constraints required by the Java Card virtual machine specification.

11.2.4 Installation Checking

CAP file installation is achieved through the cooperation of the off-card installation program and the on-card installer. Together, they load a CAP file, and, if the CAP file defines any applets, they create one or more applet instances.[3]

Installation security consists of two levels. At the first level are the standard security protections enforced by the installer and the JCRE, and at the second level are the security policies dictated by the issuers. Together they protect against the following:

- Installation data corruption

- Installation data tampering

- Incompatibility between the CAP file and on-card resources

- Illegal access from outside the CAP file

- Insufficient resources and other errors during installation and initialization

- Inconsistent state due to card tearing or power loss during the process of installation

The correctness and integrity of a CAP file are verified off-card. The Java Card installer does not perform most of the traditional Java verifications at class-loading time.[4] Before any data are written on the card, the installer first checks to see whether the card can support the CAP file. For example, the

---

[2] The Java Card platform binary compatibility rules are defined in the *Java Card 2.1 Virtual Machine Specification.*

[3] Depending on the installer implementation, applet creation can also be performed at a later stage.

[4] Java verifications at class-loading time are performed by the class verifier as described in Section 11.2.2.

installer checks whether the card's available memory resources are sufficient for the CAP file. And if the card does not support the `int` type, the installer checks whether the CAP file contains any `int` usage; that is, it checks whether the `int` flag in the CAP file is set.

When the CAP file is read in, it can be linked either on the fly or after the entire CAP file is loaded. The linking process includes resolving both internal and external references. The installer ensures that internal references are in fact local to the package's memory,[5] and external references are linked to accessible locations of other packages and the JCRE. In addition, the installer ensures that the CAP file is binary compatible with the existing software on the card.

Unlike the Java platform, the loading unit on the Java Card platform is a package (a CAP file). The installer ensures that the CAP file references only packages that are already on the card, because loading new classes incrementally is not supported.

If the CAP file defines any applets, the installer can create instances of applets by calling their `install` methods. When an applet instance is created, a context is assigned to the applet instance. Multiple instances of the same applet and instances of multiple applets defined in the same package share one context, referred to as the group context.

The installation process is transactional. If an error, card tearing, or power loss occurs during installation, the installer discards the CAP file and any applets it had created during installation and recovers the space and the previous state of the JCRE.

Beyond the minimum security requirements defined in the installer and the JCRE, Java Card technology does not standardize the installation policy. Issuers have the flexibility of configuring the card to allow installation of applets from several sources, possibly engaging different levels of protection for applets from different sources.

The simplest form of protection is to authenticate the off-card installation program by using a PIN—thus providing a measure of trust to the CAP file provider and the content of the CAP file. A more sophisticated scheme can use digital signature and data encryption. The next section provides such examples.

---

[5] Because the CAP file is verified off-card, the installer may not verify the consistency of internal references.

11.2.5 Cryptographically Enforced Chain Trust

The Java Card applet development and installation process consists of source code design and implementation; code compilation, conversion, and verification; and CAP file installation on the card.

During this process, several parties are involved, including developers, issuers, terminal vendors, card vendors, and others. If the entire process is not accomplished in a physically secure environment, files may need to be transported in an open network. Thus, Java Card system security can be further strengthened through the chain of trust, in which the identity of each party involved is authenticated and the confidentiality and integrity of data are protected.

Modern cryptography offers powerful tools to authenticate identity and to ensure confidentiality and integrity. Any Java Card file (source code, class file, CAP file, or export file) can be encrypted for secrecy during transportation between development and on-card installation. The file can be digitally signed to ensure integrity and to prove the identity of its provider. Before a CAP file is installed, the host (including the CAD) and the card should be mutually authenticated. Once the host is authenticated, it would be safe for the card to load data in plaintext. Otherwise, the data decryption and verification tasks would be required on the card, which could be very resource demanding.

To build trust through such schemes, a card issuer needs to define policies regarding the key management (key generation and exchange) and the use of cryptographic mechanisms.

11.2.6 Runtime Security Enforcement

The Java Card runtime security enforcement covers two areas: ensuring Java language type safety and enforcing applet isolation through the applet firewall.

The CAP file contains sufficient type information to enable thorough type checking at runtime. However, due to limited on-card computing resources, most JCRE implementations choose to rely on the security measures enforced by the converter and verifiers and to rely on installation checking for detecting certain kinds of illegal references. Many checks that are performed statically off-card are not repeated at runtime. The Java Card interpreter performs checks that must be handled dynamically, such as checking the runtime type of an object against its static type.

To enforce the applet firewall, when an object is accessed, the Java Card interpreter performs checks to determine whether the access can be granted. It allows applets in the same package to access each other's objects. In situations where there is a need to support cooperative applications across the package boundaries, the Java Card interpreter enables object sharing through JCRE entry point objects, global arrays, and shareable interface objects.

The Java Sandbox Model versus the Applet Firewall

Runtime security in the Java platform centers on the idea of a sandbox model. An applet may play around within its sandbox but cannot reach beyond it. In the sandbox model, classloaders can be used to provide separate name spaces (sandboxes) for various software components. For example, a browser can load applets from different Web pages by using different classloaders, thus maintaining a degree of isolation between those applet classes. In this model, access to sensitive resources is controlled by the security manager and the access controller based on the permissions granted to the requester[10]. In the Java Card platform, classloaders and the security manager are not supported. The sandbox model is complemented by the applet firewall. The JCRE assigns a context for each running applet. Access to an object is controlled by the Java Card interpreter based on the type of the accessed object and whether the currently active context is the object's owning context.

In addition, the Java Card runtime specification dictates a number of JCRE implementation requirements to ensure runtime security. Following are some notable ones.

- The JCRE must properly designate and implement JCRE entry point objects and global arrays. For example, an applet cannot store references to temporary JCRE entry point objects in class variables, instance variables, or array fields (including transient arrays).

- To prevent an applet's potentially sensitive data from being "leaked" to another applet via the global APDU buffer, the APDU buffer must be cleared to zeroes whenever an applet is selected before the JCRE accepts a new APDU command.

- The JCRE's implementation of the atomicity and transaction mechanisms must be in compliance with the specification to ensure data integrity. For example, when an applet returns with a transaction still in progress, the JCRE should automatically abort the transaction, thus triggering any necessary cleanup by the transaction system.

- Runtime failures must be properly handled. For example, a lack of resources (such as heap space) error that is recoverable should result in a

`SystemException`. Any nonrecoverable error, such as stack overflow, should cause the virtual machine to halt. When a nonrecoverable error occurs, a JCRE implementation can optionally require the card to be muted (blocked), thus preventing further use.

11.2.7 Java Card Cryptographic Support

Cryptographic mechanisms are used throughout Java Card applets and system software. The Java Card cryptography APIs allow for flexible use of these mechanisms, based on what security policy is desired and which cryptographic mechanisms are available on the card. Card issuers can configure the card for choices of algorithms, key size, and so on. Applet developers are likewise able to define their own cryptographic policies, within boundaries set by the card issuer.

11.3 Applet Security

The security of any application is determined by the security of the platform on which it runs and by security features designed into the application itself. The Java Card platform is designed to ensure that applets can be built, installed, and run in a highly secure fashion. It also enables issuers to define further security requirements and policies to meet the needs of their particular industry. For example, as an industry extension, the Open Platform enforces security rules for applet installation and management of applets on Java smart cards[9].

Application-level security needs to be programmed into applets. Because security features are built into the platform itself, applet developers can concentrate their efforts on defining a security strategy for the applets rather than on putting extra effort into programming the applets to compensate for an insecure platform.

Applet developers should define a security strategy to prevent the kinds of attacks that are likely to be made against the applet. When well defined, a security strategy provides these security objectives in applets:

- *Authentication*—Access to an applet's functions and data is controlled. The identity of the host application issuing commands to the applet should be authenticated. Also, during object sharing, the server applet should verify the identity of a client applet before granting a service.

- *Confidentiality*—The privacy of the applet's data must be protected: secure data, such as account numbers and balances, should not be accessible without proper authentication. Secret data, such as PINs and private cryptographic keys, should never be allowed to leave the card.

- *Integrity*—The correctness of the applet's data is defended. The applet's data cannot be changed without proper authentication. Data modification should be guarded through error checking. For example, the wallet balance cannot exceed its maximum limit or drop below zero.

Needless to say, different applets require different levels of security. For example, a wallet applet requires a higher degree of security and type approval than a game applet. Also, security is enforced at the cost of computing resources (performance and memory). Therefore, applet developers should evaluate the security requirements of an applet and choose appropriate mechanisms to protect its valuable assets.

PART 3

Programming
Guide and Tips

CHAPTER 12

Step-by-Step Applet Development Guide

In previous chapters, you have seen code fragments of an electronic wallet applet. This chapter walks you through the process of creating such an applet. The development steps are detailed, from designing the applet through constructing its code. At the end, the chapter provides a discussion of error checking for an applet.

12.1 Design the Applet

As with any software application development, before sitting down and writing a Java Card applet, you should first go through a *design phase*. In this phase, you define the architecture of the applet in four steps:

- Specify the functions of the applet.
- Request and assign AIDs to both the applet and the package containing the applet classes.
- Design the class structure of the applet programs.
- Define the interface between the applet and the host application.

12.1.1 Specify the Functions of the Applet

The example wallet applet stores electronic money and supports credit, debit, and check-balance functions. The Java smart card user can add money to the wallet (credit), make purchases or withdrawals (debit), and inquire about the current available balance.

To help prevent unauthorized use of the card, the applet applies a security algorithm. This algorithm requires the user to enter a PIN, a string of at most eight digits. The card user types his or her PIN on a keypad connected to the CAD. The security algorithm causes the card to block after three unsuccessful attempts to enter the PIN. The PIN is initialized according to the installation parameters when the applet is installed and created. The PIN must be verified before any credit or debit transaction can be executed.

Note: A real-world wallet applet would require a much more sophisticated security mechanism to prevent unauthorized access to the wallet.

For simplicity, let's say that the card's maximum balance is $10,000 and that no credit or debit transaction can exceed $100. Thus, Java variables of type `short` and `byte` can represent the wallet balance and the amount of each transaction, respectively.

12.1.2 Specify AIDs for the Applet

The Java classes of the wallet applet are defined in a single Java package. AIDs for the wallet applet and the applet package are defined in Table 12.1.

An AID consists of two parts: an RID (5 bytes long) and a PIX (0 to 11 bytes long). The RID (`0xa0, 0x00, 0x00, 0x00, 0x62`) in Table 12.1 is the RID for Sun Microsystems. Your organization must request an RID from the International Standards Organization (ISO). Your organization is responsible for managing the PIX assignment for packages and applets provided by your organization.

Table 12.1   AIDs for the wallet applet and the applet package

Field	Value	Length
RID	`0xa0, 0x00, 0x00, 0x00, 0x62`	5 bytes
Package PIX	`0x03, 0x01, 0x0c, 0x06`	4 bytes
Applet PIX	`0x03, 0x01, 0x0c, 0x06, 0x01`	5 bytes

12.1.3 Define the Class Structure and Method Functions of the Applet

As discussed in Chapter 7, a Java Card applet class must extend the `java-card.framework.Applet` class, whose public and protected methods are listed in Table 12.2. The applet overrides one or more of these public methods to implement the desired behavior. (For more information, refer to Chapters 7 and 9.)

An applet must define and implement the static method `install` to create an applet instance and to register the instance with the JCRE by invoking one of the two `register` methods.

The `process` method in the base `Applet` class is an abstract class. Your applet must override it. In the `process` method, the applet interprets each APDU command and performs the function specified by the command. Typically, an applet supports a set of APDU commands. See the next section for a discussion of the APDU commands needed by the electronic wallet applet.

The `select` or the `deselect` method is invoked by the JCRE when the applet is selected or deselected. Your applet can override them to provide initialization or cleanup functions. However, not every applet requires initialization or cleanup.

Table 12.2 Public and protected methods defined in the class `javacard.framework.Applet`

public static void	`install (byte[] bArray, short bOffset, byte bLength)`
public boolean	`select ()`
public void	`deselect ()`
public abstract void	`process (APDU apdu)`
public Shareable	`getShareableInterfaceObject (AID client AID, byte parameter)`
protected final void	`register()`
protected final void	`register(byte[] bArray, short bOffset, byte bLength)`
protected final boolean	`selectingApplet()`

The applet uses the `select` or `deselect` method in the base class if it does not require additional functions during selection or deselection.

The `getShareableInterfaceObject` method is called to return a shareable interface object. The use of this method is covered in Chapter 9. For simplicity, the wallet applet in this chapter does not implement the object sharing function. Interested readers can add the function to the wallet applet by using the code examples in Chapter 9.

Two `register` methods and the `selectingApplet` method are protected final methods. They are invoked only by applets for registering an applet instance with the JCRE or detecting an applet SELECT APDU command.

12.1.4 Define the Interface between the Applet and Its Host Application

An applet running in a Java smart card communicates with the host application at the CAD side by using the application protocol data units (APDUs). In essence, the interface between an applet and its host application is a set of APDU commands that are agreed on and supported by both the applet and the host application.

A Java Card applet should support a set of APDU commands comprising a SELECT APDU command and one or more process APDU commands.

- The SELECT command instructs the JCRE to select the applet on the card.

- The set of process commands defines the commands that the applet supports. They must be defined according to the intended behavior of the applet.

Java Card technology specifies the encoding of the SELECT APDU command used for selecting applets. As an applet developer, you are free to define the encoding of the process commands of an applet as long as they comply with the structure outlined in ISO 7816-4. That is, the SELECT command and each process command are pairs of command and response APDUs.

For each command APDU, the applet should first decode the value of each field in the header. If the optional data field is included, the applet should also determine the data format and the content. Knowing how to interpret the command and read the data, the applet can then execute the function requested by the command.

For the response APDU, the applet should define a set of status words to indicate the result of processing the corresponding command APDU. During normal processing, the applet returns the success status word (0x9000, as specified in ISO 7816). If an error occurs, the applet must return a status word other than 0x9000 to denote its internal state or a diagnosis of the error. If the optional data field is required in the response APDU, the applet should define what to return.

The wallet applet example supports credit, debit, and check-balance functions. In addition, it supports the VERIFY command for PIN verification. The

SELECT command and four process APDU commands for the wallet applet are defined in Tables 12.3–12.12.

12.1.4.1 SELECT APDU

Table 12.3   SELECT APDU—command APDU

CLA	INS	P1	P2	Lc	Data field	Le
0x0	0xA4	0x04	0x0	0x0A	0xa0, 0x00, 0x00, 0x00, 0x62, 0x03, 0x01, 0x0c, 0x06, 0x01	N/A

The command header (CLA, INS, P1, and P2) must be coded as in Table 12.3 so that the JCRE can identify it as a SELECT APDU. The data field contains the AID of the wallet applet. The JCRE searches its internal registry table against the AID bytes. If a match is found, the wallet applet is selected, and the SELECT APDU is forwarded to the applet's process method for further processing.

Table 12.4   SELECT APDU—response APDU

Optional data	Status word	Meaning of status word
No data	0x9000	Successful processing
	0x6999	Applet selection failed: the applet could not be found or selected

12.1.4.2 VERIFY APDU

Table 12.5   VERIFY APDU—command APDU

CLA	INS	P1	P2	Lc	Data field	Le
0xB0	0x20	0x0	0x0	Length of the PIN data	PIN data	N/A

- CLA byte denotes the structure of the command.
- INS byte (0x20) indicates a VERIFY instruction.
- P1 and P2 are not used and are both set to 0.
- The data field contains the PIN.

Table 12.6   VERIFY APDU—response APDU

Optional data	Status word	Meaning of status word
N/A	0x9000	Successful processing
	0x6300	Verification failed

12.1.4.3 CREDIT APDU

Table 12.7   CREDIT APDU—command APDU

CLA	INS	P1	P2	Lc	Data field	Le
0xB0	0x30	0x0	0x0	1	Credit amount	N/A

The data field contains the credit amount.

Table 12.8   CREDIT APDU—response APDU

Optional data	Status word	Meaning of status word
N/A	0x9000	Successful processing
	0x6301	PIN verification required
	0x6A83	Invalid credit amount
	0x6A84	Exceed the maximum amount

12.1.4.4 DEBIT APDU

Table 12.9   DEBIT APDU—command APDU

CLA	INS	P1	P2	Lc	Data field	Le
0xB0	0x40	0x0	0x0	1	Debit amount	N/A

The data field contains the debit amount.

Table 12.10 DEBIT APDU—response APDU

Optional data	Status word	Meaning of status word
N/A	0x9000	Successful processing
	0x6301	PIN verification required
	0x6A83	Invalid debit amount
	0x6A85	Negative balance

12.1.4.5 GET BALANCE APDU

Table 12.11 GET BALANCE APDU—command APDU

CLA	INS	P1	P2	Lc	Data field	Le
0xB0	0x50	0x0	0x0	N/A	N/A	2

The data field of the response APDU contains the balance amount.

Table 12.12 GET BALANCE APDU—response APDU

Data	Status word	Meaning of status word
Balance amount	0x9000	Successful processing

In addition to the status words declared in each response APDU command, the interface `javacard.framework.ISO7816` defines a set of ISO status words that signal common errors in applets, such as an APDU command formatting error.

12.2 Construct the Applet Code

Once you've completed the applet design phase, the next phase of writing applets is to construct the applet code. This section provides the wallet applet implementation.

12.2.1 Wallet Applet Code

```
package com.sun.javacard.samples.wallet;
import javacard.framework.*;

public class WalletApp extends Applet {

    // codes of CLA byte in the command APDUs
    final static byte Wallet_CLA = (byte)0xB0;

    // codes of INS byte in the command APDUs
    final static byte VERIFY = (byte) 0x20;
    final static byte CREDIT = (byte) 0x30;
    final static byte DEBIT = (byte) 0x40;
    final static byte GET_BALANCE = (byte) 0x50;

    // maximum wallet balance
    final static short MAX_BALANCE = 10000;
    // maximum transaction amount
    final static byte MAX_TRANSACTION_AMOUNT = 100;

    // maximum number of incorrect tries before the
    // PIN is blocked
    final static byte PIN_TRY_LIMIT =(byte)0x03;
    // maximum size PIN
    final static byte MAX_PIN_SIZE =(byte)0x08;

    // Applet-specific status words:
    final static short SW_VERIFICATION_FAILED = 0x6300;
    final static short SW_PIN_VERIFICATION_REQUIRED = 0x6301;
    final static short SW_INVALID_TRANSACTION_AMOUNT = 0x6A83;
    final static short SW_EXCEED_MAXIMUM_BALANCE = 0x6A84;
    final static short SW_NEGATIVE_BALANCE = 0x6A85;

    // instance variables declaration
    OwnerPIN pin;
    short balance;

    /**
     * called by the JCRE to create an applet instance
```

```
   */
public static void install(byte[] bArray,
                           short bOffset,
                           byte bLength) {

    // create a Wallet applet instance
    new WalletApp(bArray, bOffset, bLength);

} // end of install method

/**
  * private constructor - called by the install method to
  * instantiate a WalletApp instance
  */
private WalletApp (byte[] bArray, short bOffset, byte bLength){

    pin = new OwnerPIN(PIN_TRY_LIMIT, MAX_PIN_SIZE);

    // bArray contains the PIN initialization value
    pin.update(bArray, bOffset, bLength);

    // register the applet instance with the JCRE
    register();

} // end of the constructor

/**
  * initialize the applet when it is selected
  */
public boolean select() {

    // the applet declines to be selected
    // if the pin is blocked
    if (pin.getTriesRemaining() == 0)
       return false;

    return true;

} // end of select method
```

```java
/**
 * perform any cleanup and bookkeeping tasks before
 * the applet is deselected
 */
public void deselect() {

    // reset the pin
    pin.reset();
}

/**
 * process APDUs
 */
public void process(APDU apdu) {

    // APDU object carries a byte array (buffer) to
    // transfer incoming and outgoing APDU header
    // and data bytes between the card and the host

    // at this point, only the first five bytes
    // [CLA, INS, P1, P2, P3] are available in
    // the APDU buffer
    byte[] buffer = apdu.getBuffer();

    // return if the APDU is the applet SELECT command
    if (selectingApplet())
        return;

    // verify the CLA byte
    if (buffer[ISO7816.OFFSET_CLA] != Wallet_CLA)
        ISOException.throwIt(ISO7816.SW_CLA_NOT_SUPPORTED);

    // check the INS byte to decide which service method to call
    switch (buffer[ISO7816.OFFSET_INS]) {
        case GET_BALANCE: getBalance(apdu); return;
        case DEBIT:    debit(apdu); return;
        case CREDIT:   credit(apdu); return;
        case VERIFY:   verify(apdu); return;
        default:       ISOException.throwIt
                       (ISO7816.SW_INS_NOT_SUPPORTED);
    }
```

```java
} // end of process method

/**
 * add money to the wallet
 */
private void credit(APDU apdu) {

    // verify authentication
    if (!pin.isValidated())
        ISOException.throwIt(SW_PIN_VERIFICATION_REQUIRED);

    byte[] buffer = apdu.getBuffer();

    // get the number of bytes in the
    // data field of the command APDU
    byte numBytes = buffer[ISO7816.OFFSET_LC];

    // recieve data
    // data are read into the apdu buffer
    // at the offset ISO7816.OFFSET_CDATA
    byte byteRead = (byte)(apdu.setIncomingAndReceive());

    // error if the number of data bytes
    // read does not match the number in the Lc byte
    if (( numBytes != 1 ) || (byteRead != 1))
        ISOException.throwIt(ISO7816.SW_WRONG_LENGTH);

    // get the credit amount
    byte creditAmount = buffer[ISO7816.OFFSET_CDATA];

    // check the credit amount
    if (( creditAmount > MAX_TRANSACTION_AMOUNT)
        || ( creditAmount < 0 ))
        ISOException.throwIt(SW_INVALID_TRANSACTION_AMOUNT);

    // check the new balance
    if ((short)( balance + creditAmount)  > MAX_BALANCE)
        ISOException.throwIt(SW_EXCEED_MAXIMUM_BALANCE);

    // credit the amount
    balance = (short)(balance + creditAmount);
```

```
        return;

    } // end of deposit method

    /**
     * withdraw money from the wallet
     */
    private void debit(APDU apdu) {

        // verify authentication
        if (! pin.isValidated())
            ISOException.throwIt(SW_PIN_VERIFICATION_REQUIRED);

        byte[] buffer = apdu.getBuffer();

        byte numBytes = (byte)(buffer[ISO7816.OFFSET_LC]);

        byte byteRead = (byte)(apdu.setIncomingAndReceive());

        if (( numBytes != 1 ) || (byteRead != 1))
            ISOException.throwIt(ISO7816.SW_WRONG_LENGTH);

        // get debit amount
        byte debitAmount = buffer[ISO7816.OFFSET_CDATA];

        // check debit amount
        if (( debitAmount > MAX_TRANSACTION_AMOUNT)
            || ( debitAmount < 0 ))
            ISOException.throwIt(SW_INVALID_TRANSACTION_AMOUNT);

        // check the new balance
        if ((short)( balance - debitAmount ) < (short)0)
            ISOException.throwIt(SW_NEGATIVE_BALANCE);

        balance = (short) (balance - debitAmount);

    } // end of debit method

    /**
     * the method returns the wallet's balance
```

```java
    */
    private void getBalance(APDU apdu) {

        byte[] buffer = apdu.getBuffer();

        // inform the JCRE that the applet has data to return
        short le = apdu.setOutgoing();

        // set the actual number of the outgoing data bytes
         apdu.setOutgoingLength((byte)2);

        // write the balance into the APDU buffer at the offset 0
        Util.setShort(buffer, (short)0, balance);

        // send the 2-byte balance at the offset
        // 0 in the apdu buffer
        apdu.sendBytes((short)0, (short)2);

    } // end of getBalance method

    /**
     * verify the PIN
     */
    private void verify(APDU apdu) {

        byte[] buffer = apdu.getBuffer();

        // receive the PIN data for validation.
        byte byteRead = (byte)(apdu.setIncomingAndReceive());

        // check pin
        // the PIN data is read into the APDU buffer
        // starting at the offset ISO7816.OFFSET_CDATA
        // the PIN data length = byteRead
        if (pin.check(buffer, ISO7816.OFFSET_CDATA,byteRead)
            == false)
           ISOException.throwIt(SW_VERIFICATION_FAILED);

    } // end of verify method

} // end of class Wallet
```

12.2.2 Implement Error Checking

The next step in coding a Java Card applet is to provide for error checking. Error checking is essential in any software development and typically requires a significant amount of the total development work.

Error checking is particularly important in smart card application development. An undetected error can cause the card to be blocked or result in the loss of critical data stored in the card.

Once an applet is installed in a smart card, it interfaces with the outside world only through APDU commands. Even though ISO 7816 sets the protocol standard, the applet and the host application must agree on the significance of the value in each field of an APDU command.

In the wallet applet code, much attention is devoted to detecting illegal or ill-formatted commands. In this example, the APDU commands are examined to ensure that the APDU header bytes (CLA, INS, P1, and P2) are set correctly, that the Lc or Le field matches the data field length, that the PIN has been verified before a transaction, and that the balance and transaction amounts are valid.

In general, before performing the task indicated by an APDU command, an applet must validate the command according to the requirements of the applet. An applet should confirm the following before attempting to carry out a command:

- The APDU command is supported by the applet.

- The APDU command is well formatted.

- The APDU command meets the security or other internal conditions of the applet.

While executing the task, the applet should also detect whether the task can be performed successfully without leaving the applet in an invalid state.

As important as error checking is, it is just as important that the applet report to the host errors that occur. This ensures that the host application knows what is going on inside the applet. When an error is detected, a Java Card applet will normally terminate the process and throw an ISOException containing a status word to indicate the processing state of the applet. If the ISOException is not handled by the applet, it will be caught by the JCRE, which then retrieves the status word and reports it to the host.

12.3   What's the Next Step?

The next step during the applet development process is to test the wallet applet in a Java Card simulation or emulation environment. You can find instructions on how to complete applet testing at the Web site *http://java.sun.com/docs/books/series/javacard*. You can also download the Java Card development tools, the Java Card API classes, and related documents from the Java Card Web site *http://java.sun.com/docs/books/javacard*.

CHAPTER 13

Applet Optimization

Smart cards represent the smallest computing platform in use today. A major factor influencing the design and implementation of Java Card applets is the limited availability of computing resources (data and program memory and CPU cycles) in the smart card environment.

This chapter focuses on applet optimizations. It provides a number of recommendations that you, the applet developer, can apply in designing and implementing applets. In many cases, a discussion is provided with the recommendation to help you understand various design trade-offs.

13.1 Optimizing an Applet's Overall Design

When optimizing an applet, you should first review the applet's overall design to identify any optimization opportunities. The reason is that optimizations can usually be applied at the global level and thus provide the most payoff.

To optimize an applet's overall design, you should apply the object-oriented features of the Java language. A Java Card applet consists of one or more classes. A class provides an organized way to define the variables and methods common to all objects of a certain kind. Thus, classes provide the benefits of modularity and reusability. Modularity and reusability can be further achieved by using inheritance. Inheritance allows you to define generic and common behavior in a superclass and to add specialized behavior to each subclass. When defining classes and their inheritance hierarchy, you should consider all applets coexisting in a card and decide whether common functions can be reused.

Optimization is often a balancing act. To optimize an applet's overall design, you should also consider the memory limitations of smart cards. Each class requires a data structure to represent it, and this involves overhead. Class inheritance also adds overhead, particularly when the inheritance hierarchy becomes complex. Therefore, an applet whose architecture maximizes flexibility through a greater number of classes and methods, nonoptimized data representation, and multiple levels of indirection creates significant overhead. On the other hand, a compact applet architecture with fewer classes and methods, packed data representation, and hard-coded logic might consume less memory. But such an architecture limits opportunities for interapplet code sharing. Also, debugging and updating such applet code become very difficult. There is no clear measure to indicate what approach you should take and how far you should go. Applet developers need to balance the design choices based on the applet's requirements and how the applet will be used. Typically, an applet would have between 5 and 10 classes and should have no more than two or three levels of class inheritance.

13.2   On-Card Execution Time

In a smart card system, cryptographic operations and EEPROM writes account for most of the on-card processing time. Therefore, it is usually not feasible to deploy computationally expensive cryptographic operations on voluminous data. For example, RSA is not commonly used for data encryption in smart cards, despite its very good security, due to the long execution time it requires. Its main application is in digital signatures, which are computed from encrypting hash values (small "fingerprints" of larger sets of data)[1].

To minimize EEPROM writes, transient arrays (in RAM) can be used to store intermediate results or frequently updated temporary data. Writing to RAM is 1,000 times faster than writing to EEPROM. Also, RAM is not subject to wear as is EEPROM. However, RAM is a very scarce resource on a card. Its use should be economized in every possible way.

13.3   Method Invocations

During execution, the Java Card virtual machine uses a data structure in RAM, called a *stack*, for holding method parameters, return values, local variables, and partial results. In many cards, the size of the stack is around 200 bytes. Therefore, to reduce the stack usage, you should optimize the use of method parameters and local variables. You should also limit nested method invocations, which could easily lead to stack overflow. In particular, applets should not use recursive calls.

13.4 Creating Objects in Applets

As explained in Chapter 7, an applet is created when its `install` method is called. The `install` method uses `new` to instantiate an applet instance. It is recommended, that, when possible, an applet should create in its constructor all objects it will need in its lifetime. This has two advantages. First, the applet can budget space to avoid an out-of-memory problem during execution. Second, the `install` method is enclosed within a transaction. In this way, should the applet installation fail due to memory allocation or other problems, the space allocated by the applet can be reclaimed. Needless to say, an applet may need to create more objects when it runs. An applet should always check that an object is created only once.

In any case, when a new object is created, the applet should assign the object reference to a permanent location, such as a class field (static field) or an object field (instance field) or a permanent array element. In this way, the object can be used throughout the applet's lifetime.

13.5 Reusing Objects

In the Java platform, objects are created as needed and are garbage collected when they are not referenced by other objects or by the virtual machine. When the virtual machine terminates, all objects are destroyed.

In a Java Card implementation, garbage collection may not be supported. In such an implementation, both persistent objects (allocated in EEPROM) and transient objects (allocated in RAM) exist throughout the lifetime of the card. Therefore, applets should not instantiate objects with the expectation that their storage will be reclaimed. For example, in the following code fragment, an object is created whenever the method is invoked. Such an object is singly referenced by a local variable and becomes unreachable after the method returns. Sooner or later, these dangling objects would consume all memory space and make the card unusable.

```
public void myMethod() {

    Object a = new Object();
}
```

Therefore, in the Java Card platform, the general rule is that a single instantiation of an object should be reused by writing new values to the member variables. This model is different from the one you may be accustomed to in Java technology.

The exception classes in the Java Card APIs are implemented in a manner that maximizes object recycling by using the system instance each time the method throwIt is invoked:

```
public class ISOException extends CardRuntimeException {

    private static ISOException systemInstance;

    // called once by the JCRE to create a system instance.
    // this instance is shared by all applets.
    public ISOException (short sw) {

        super(sw);
        if (systemInstance == null)
            systemInstance = this;
    }

    public static void throwIt(short sw) {

        systemInstance.setReason(sw);
        throw systemInstance;
    }
}
```

The throwIt method is declared static so that it can be invoked by any applet. When calling the throwIt method, an applet customizes the ISOException object with a reason code:

```
if (apdu_buffer[ISO7816.OFFSET_P1] != 0)
    ISOException.throwIt(ISO7816.SW_INCORRECT_P1P2);
```

13.6 Eliminating Redundant Code

Eliminating redundant code is an often-used and effective optimization technique. Redundant code exists when two or more segments of code duplicate an identical function. An optimization can be achieved when redundant segments of code are factored out into a separate method.

To increase reusability and modularity (and thus eliminate code redundancy), programmers are often encouraged to write small methods with only 10 to 15 lines of code. However, a trade-off exists in eliminating redundant code. Creating more methods adds extra overhead, including the data structures to represent the methods, and method invocation bytecodes. Therefore, factoring the code to eliminate redundancy may actually increase the overall code size.

Applet developers should identify code segments that really warrant separation for the purpose of reusability. On the one hand, small methods possibly should be inlined, especially if invoked only once by the applet. On the other hand, if the size of the redundant code is large enough and such code repeats in several places, factoring it into a separate method can save a considerable amount of memory.

13.7 Accessing Arrays

Typically, accessing array elements requires more bytecodes than accessing local variables. To optimize memory usage, if the same element of an array is accessed multiple times from different locations in the same method, save the array value in a local variable on the first access, and then use the variable in subsequent accesses. Consider the following code example in the wallet applet's process method:

```
public void process(APDU apdu) {

    if (buffer[ISO7816.OFFSET_INS] == VERIFY)
        verifyPIN(apdu);
    else if (buffer[ISO7816.OFFSET_INS] == CREDIT)
        credit(apdu);
    else if (buffer[ISO7816.OFFSET_INS] == DEBIT)
        debit(apdu);
    else if (buffer[ISO7816.OFFSET_INS] == CHECKBALANCE)
        checkBalance(apdu);
    else if (ins == UPDATEPIN)
        updatePIN(apdu);
    else
        ISOException.throwIt(ISO7816.SW_INS_NOT_SUPPORTED);
}
```

The element of array `buffer` indexed at `ISO7816.OFFSET_INS` is accessed and checked repeatedly to determine what task is specified in the APDU command and thus which service function to invoke. This code can be optimized to save memory if the indexed array element is cached in a local variable:

```
public void process(APDU apdu) {

    byte ins = buffer[ISO7816.OFFSET_INS]; // cache it

    if (ins == VERIFY)
        verifyPIN(apdu);
    else if (ins == CREDIT)
        credit(apdu);
    else if (ins == DEBIT)
        debit(apdu);
    else if (ins == CHECKBALANCE)
        checkBalance(apdu);
    else if (ins == UPDATEPIN)
        updatePIN(apdu);
    else
        ISOException.throwIt(ISO7816.SW_INS_NOT_SUPPORTED);
}
```

To ease array manipulation in applets, the class `javacard.framework.Util` provides a number of convenient methods. The `arrayCompare` method allows you to compare the elements of two arrays, with a return value indicating whether one array is less than, equal to, or greater than the other.

The `arrayCopy` method copies an array to another location. This method ensures that the copy operation is transactional, which means that an error that occurs in the middle of the operation does not result in a partially copied array. But the `arrayCopy` method requires more EEPROM writes and thus takes longer execution time. If the data in the destination array need not be preserved in case of an error, you should instead use the nonatomic version of the same method, `arrayCopyNonAtomic`. A similar method, `arrayFillNonAtomic`, nonatomically fills the elements of a byte array with a specified value.

Two consecutive byte array elements may be returned as a short value using the `getShort` method. Likewise, two consecutive byte array elements may be set using the first and second bytes in a short value using the `setShort` method.

13.8   The `switch` Statement versus the `if-else` Statement

The nested if-else statements in the wallet's process method (page 188) can be transformed to an equivalent switch statement:

```
public void process(APDU apdu) {

    byte ins = buffer[ISO7816.OFFSET_INS];
    switch (ins) {
        case VERIFY: verifyPIN(apdu); break;
        case CREDIT: credit(apdu); break;
        case DEBIT:  debit(apdu); break;
        case CHECKBALANCE: checkBalance(apdu); break;
        case UPDATEPIN: updatePIN(apdu); break;
        default: ISOException.throwIt(ISO7816.SW_INS_NOT_SUPPORTED);
    }
}
```

In general, a switch statement executes faster and takes less memory than an equivalent if-else statement. But in some cases, a switch statement might actually take up more memory. So you should try it both ways and use empirical evidence to determine which statement is more efficient.

When writing an applet, there are many optimization opportunities in which you can reconstruct a cascaded if-else statement or a switch statement to reduce code size. For example, in the wallet applet, assume that the PIN must be verified before other functions can be executed:

```
byte ins = buffer[ISO7816.OFFSET_INS]; // cache it

if (ins == VERIFY)
    verifyPIN(apdu);
else if (ins == CREDIT)
    if (isPinValided() == false)
        throw ISOException(SW_PIN_NOT_VALIDATED);
    credit(apdu);
else if (ins == DEBIT)
    if (isPinValided() == false)
        throw ISOException(SW_PIN_NOT_VALIDATED);
    debit(apdu);
```

```
else if (ins == CHECKBALANCE)
   if (isPinValided() == false )
      throw ISOException(SW_PIN_NOT_VALIDATED);
   checkBalance(apdu);
else if (ins == UPDATEPIN)
   if (isPinValided() == false)
      throw ISOException(SW_PIN_NOT_VALIDATED);
   updatePIN(apdu);
else
   ISOException.throwIt(ISO7816.SW_INS_NOT_SUPPORTED);
```

Notice that the code checking whether the PIN has been validated is duplicated in a number of places. Memory can be saved if the duplicated code can be eliminated. Compare the preceding code with the following:

```
byte ins = buffer[ISO7816.OFFSET_INS]; // cache it

if (ins == VERIFY)
   verifyPIN(apdu);
else {
   if (isPinValided() == false)
      throw ISOException(SW_PIN_NOT_VALIDATED);

   if (ins == CREDIT)
      credit(apdu);
   else if (ins == DEBIT)
      debit(apdu);
   else if (ins == CHECKBALANCE)
      checkBalance(apdu);
   else if (ins == UPDATEPIN)
      updatePIN(apdu);
   else
      ISOException.throwIt(ISO7816.SW_INS_NOT_SUPPORTED);
}
```

Factoring out common code and relocating it to a commonly accessible area eliminates redundancy in a method. This scheme is particularly useful in an applet's process method, in which selections of service functions are coded as cascaded if-else or switch statements that check incoming APDUs.

13.9 Arithmetic Statements

You might think that a compound arithmetic statement instead of separate assignments would use fewer bytecode instructions. The truth is quite opposite: a compound statement is actually more efficient.

```
x = a + b; x = x - c;
x = a + b - c;
```

The reason is that separate assignments require additional bytecode instructions to first store the intermediate value (a + b) in a variable and then load it back onto the stack for the next calculation.

Although it is a good idea to combine two or three operations into a single compound statement, a compound statement with too many levels of nested arithmetic operations can degrade the readability of source code and can be error prone.

13.10 Optimizing Variables in Applets

Variables in a Java Card applet can be of various kinds: instance variables, class variables, local variables, or method parameters. Local variables must be initialized before they can be accessed. Initialization is enforced by the Java compiler. In contrast, if no initializers are defined for instance or static variables in an applet, the virtual machine automatically applies the default initializers, setting their values to zero, false, or null. Therefore, you do not need to write code to initialize instance and static variables in an applet if they need no preassigned values other than the default ones (see the following code). This is different from programming in C, in which a variable might contain an arbitrary value if not explicitly initialized in the code.

```
public class MyApp extends Applet {
    // no initialization is needed for the following fields
    static int a = 0;
    boolean b = false;
    byte[] buffer = null;
}
```

Static fields (class variables) can be declared either final or nonfinal. Final static fields are used to represent constants. In the Java Card system, static fields (both final and nonfinal) may be initialized only to primitive compile-time constants or to arrays of primitive compile-time constants.

```
// primitive data type
static final byte a = 1;
// primitive array type
static byte b[] = {1, 2, 3};
```

The Java Card system supports two optimizations for handling static fields. In the first, *final static fields of primitive data types* are inlined in the bytecodes of a CAP file. That is, the converter replaces the bytecodes that reference final static fields with bytecodes that load constants. This optimization saves data space taken up by primitive final static fields. However, because constants are inlined in bytecodes, this optimization may or may not save code space. Compared to referencing a static field, loading a byte constant is cheaper, loading a short constant (2 bytes) has no impact on code size, and loading an int constant (4 bytes) is actually more expensive. But most constants used in a Java Card system can be represented in a single byte. Thus, overall, inlining constants probably will save significant code space. For example, the byte type constants in the interface ISO7816 need not be stored, and numerous references to them from applets and the JCRE are replaced by less expensive bytecode.

In the second optimization, the converter preprocesses static field initialization. It creates in the CAP file binary images of static fields with their initialized values (an exception is static final primitive fields, which are inlined in bytecodes). Later, when the CAP file is installed, these static images are loaded onto the card. This converter optimization saves at least 7 bytes for each element initialized in a static array and at least 3 bytes for each static primitive field initialized. Many applets have predefined parameters (usually stored in arrays). For example, in a wallet applet, applet parameters could be the applet version number, currency code and exponent, security and authentication method descriptions, and so on. Declaring these parameter arrays as static or final static takes advantage of the converter optimization and can eliminate a significant number of array initialization bytecodes. However, if these parameters are not shared by all instances of the same applet—if instead the values of the parameters are customized for each applet and there will be multiple instances of the same applet coexisting on the card—they must be stored in instance arrays. In this case, an applet could declare static arrays to hold the common set of values while declaring instance arrays to store those parameters whose values are applet dependent.

Normally, an applet should not initialize static fields inside an instance method unless the initialization depends on the logic implemented in the method. The reason is that the instance method may or may not be invoked at runtime. Therefore, the converter cannot forego optimization on such static field initialization.

CHAPTER 14

Working with int Data Type

The numeric integer types in the Java programming language are byte, short, int, and long, whose values are 8 bits, 16 bits, 32 bits, and 64 bits, respectively. All these types are signed two's-complement integers. Another integer type in the Java programming language is char, whose value is represented as a 16-bit unsigned integer representing a Unicode character.

The Java Card platform does not support types char or long or operations on these types. The int keyword and its 32-bit integer data type are optionally supported. A Java Card virtual machine that does not support int data type rejects programs using that type.

This chapter discusses issues related to using int when writing Java Card applets. It contains three sections: 32-bit arithmetic operations, array size and array index, and storing and computing int values.

14.1   32-Bit Arithmetic Operations

Arithmetic operations are one of the most commonly used operations of high-level programming languages, such as Java, C, or BASIC. An arithmetic operation consists of an arithmetic operator that performs a calculation on one or more operands.

In the Java programming language, the defined arithmetic operators are addition, subtraction, multiplication, division, and remainder. In a loose sense, bit-wise operators are also considered to be arithmetic operators. In this chapter, the term arithmetic operator refers to both arithmetic and bit-wise operators, as shown in Table 14.1.

The Java Card platform supports all Java arithmetic operators, except that they cannot operate on unsupported data types, such as long, float, and double. Applets can use the int type if the target Java Card virtual machine implementation supports int.

Table 14.1 Arithmetic operators

Operator name (arithmetic operators)	Java syntax	Operator names (bit-wise operator)	Java syntax
addition	+	bit-wise AND	&
subtraction	-	bit-wise inclusive OR	|
multiplication	*	bit-wise exclusive or (XOR)	^
division	/	bit-wise arithmetic right shift	>>
remainder	%	bit-wise logical right shift	>>>
		bit-wise shift left	<<
		bit-wise complement	~

An arithmetic operation should render the same result when computed on the Java Card platform and on the Java platform. However, if the int type is not supported, the Java Card virtual machine might not preserve the mathematical semantics of some arithmetic operations. Consider the following example:

```
// SHORT.MAX_VALUE = (short)0x7FFF = 32767;
short a = SHORT.MAX_VALUE;
short b = 1;
short c = 2;
a = (short) ((a + b) / c);
```

A Java virtual machine would execute the preceding arithmetic operation and compute a value of (32767 + 1) / 2 = 16384. However, a Java Card virtual machine without int type support would calculate a negative value: -16348.

To prevent discrepancies in computations that could cause serious consequences, the Java Card subset checker—a function typically implemented in the converter—reports an error if an applet contains an arithmetic operation like the one in the preceding example. The error message would be worded something like this:

```
unsupported int type of intermediate value, must cast intermediate
value to type byte or short
```

What does this error message mean? And why would the preceding example yield a different result when computed by the Java Card virtual machine? The answer to these questions lies in the differences in which a Java virtual machine and a Java Card virtual machine handle arithmetic operations.

Programs written in the Java programming language are executed on a target machine, called a Java virtual machine. A Java program must be compiled into Java bytecode instructions in order to be run on a Java virtual machine. To avoid defining an extensive set of bytecode instructions that operate separately on type byte, short, and int, the Java bytecode instruction set includes 32-bit integer arithmetic bytecode instructions that take uniform int operands and compute int results.[1] For example, the iadd instruction adds two int values, and the sum is also an int value. If operands of type byte or short are added with the iadd, their values are widened and sign-extended to 32-bit int.

Each of the following three examples (A, B, and C) contains an arithmetic operation a + b, whose operands are of type int, short, and byte, respectively.

```
Example A:
int a, b, c;
c = a + b;

Example B:
short a, b; int c;
c = a + b;

Example C:
byte a, b; int c;
c = a + b;
```

All three of these arithmetic operations are compiled to use the iadd instruction that adds two int values. At runtime, the Java virtual machine uses a last-in-first-out (LIFO) stack called the operand stack. The Java virtual machine loads constants or values from local variables and fields onto the operand stack. The values on the operand stack are used as operands in arithmetic and other Java virtual machine instructions. These instructions take values from the operand stack, operate on them, and push the result back onto the operand stack. The operand stack is also used to prepare parameters to be passed to methods and to receive method results[16].

---

[1] Separate instructions are defined to calculate arithmetic operations having operands type long, float, and double, respectively. These instructions are not discussed, because they operate on types that are not supported on the Java Card platform.

In the three examples, the variables a and b are pushed onto the stack by byte-code instructions setting up the calculation. Because an iadd instruction can operate only on 32-bit int values, if the variables a and b are type short or byte as in examples B and C, they are widened and sign-extended to become 32-bit int values as they are pushed onto the operand stack. When executing the iadd instruction, both int values a and b are popped from the operand stack and added, and their sum is pushed back onto the operand stack. The sum is also a 32-bit integer. The states of the operand stack when computing the operation a + b is depicted in Figure 14.1. The vertical arrows indicate the direction in which the stack grows.

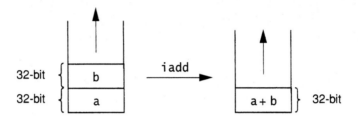

Figure 14.1 Operand stack in 32-bit addition

The Java bytecode instruction set is designed for desktop computers, which have 32-bit or 64-bit processors and are rich in memory compared to smart cards. Smart cards typically have 8-bit or 16-bit processors. As such, they perform 8-bit or 16-bit arithmetic operations more efficiently than 32-bit arithmetic operations. And because 8-bit or 16-bit operations do not require byte or short values to be widened to 32 bits, they use less stack space (in scarce RAM).

Therefore, besides supporting Java 32-bit integer arithmetic instructions, the Java Card bytecode instruction set provides additional integer arithmetic instructions to handle 16-bit values. For example, the sadd instruction is used for adding two 16-bit values. In the case of a Java Card virtual machine that supports ints, the 32-bit iadd instruction is also supported for adding two 32-bit values.

In the Java Card platform, the 32-bit arithmetic instructions have the same semantics as defined in the Java platform. That is, when operating on byte or short values, 32-bit instructions require such values to be widened and sign-extended to int. The 16-bit arithmetic instructions take uniform 16-bit short operands and output results of 16-bit short type. When operating on 8-bit values, 16-bit instructions require byte operands to be widened and sign-extended to short.

Most smart card applications use only data values of type byte or short. The 16-bit arithmetic instructions provide faster execution and less stack usage than 32-bit arithmetic instructions.

Among the responsibilities of the converter is to transform the Java byte-code instructions in class files to Java Card bytecode instructions and to write the output in a CAP file. The compilation and conversion processes are illustrated in Figure 14.2.

Figure 14.2 Compilation and conversion processes

The converter can optimize 32-bit arithmetic bytecode to 16-bit arithmetic bytecode when it sees that the operand(s) are type byte or short. For example, in examples B and C, the converter optimizes the iadd instruction to the sadd instruction. The optimized Java Card bytecode instructions after the conversion for all three examples are illustrated in Table 14.2.

Both load_a and load_b are pseudo bytecode instructions. To simplify this discussion, the actual bytecode for loading variables is not described here.

At runtime, a Java Card virtual machine also uses a stack structure for storing values. The state of the Java Card stack for computing 16-bit addition is shown in Figure 14.3. (The state of the Java Card stack for computing 32-bit addition is the same as that of the Java stack, as shown in Figure 14.1.)

Table 14.2 Optimized bytecode in example A, B, and C

Example	Java bytecode instructions	Java Card bytecode instructions
Example A	load_a; load_b; iadd;	load_a; load_b; iadd;
Examples B and C	load_a; load_b; iadd;	load_a; load_b; sadd;

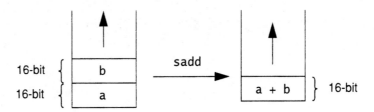

Figure 14.3 Operand stack in 16-bit addition

Note that when the optimized 16-bit arithmetic bytecodes are used, the result may lose precision. Incorrect results are possible because an arithmetic operation may produce overflow[2] to a result that would require 32-bit representation.

To illustrate this, let's assign the variable a to be the maximum value that can be represented by a 16-bit signed short and the variable b to 1.

```
short a = SHORT.MAX_VALUE; // MAX_VALUE = 0x7FFF = 32767;
short b = 1;
```

When the variable b is added to a, the sum overflows from the 16-bit range to the 32-bit range. In the Java platform, the effect of overflow is to create a larger positive 32-bit number 32768, because 32-bit addition is used.

By contrast, in the Java Card platform, when sadd is used instead of iadd, the addition creates overflow into the leftmost significant bit. Java integer values are signed. This means that the leftmost significant bit is used to indicate a positive number when it is set to 0 or a negative number when it is set to 1. Therefore, the sum of 16-bit addition causes an overflow into the sign bit, and the result is interpreted as a negative value: −32768. The processes of calculating a + b using 32-bit addition and 16-bit addition are demonstrated side by side in Table 14.3.

Table 14.3 Compute a + b using 32-bit addition and 16-bit addition

32-bit addition	16-bit addition
a + b = 0x00007FFF + 1 = 0x00008000 = 32768	a + b = 0x7FFF + 1 = 0x8000 = −32768

---

[2] Underflow is considered the same as overflow.

Table 14.4 Compute `(short)(a + b)` using 32-bit and 16-bit addition

32-bit addition	16-bit addition

`(short) (a + b)`
`= (short) (0x00007FFF + 1)`
`= (short) 0x00008000`
`= 0x8000`
`= -32768`
	`(short) (a + b)`
	`= 0x7FFF + 1`
	`= 0x8000`
	`= -32768`

To ensure semantic equivalency of 32-bit and 16-bit addition, the sum of a + b must be explicitly cast to byte or short.

As shown in Table 14.4, in 16-bit addition, the casting operator is a no-op—it does not affect the result, whereas in 32-bit addition, it truncates the most significant 16 bits of the sum to a short value, thereby eliminating any potential overflow problem. Even though the example in Table 14.4 is described in terms of addition, all 32-bit and 16-bit arithmetic operations render the same result if their results are immediately cast to byte or short.

Because the Java language is strongly typed, an explicit type cast (either an assignment conversion or a method invocation conversion) is required by the Java compiler when an arithmetic operation result is assigned to a variable of type byte or short or when the result is used as a method parameter or a return value of type byte or short (see the following code examples).

```
Assignment conversions:
short a, b, c;
c = a + b;      // compile-time error
c = (short)(a + b); // ok
```

```
Method invocation conversions:
public short aMethod(short b) {
    ...
    return a + b;      // compile-time error
    return (short)(a + b);// ok
}
```

```
aMethod(a+b);       // compile-time error
aMethod((byte)(a+b)); // ok
```

Table 14.5 `c = (short) ((a + b) / c)`

32-bit operations	16-bit operations
`c = (short) ((0x00007FFF + 1) / 2)`	`c = (short) ((0x7FFF + 1) / 2)`
`c = (short) (0x00008000 / 2)`	`c = (short) (0x8000 / 2)`
`c = (short) (0x00004000)`	`c = (short) (0xC000)`
`c = 0x4000`	`c = 0xC000`
`c = 16384`	`c = -16384`

The target—the local variable, the field, the method parameter, or the return value—has a specific required type. In the example, when the 32-bit `int` sum of a + b cannot be stored in a 16-bit `short` variable, the compiler forces developers to explicitly cast the value of a larger type to a smaller type so that the assignment instruction can proceed.

However, when the result of an arithmetic operation is not assigned immediately, it is called an intermediate value. An intermediate value can be further consumed as an operand in successive instructions, such as nested arithmetic expressions or comparison, switch, or array access statements.

Because no explicit type conversion is required by the compiler, 32-bit intermediate results contain the true mathematical results by having additional 16 high-order bits on the left to contain possible overflow, whereas 16-bit results may lose precision due to overflow.

Let's revisit the example `(short) ((a + b) / c)` on page 196. Both 32-bit and 16-bit arithmetic computations of this expression are shown in Table 14.5.

In the example, 16-bit addition `(a + b)` creates an intermediate value that overflows the 16-bit range and becomes negative. The next operation (division) is affected by the overflow from the `(a + b)` computation. Therefore, the final result is affected by overflow, even though the entire expression `(a + b)/c` is cast to `short`. In such a case, the converter must enforce the casting rule on intermediate values to ensure mathematical equivalence.

In the course of conversion, the converter always tries its best to optimize bytecode, performing the 32-bit to 16-bit arithmetic bytecode optimization when possible. But such optimization must ensure that the optimized Java Card bytecode is semantically equivalent to the original Java bytecode so that programs behave consistently on a Java Card virtual machine and on a Java virtual machine.

Table 14.6 `c = (short) (((short)(a + b)) / c)`

32-bit operations	16-bit operations
`c = (short)(((short)(0x00007FFF + 1))/2)` `c = (short) (((short)0x00008000) / 2)` `c = (short) (0xFFFF8000 / 2)` `c = (short) 0xFFFFC000` `c = 0xC000` `c = -16384`	`c = (short)(((short)(0x7FFF + 1))/2)` `c = (short) (((short) 0x8000) / 2)` `c = (short) (0x8000 / 2)` `c = (short) 0xC000` `c = 0xC000` `c = -16384`

When converting the example in Table 14.5, the converter detects that the sum of a + b might overflow beyond 16-bit representation.[3] In this case, no optimization is applied. This converter retains the iadd instruction for computing a + b. However, if int type is not supported on the target Java Card virtual machine, 32-bit arithmetic bytecode instructions are also not supported. In this case, the converter must issue an error.

To support the 32-bit to 16-bit bytecode optimization and to obtain mathematically equivalent results, an explicit type cast is required. The example in Table 14.5 is recalculated in Table 14.6 by casting the sum a + b to short.

An intermediate value that may lose precision due to overflow also affects the result of comparison, switch, or array access instructions when used as an operand in these operations.

So the rule of thumb is that to preserve the semantics of arithmetic operations when type int is not supported, the results of intermediate or unassigned arithmetic operations must be explicitly cast to either a byte or a short value. The Java Card casting rule is demonstrated in the following examples, where the cast operators enforced by the converter are in boldface.

```
short a, b, c;

c= (short) ((byte)(a/b) >> 2);
```

---

[3] Because the actual values used in an arithmetic operation are not always known at conversion time, the converter must assume the worst-case value for each operand. The worst case is determined on the basis of the input operand type.

```
byte array[] = new byte[(byte)(a * b)];

c = array[(short)(a + b)];

if (((short)(a >> b)) < 10) { ... }

switch ((byte) (a + b)) { ... }
```

Even though it is always a safe bet to apply the casting rule to all intermediate values, casting each intermediate value in a nested complex expression, such as the following one, can be cumbersome.

```
short a, b, c, d;
a = (short)(((short)((short)(((short)(a+b))+c))) &
    ((short)(((short)(a-b)) % c)));
```

A sophisticated converter can provide some relief by not requiring all intermediate values to be cast. Consider an example of adding a, b, and c. Both the 32-bit and the 16-bit computation are shown in Table 14.7.

The example in Table 14.7 differs from the example in Table 14.5 on page 202 in that the sum of a + b is used as an operand in addition instead of division. The addition operator is not sensitive to overflow as the division operator is. The final result is cast to type short, removing possible overflow in the addition operation. Thus, the results for both 16-bit and 32-bit operations are the same.

As demonstrated in the preceding example, not all arithmetic operators are sensitive to overflow. That is, such operators can take operands that carry potential

Table 14.7 c = (short) (a + b + c)

```
short a = SHORT.MAX_VALUE;
short b = 1;
short c = 1;
a = (short)(a + b + c);
```

32-bit operations	16-bit operations
c = (short) (0x00007FFF + 1 + 1)	c = (short) (0x7FFF + 1 + 1)
c = (short) (0x00008000 + 1)	c = (short) (0x8000 + 1)
c = (short) 0x00008001	c = (short) 0x8001
c = 0x8001	c = -32767
c = -32767	

Table 14.8   Arithmetic operators with potential overflow

Java operation	Description
a + b	addition
a - b	subtraction or negation
a * b	multiplication
a / b	division
a << b	bit-wise left shift

overflow. In addition, not all arithmetic operations produce results that have the potential for overflow. Thus, arithmetic operators can be categorized into operators with the potential to create overflow (in Table 14.8) and operators sensitive to overflow (in Table 14.9).

The result of an operation in Table 14.8 may lose precision due to overflow if the operation is optimized for the Java Card platform, using 16-bit arithmetic bytecode. An erroneous result can occur if such a result is input to any of the operators in Table 14.9 that are sensitive to overflow.

Table 14.9   Java operations that are sensitive to overflow

Java operation	Description	Which input operand(s) cannot lose precision
a / b	division	both operands a and b
a % b	remainder	both operands a and b
-a	negation	operand a
a >> b	bit-wise right shift	operand a
a >>> b	bit-wise logical right shift	operand a
a comparison_op b	boolean comparison statement	comparison operands a and b
switch (a)	while loop	integer evaluation operand a
new [a]	array creation	array size operand a
b[a]	array access	array index operand a

Therefore, the Java Card casting rule can be revised: When type int is not supported on the target Java Card virtual machine, the intermediate values of arithmetic calculations in Table 14.8 must be explicitly cast to either a byte or a short value when such intermediate values are used as operands in the operations listed in Table 14.9.

In the following code examples, the type casting rule is not applied to all intermediate values. The places where the casting operators are enforced by the converter are in boldface.

```
short a, b, c;
c = (short) ((byte)(a * b) / c);
c = (short) (a * b - c);// no cast required on result of a * b

c = (short) ((byte) (a * b) / c);
c = (short) (a & b / c); // no cast required on result of a & b

c = (byte) ((short)(a + b) << c);
c = (byte) (c << (a + b));// no cast required on result of a + b

if ((short)(a * b * c) < 10) {…}
switch ((byte) (c >>> b)) {…}

short array[] = new short[(byte)(a * b)];
c = array[(byte) (a / b)];
array[(byte)(a / b)] = c;

short a, b, c, d;
// no cast required on result of (a + b + c) << 5
a = (short) (((a + b + c) << 5) &((short)(a-b) % c));
```

Of course, the casting rule enforced by the compiler still applies. In the preceding examples, assignment conversion is required by casting results of arithmetic operations to byte or short.

14.2 Array Size and Array Index

Java Card technology supports one-dimensional arrays. Due to the limited resources on smart cards, arrays can hold a maximum of 32,767 elements. The number 32,767 is the maximum value that can be represented in a short variable.

The following examples are lines of Java code that create arrays or access array elements:

```
int a, b;
int[] array = new int[a];
a = array[a + b];
for (int i = 0; i < a; i++)
    array[i] = i;
```

In the examples, the runtime values of a and b are not known at conversion time. To prevent loading erroneous code that might create arrays with sizes larger than the supported range or that might access an array element out of bounds, the converter requires that only variables of type short or byte be used as an array index or to specify an array size. This restriction applies to all array access operations in the Java Card platform regardless of whether the 32-bit integers are supported.

In the following, the array access examples are corrected to pass the converter inspection (the changes are in boldface).

```
int a, b;
int[] array = new int[(short)a];
a = array[(short)(a + b)];
for (int i = 0; i < a; i++)
    array[(short)i] = i;
```

14.3 Storing and Computing **int** Values

Java Card applets often need to deal with large numbers. For example, a wallet applet might support a balance of up to $1000. If the minimum monetary unit *cent* is used as the base representation, an int value is required to store a balance that can have the maximum value of 1000 * 100 = 100,000 cents. This section discusses how to store a large number and perform mathematical computation on large numbers in applets when the int type is not supported by a Java Card virtual machine.

When large data types are not available, smart card applications use a sequence of bytes for storing a large number. Applying this technique to programming in the Java language, applets can create a byte array of four elements to represent an int number whose value is constructed by concatenating the elements of the array (Figure 14.4).

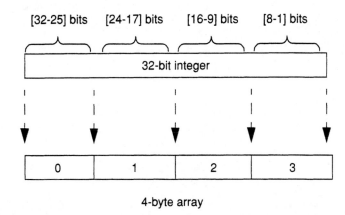

Figure 14.4 Storing an int value in a 4-byte array using big endian order

Figure 14.4 assumes that the array bytes are encoded in big endian order; that is, the first element represents the most significant byte. Alternatively, small endian order could be used to represent an int number in which the first element represents the least significant byte.

The Java language does not have built-in arithmetic operators that take byte arrays as operands and internally compute the result from byte arrays. The class BigIntNumber provides addition, subtraction, and comparison functions for two unsigned integer numbers in the byte array format. (The class BigIntNumber could also be modified to support signed integers.) The functions in the BigIntNumber class assume that input operands and results are uniform-size integers stored in big endian order. A user of this class can specify the number of bytes that make up an integer. This way, the BigIntNumber class can be applied to numbers of any range. For example, 4 bytes in an array represents an unsigned 32-bit value, and 8 bytes in an array represents an unsigned 64-bit value. To make optimum use of space, an applet often creates one array for storing multiple fields (values). For example, a byte array in the wallet applet might contain the balance as well as other data. Therefore, the functions in the BigIntNumber class also allow a user to specify the starting position where the number starts in its containing array.

```
/**
 * Class BigIntNumber provides addition, subtraction, and
 * comparison functions for unsigned integers represented in
 * byte array format in big endian order.
 */
public class BigIntNumber {
```

```
/**
 * Add two unsigned integers represented in array A and B.
 * The sum is stored in array C.
 * @param A the left operand
 * @param AOff the starting position in array A
 * @param B the right operand
 * @param BOff the starting position in array B
 * @param C the result of (A + B)
 * @param COff the starting position in array C
 * @param len the number of bytes in the operands as well
 * in the computed result. The parameter len cannot be
 * a negative number.
 * @return false if the result overflows
 * If overflow occurs, the sum would be the true
 * mathematical result with the most significant bytes
 * discarded to fit into array C of the specified length.
 * @throws ArrayOutOfBoundException if accessing array
 * out of bound
 */
public static boolean add(byte[] A, byte AOff,
                          byte[] B, byte BOff,
                          byte[] C, byte COff,
                          byte len) {

    short result = 0;

    for (len = (byte)(len - 1); len >= 0; len--) {

        // add two unsigned bytes and the carry from the
        // previous byte computation
        result = (short)(getUnsignedByte(A, AOff, len) +
                    getUnsignedByte(B, BOff, len) +
                    result);

        // store the result in byte array C
        C[(short)(len + COff)] = (byte) result;

        // has a carry?
        if (result > 0x00FF)
            result = 1;
```

```
        else
            result = 0;
    }


    // produce overflow in the sum
    if (result == 1)
        return false;
    return true;
}



/**
 * Subtract two unsigned integers represented in
 * array A and B. The result is stored in array C.
 * @param A the left operand
 * @param AOff the starting position in A
 * @param B the right operand
 * @param BOff the starting position in B
 * @param C the result of (A-B)
 * @param COff the starting position in C
 * @param len the number of bytes in the operands as well
 * in the computed result. The parameterlen cannot be
 * a negative number.
 * @return false if the result underflows
 * If underflow occurs, the result would be the
 * mathematical result of A + ~B + 1.
 * @throws ArrayOutOfBoundException if array access
 * out of bound
 */
public static boolean subtract (byte[] A, byte AOff,
                                byte[] B, byte BOff,
                                byte[] C, byte COff,
                                byte len) {

    byte borrow = 0;
    short result;

    for (len = (byte)(len -1); len >= 0; len--) {
```

```
        // subtract one unsigned byte from the other
        // also subtract the borrow from the previous
        // byte computation
        result = (short)(getUnsignedByte(A, AOff, len) -
                         getUnsignedByte(B, BOff, len) -
                         borrow);

        // need to borrow?
        if (result < 0) {
            borrow = 1;
            result = (short)(result + 0x100);
        } else {
            borrow = 0;
        }

        // store the result in C
        C[(byte)(len + COff)] = (byte)result;
    }

    // is the result underflow
    if (borrow == 1)
        return false;
    return true;
}


/**
 * Compare two unsigned integers represented in array A and B
 * @param A the left operand
 * @param AOff the starting position in A
 * @param B the right operand
 * @param BOff the starting position in B
 * @param len the number of bytes in the operands
 * The parameter len cannot be a negative number.
 * @return the result of the comparison as follows:
 * 0 if identical
 * -1 if the left operand is smaller than the right operand
 * 1 if the left operand is bigger than the right operand
```

```
    * @throws ArrayOutOfBoundException if array access out
    * of bound
    */
public static byte compare(byte[] A, byte AOff,
                           byte[] B, byte BOff,
                           byte len) {

    byte count = (byte)0;

    for(; count < len; count++) {

        short C = getUnsignedByte(A, AOff, count);
        short D = getUnsignedByte(B, BOff, count);

        if (C > D) return 1;
        if (C < D) return -1;

    }
    return 0;
}


/**
 * Get the unsigned byte at the index (AOff + count)
 */
private static short getUnsignedByte(byte[] A,
                                     byte AOff,
                                     byte count){

    return (short) (A[(short)(count + AOff)] & 0x00FF);
}
}
```

14.4 Summary

To summarize, this chapter discusses the following issues related to using `int` when writing Java Card applets:

- *32-bit arithmetic operations*—When the `int` data type is not supported, intermediate results of arithmetic expressions might need to be cast to type `byte` or `short`. The first section of the chapter explains why the casting rule is required and when it should be applied.

- *Array size and array index*—The Java Card language subset specifies that arrays can hold up to 32,767 fields. This requires that only variables of type `byte` or `short` be used as an array index or to specify the size of an array during array creation. The second section of this chapter points out examples where code does not conform to the language subset and needs to be corrected.

- *Storing and computing `int` values*—Many applets need to store large integer numbers that are beyond 8-bit (`byte`) or 16-bit (`short`) representation. The end of this chapter demonstrates how to store and compute large integers in applets by using the `BigIntNumber` class.

PART 4

Appendices

Java Card Language Subset

(from Chapter 2 of the Java Card Virtual Machine Specification)[1]

Applets written for the Java Card platform are written in the Java programming language. They are compiled using Java compilers. Java Card technology uses a subset of the Java language, and familiarity with the Java platform is required to understand the Java Card platform.

A.1 Unsupported Items

The items listed in this section are elements of the Java programming language and platform that are not supported by the Java Card platform.

A.1.1 Unsupported Features

Dynamic Class Loading

Dynamic class loading is not supported in the Java Card platform. An implementation of the Java Card platform is not able to load classes dynamically. Classes are either masked into the card during manufacturing or downloaded through an installation process after the card has been issued. Programs executing on the card may only refer to classes that already exist on the card, since there is no way to download classes during the normal execution of application code.

---

[1] *The Java Card Virtual Machine Specification* can be downloaded from the Web site at http://java.sun.com/products/javacard.

Security Manager

Security management in the Java Card platform differs significantly from that of the Java platform. In the Java platform, there is a Security Manager class (java.lang.SecurityManager) responsible for implementing security features. In the Java Card platform, language security policies are implemented by the virtual machine. There is no Security Manager class that makes policy decisions on whether to allow operations.

Garbage Collection & Finalization

Java Card technology does not require a garbage collector. Nor does Java Card technology allow explicit deallocation of objects, since this would break the Java programming language's required pointer-safety. Therefore, application programmers cannot assume that objects that are allocated are ever deallocated. Storage for unreachable objects will not necessarily be reclaimed.

Finalization is also not required. finalize() will not necessarily be called automatically by the Java Card virtual machine, and programmers should not rely on this behavior.

Threads

The Java Card virtual machine does not support multiple threads of control. Java Card programs cannot use class Thread or any of the thread-related keywords in the Java programming language.

Cloning

The Java Card platform does not support cloning of objects. Java Card API class Object does not implement a clone method, and there is no Cloneable interface provided.

Access Control in Java Packages

The Java Card language subset supports the package access control defined in the Java language. However, the cases that are not supported are as follows.

- If a class implements a method with package access visibility, a subclass cannot override the method and change the access visibility of the method to protected or public.
- An interface that is defined with package access visibility cannot be extended by an interface with public access visibility.
- A public or protected method in a public class cannot contain a formal parameter of type reference to a package-visible class.

- A package-visible class that is extended by a public class cannot define any public or protected methods.

A.1.2 Keywords

The following keywords indicate unsupported options related to native methods, threads and memory management.

native   synchronized   transient   volatile

A.1.3 Unsupported Types

The Java Card platform does not support types char, double, float or long, or operations on those types. It also does not support arrays of more than one dimension.

A.1.4 Classes

In general, none of the Java core API classes are supported in the Java Card platform. Some classes from the java.lang package are supported (see Section A.2.4), but none of the rest are. For example, classes that are *not* supported are String, Thread (and all thread-related classes), wrapper classes such as Boolean and Integer, and class Class.

A.1.5 System

Class java.lang.System is not supported. Java Card technology supplies a class javacard.framework.JCSystem, which provides an interface to system behavior.

A.2 Supported Items

If a language feature is not explicitly described as unsupported, it is part of the supported subset. Notable supported features are described in this section.

A.2.1 Features

Packages

Software written for the Java Card platform follows the standard rules for the Java platform packages. Java Card API classes are written as Java source files, which include package designations. Package mechanisms are used to identify and control access to classes, static fields and static methods. Except as noted in "Access Control in Java Packages" (A.1.1), packages in the Java Card platform are used exactly the way they are in the Java platform.

Dynamic Object Creation

The Java Card platform programs supports dynamically created objects, both class instances and arrays. This is done, as usual, by using the new operator. Objects are allocated out of the heap.

As noted in "Garbage Collection & Finalization" (Section A.1.1), a Java Card virtual machine will not necessarily garbage collect objects. Any object allocated by a virtual machine may continue to exist and consume resources even after it becomes unreachable.

Virtual Methods

Since Java Card objects are Java programming language objects, invoking virtual methods on objects in a program written for the Java Card platform is exactly the same as in a program written for the Java platform. Inheritance is supported, including the use of the super keyword.

Interfaces

Java Card classes may define or implement interfaces as in the Java programming language. Invoking methods on interface types works as expected. Type checking and the instanceof operator also work correctly with interfaces.

Exceptions

Java Card programs may define, throw and catch exceptions, as in Java programs. Class Throwable and its relevant subclasses are supported. (Some Exception and Error subclasses are omitted, since those exceptions cannot occur in the Java Card platform. See *the Java Card Virtual Machine Specification* section 2.3.3 for specification of errors and exceptions.)

A.2.2   Keywords

The following keywords are supported. Their use is the same as in the Java programming language.

abstract	default	if	private	this
boolean	do	implements	protected	throw

break	else	import	public	throws
byte	extends	instanceof	return	try
case	final	int	short	void
catch	finally	interface	static	while
class	for	new	super	
continue	goto	package	switch	

A.2.3   Types

Java programming language types boolean, byte, short, and int are supported. Objects (class instances and single-dimensional arrays) are also supported. Arrays can contain the supported primitive data types, objects, and other arrays.

Some Java Card implementations might not support use of the int data type. (Refer to A.3.1.)

A.2.4   Classes

Most of the classes in the java.lang package are not supported in Java Card. The following classes from java.lang are supported on the card in a limited form.

Object

Java Card classes descend from java.lang.Object, just as in the Java programming language. Most of the methods of Object are not available in the Java Card API, but the class itself exists to provide a root for the class hierarchy.

Throwable

Class Throwable and its subclasses are supported. Most of the methods of Throwable are not available in the Java Card API, but the class itself exists to provide a common ancestor for all exceptions.

A.3   Optionally Supported Items

This section describes the optional features of the Java Card platform. An optional feature is not required to be supported in a Java Card compatible implementation. However, if an implementation does include support for an optional feature, it must be supported fully, and exactly as specified in this document.

A.3.1   `int`

The `int` keyword and 32-bit integer data types need not be supported in a Java Card implementation. A Java Card virtual machine that does not support the `int` data type will reject programs which use the `int` data type or 32-bit intermediate values.

The result of an arithmetic expression produced by a Java Card virtual machine must be equal to the result produce by a Java virtual machine, regardless of the input values. A Java Card virtual machine that does not support the `int` data type must reject expressions that could produce a different result.

A.4   Limitations of the Java Card Virtual Machine

The limitations of resource-constrained hardware prevent Java Card programs from supporting the full range of functionality of certain Java platform features. The features in question are supported, but a particular virtual machine may limit the range of operation to less than that of the Java platform.

To ensure a level of portability for application code, this section establishes a minimum required level for partial support of these language features.

The limitations here are listed as maximums from the application programmer's perspective. Applets that do not violate these maximum values can be converted into Java Card CAP files, and will be portable across all Java Card implementations. From the Java Card virtual machine implementer's perspective, each maximum listed indicates a minimum level of support that will allow portability of applets.

A.4.1   Classes

Classes in a Package

A package can contain at most 255 public classes and interfaces.

Interfaces

A class can implement at most 15 interfaces, including interfaces implemented by superclasses.

An interface can inherit from at most 15 superinterfaces.

Static Fields

A class can have at most 256 public or protected static fields.

Static Methods

A class can have at most 256 public or protected static methods.

A.4.2   Objects

Methods

A class can implement a maximum of 128 public or protected instance methods, and a maximum of 128 instance methods with package visibility. These limits include inherited methods.

Class Instances

Class instances can contain a maximum of 255 fields, where an `int` data type is counted as occupying two fields.

Arrays

Arrays can hold a maximum of 32767 fields.

A.4.3   Methods

The maximum number of local variables that can be used in a method is 255, where an `int` data type is counted as occupying two local variables.

A method can have at most 32767 Java Card virtual machine bytecodes. The number of Java Card bytecodes may differ from the number of Java bytecodes in the Java virtual machine implementation of that method.

A.4.4   Switch Statements

The format of the Java Card virtual machine switch instructions limits switch statements to a maximum of 65536 cases. This limit is far greater than the limit imposed by the maximum size of methods (Section A.4.3).

A.4.5   Class Initialization

There is limited support for initialization of static field values in `<clinit>` methods. Static fields of applets may only be initialized to primitive compile-time constant values, or arrays of primitive compile-time constants. Static fields of user libraries may only be initialized to primitive compile-time constant values. Primitive constant data types include `boolean`, `byte`, `short`, and `int`.

Java Card 2.1 Application Programming Interface

package
java.lang

Description
Provides classes that are fundamental to the design of the Java Card technology subset of the Java programming language.

Class Summary	
Classes	
Object	Class Object is the root of the Java Card class hierarchy.
Throwable	The Throwable class is the superclass of all errors and exceptions in the Java Card subset of the Java language.
Exceptions	
ArithmeticException	A JCRE owned instance of ArithmethicException is thrown when an exceptional arithmetic condition has occurred.
ArrayIndexOutOfBoundsException	A JCRE owned instance of IndexOutOfBoundsException is thrown to indicate that an array has been accessed with an illegal index.
ArrayStoreException	A JCRE owned instance of ArrayStoreException is thrown to indicate that an attempt has been made to store the wrong type of object into an array of objects.
ClassCastException	A JCRE owned instance of ClassCastException is thrown to indicate that the code has attempted to cast an object to a subclass of which it is not an instance.
Exception	The class Exception and its subclasses are a form of Throwable that indicates conditions that a reasonable applet might want to catch.
IndexOutOfBoundsException	A JCRE owned instance of IndexOutOfBoundsException is thrown to indicate that an index of some sort (such as to an array) is out of range.
NegativeArraySizeException	A JCRE owned instance of NegativeArraySizeException is thrown if an applet tries to create an array with negative size.
NullPointerException	A JCRE owned instance of NullPointerException is thrown when an applet attempts to use null in a case where an object is required.
RuntimeException	RuntimeException is the superclass of those exceptions that can be thrown during the normal operation of the Java Card Virtual Machine.
SecurityException	A JCRE owned instance of SecurityException is thrown by the Java Card Virtual Machine to indicate a security violation.

java.lang
ArithmeticException

Syntax

```
public class ArithmeticException extends RuntimeException
```

```
Object
  |
  +--Throwable
        |
        +--Exception
              |
              +--RuntimeException
                    |
                    +--java.lang.ArithmeticException
```

Description

A JCRE owned instance of ArithmethicException is thrown when an exceptional arithmetic condition has occurred. For example, a "divide by zero" is an exceptional arithmetic condition.

JCRE owned instances of exception classes are temporary JCRE Entry Point Objects and can be accessed from any applet context. References to these temporary objects cannot be stored in class variables or instance variables or array components. See *Java Card Runtime Environment (JCRE) 2.1 Specification* for details.

This Java Card class's functionality is a strict subset of the definition in the *Java Platform Core API Specification*.

Constructors

ArithmeticException()

```
public ArithmeticException()
```

Constructs an ArithmeticException.

java.lang
ArrayIndexOutOfBounds-
Exception

Syntax

```
public class ArrayIndexOutOfBoundsException extends
    IndexOutOfBoundsException
```

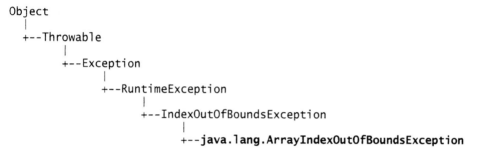

```
Object
  |
  +--Throwable
       |
       +--Exception
            |
            +--RuntimeException
                 |
                 +--IndexOutOfBoundsException
                      |
                      +--java.lang.ArrayIndexOutOfBoundsException
```

Description

A JCRE owned instance of IndexOutOfBoundsException is thrown to indicate that an array has been accessed with an illegal index. The index is either negative or greater than or equal to the size of the array.

JCRE owned instances of exception classes are temporary JCRE Entry Point Objects and can be accessed from any applet context. References to these temporary objects cannot be stored in class variables or instance variables or array components. See *Java Card Runtime Environment (JCRE) 2.1 Specification* for details.

This Java Card class's functionality is a strict subset of the definition in the *Java Platform Core API Specification*.

Constructors

ArrayIndexOutOfBoundsException()

```
public ArrayIndexOutOfBoundsException()
```

Constructs an ArrayIndexOutOfBoundsException.

java.lang
ArrayStoreException

Syntax

```
public class ArrayStoreException extends RuntimeException

Object
  |
  +--Throwable
       |
       +--Exception
            |
            +--RuntimeException
                 |
                 +--java.lang.ArrayStoreException
```

Description

A JCRE owned instance of ArrayStoreException is thrown to indicate that an attempt has been made to store the wrong type of object into an array of objects. For example, the following code generates an ArrayStoreException:

```
Object x[] = new AID[3];
x[0] = new OwnerPIN( (byte) 3, (byte) 8);
```

JCRE owned instances of exception classes are temporary JCRE Entry Point Objects and can be accessed from any applet context. References to these temporary objects cannot be stored in class variables or instance variables or array components. See *Java Card Runtime Environment (JCRE) 2.1 Specification* for details.

This Java Card class's functionality is a strict subset of the definition in the *Java Platform Core API Specification*.

Constructors

ArrayStoreException()

public ArrayStoreException()

Constructs an ArrayStoreException.

java.lang
ClassCastException

Syntax

```
public class ClassCastException extends RuntimeException
```

```
Object
  |
  +--Throwable
       |
       +--Exception
            |
            +--RuntimeException
                 |
                 +--java.lang.ClassCastException
```

Description

A JCRE owned instance of `ClassCastException` is thrown to indicate that the code has attempted to cast an object to a subclass of which it is not an instance. For example, the following code generates a `ClassCastException`:

```
Object x = new OwnerPIN((byte)3,(byte)8);
JCSystem.getAppletShareableInterfaceObject((AID)x,(byte)5);
```

JCRE owned instances of exception classes are temporary JCRE Entry Point Objects and can be accessed from any applet context. References to these temporary objects cannot be stored in class variables or instance variables or array components. See *Java Card Runtime Environment (JCRE) 2.1 Specification* for details.

This Java Card class's functionality is a strict subset of the definition in the *Java Platform Core API Specification*.

Constructors

ClassCastException()

```
public ClassCastException()
```

Constructs a `ClassCastException`.

java.lang
Exception

Syntax

```
public class Exception extends Throwable
```

```
Object
  |
  +--Throwable
         |
         +--java.lang.Exception
```

Direct Known Subclasses: CardException, RuntimeException

Description

The class Exception and its subclasses are a form of Throwable that indicates conditions that a reasonable applet might want to catch.

This Java Card class's functionality is a strict subset of the definition in the *Java Platform Core API Specification*.

Constructors

Exception()

```
public Exception()
```

Constructs an Exception instance.

java.lang
IndexOutOfBoundsException

Syntax

```
public class IndexOutOfBoundsException extends RuntimeException

Object
  |
  +--Throwable
        |
        +--Exception
              |
              +--RuntimeException
                    |
                    +--java.lang.IndexOutOfBoundsException
```

Direct Known Subclasses: `ArrayIndexOutOfBoundsException`

Description

A JCRE owned instance of `IndexOutOfBoundsException` is thrown to indicate that an index of some sort (such as to an array) is out of range.

JCRE owned instances of exception classes are temporary JCRE Entry Point Objects and can be accessed from any applet context. References to these temporary objects cannot be stored in class variables or instance variables or array components. See *Java Card Runtime Environment (JCRE) 2.1 Specification* for details.

This Java Card class's functionality is a strict subset of the definition in the *Java Platform Core API Specification*.

Constructors

IndexOutOfBoundsException()

```
public IndexOutOfBoundsException()
```

Constructs an `IndexOutOfBoundsException`.

java.lang
NegativeArraySizeException

Syntax

```
public class NegativeArraySizeException extends RuntimeException
```

```
Object
  |
  +--Throwable
        |
        +--Exception
              |
              +--RuntimeException
                    |
                    +--java.lang.NegativeArraySizeException
```

Description

A JCRE owned instance of `NegativeArraySizeException` is thrown if an applet tries to create an array with negative size.

JCRE owned instances of exception classes are temporary JCRE Entry Point Objects and can be accessed from any applet context. References to these temporary objects cannot be stored in class variables or instance variables or array components. See *Java Card Runtime Environment (JCRE) 2.1 Specification* for details.

This Java Card class's functionality is a strict subset of the definition in the *Java Platform Core API Specification*.

Constructors

NegativeArraySizeException()

```
public NegativeArraySizeException()
```

Constructs a `NegativeArraySizeException`.

java.lang
NullPointerException

Syntax

```
public class NullPointerException extends RuntimeException
```

```
Object
  |
  +--Throwable
        |
        +--Exception
              |
              +--RuntimeException
                    |
                    +--java.lang.NullPointerException
```

Description

A JCRE owned instance of NullPointerException is thrown when an applet attempts to use null in a case where an object is required. These include:

- Calling the instance method of a null object.
- Accessing or modifying the field of a null object.
- Taking the length of null as if it were an array.
- Accessing or modifying the slots of null as if it were an array.
- Throwing null as if it were a Throwable value.

JCRE owned instances of exception classes are temporary JCRE Entry Point Objects and can be accessed from any applet context. References to these temporary objects cannot be stored in class variables or instance variables or array components. See *Java Card Runtime Environment (JCRE) 2.1 Specification* for details.

This Java Card class's functionality is a strict subset of the definition in the *Java Platform Core API Specification*.

Constructors

NullPointerException()

```
public NullPointerException()
```

Constructs a NullPointerException.

java.lang
Object

Syntax
`public class Object`

Description
Class `Object` is the root of the Java Card class hierarchy. Every class has `Object` as a superclass. All objects, including arrays, implement the methods of this class. This Java Card class's functionality is a strict subset of the definition in the *Java Platform Core API Specification*.

Constructors

Object()

> `public Object()`

Methods

equals(Object)

> `public boolean equals(Object obj)`

> Compares two Objects for equality.

> The `equals` method implements an equivalence relation:

> - It is *reflexive*: for any reference value x, x.`equals(x)` should return `true`.
> - It is *symmetric*: for any reference values x and y, x.`equals(y)` should return `true` if and only if y.`equals(x)` returns `true`.
> - It is *transitive*: for any reference values x, y, and z, if x.`equals(y)` returns `true` and y.`equals(z)` returns `true`, then x.`equals(z)` should return `true`.
> - It is *consistent*: for any reference values x and y, multiple invocations of x.`equals(y)` consistently return `true` or consistently return `false`.
> - For any reference value x, x.`equals(null)` should return `false`.

The equals method for class Object implements the most discriminating possible equivalence relation on objects; that is, for any reference values x and y, this method returns true if and only if x and y refer to the same object (x==y has the value true).

Parameters:

    obj—the reference object with which to compare.

Returns: true if this object is the same as the obj argument; false otherwise.

java.lang
RuntimeException

Syntax

```
public class RuntimeException extends Exception

Object
  |
  +--Throwable
        |
        +--Exception
              |
              +--java.lang.RuntimeException
```

Direct Known Subclasses: ArithmeticException, ArrayStoreException, CardRuntimeException, ClassCastException, IndexOutOfBoundsException, NegativeArraySizeException, NullPointerException, SecurityException

Description

RuntimeException is the superclass of those exceptions that can be thrown during the normal operation of the Java Card Virtual Machine.

A method is not required to declare in its throws clause any subclasses of Runtime-Exception that might be thrown during the execution of the method but not caught.

This Java Card class's functionality is a strict subset of the definition in the *Java Platform Core API Specification*.

Constructors

RuntimeException()

```
public RuntimeException()
```

Constructs a RuntimeException instance.

java.lang
SecurityException

Syntax

```
public class SecurityException extends RuntimeException

Object
  |
  +--Throwable
        |
        +--Exception
              |
              +--RuntimeException
                    |
                    +--java.lang.SecurityException
```

Description

A JCRE owned instance of `SecurityException` is thrown by the Java Card Virtual Machine to indicate a security violation.

This exception is thrown when an attempt is made to illegally access an object belonging to a another applet. It may optionally be thrown by a Java Card VM implementation to indicate fundamental language restrictions, such as attempting to invoke a private method in another class.

For security reasons, the JCRE implementation may mute the card instead of throwing this exception.

JCRE owned instances of exception classes are temporary JCRE Entry Point Objects and can be accessed from any applet context. References to these temporary objects cannot be stored in class variables or instance variables or array components. See *Java Card Runtime Environment (JCRE) 2.1 Specification* for details.

This Java Card class's functionality is a strict subset of the definition in the *Java Platform Core API Specification*.

Constructors

SecurityException()

```
public SecurityException()
```

Constructs a `SecurityException`.

java.lang
Throwable

Syntax

```
public class Throwable

Object
  |
  +--java.lang.Throwable
```

Direct Known Subclasses: Exception

Description

The Throwable class is the superclass of all errors and exceptions in the Java Card subset of the Java language. Only objects that are instances of this class (or of one of its subclasses) are thrown by the Java Card Virtual Machine or can be thrown by the Java throw statement. Similarly, only this class or one of its subclasses can be the argument type in a catch clause.

This Java Card class's functionality is a strict subset of the definition in the *Java Platform Core API Specification.*

Constructors

Throwable()

```
public Throwable()
```

Constructs a new Throwable.

package
javacard.framework

Description

Provides framework of classes and interfaces for the core functionality of a Java Card applet.

Class Summary	
Interfaces	
ISO7816	ISO7816 encapsulates constants related to ISO 7816-3 and ISO 7816-4.
PIN	This interface represents a PIN.
Shareable	The Shareable interface serves to identify all shared objects.
Classes	
AID	This class encapsulates the Application Identifier(AID) associated with an applet.
APDU	Application Protocol Data Unit (APDU) is the communication format between the card and the off-card applications.
Applet	This abstract class defines an applet in Java Card.
JCSystem	The JCSystem class includes a collection of methods to control applet execution, resource management, atomic transaction management and inter-applet object sharing in Java Card.
OwnerPIN	This class represents an Owner PIN.
Util	The Util class contains common utility functions.
Exceptions	
APDUException	APDUException represents an APDU related exception.
CardException	The CardException class defines a field **reason** and two accessor methods getReason() and setReason().
CardRuntimeException	The CardRuntimeException class defines a field **reason** and two accessor methods getReason() and setReason().
ISOException	ISOException class encapsulates an ISO 7816-4 response status word as its **reason** code.
PINException	PINException represents a OwnerPIN class access-related exception.
SystemException	SystemException represents a JCSystem class related exception.
TransactionException	TransactionException represents an exception in the transaction subsystem.
UserException	UserException represents a User exception.

javacard.framework
AID

Syntax

```
public final class AID
```

```
Object
   |
   +--javacard.framework.AID
```

Description

This class encapsulates the Application Identifier(AID) associated with an applet. An AID is defined in ISO 7816-5 to be a sequence of bytes between 5 and 16 bytes in length.

The JCRE creates instances of AID class to identify and manage every applet on the card. Applets need not create instances of this class. An applet may request and use the JCRE owned instances to identify itself and other applet instances.

JCRE owned instances of AID are permanent JCRE Entry Point Objects and can be accessed from any applet context. References to these permanent objects can be stored and re-used.

An applet instance can obtain a reference to JCRE owned instances of its own AID object by using the JCSystem.getAID() method and another applet's AID object via the JCSystem.lookupAID() method.

An applet uses AID instances to request to share another applet's object or to control access to its own shared object from another applet. See *Java Card Runtime Environment (JCRE) 2.1 Specification* for details.

See Also: JCSystem, SystemException

Constructors

AID(byte[], short, byte)

```
public AID(byte[] bArray, short offset, byte length)
```

The JCRE uses this constructor to create a new AID instance encapsulating the specified AID bytes.

Parameters:

> bArray—the byte array containing the AID bytes.
>
> offset—the start of AID bytes in bArray.
>
> length—the length of the AID bytes in bArray.

Throws: SystemException—with the following reason code:
- SystemException.ILLEGAL_VALUE if the length parameter is less than 5 or greater than 16.

Methods

equals(byte[], short, byte)

```
public boolean equals(byte[] bArray, short offset, byte length)
```

Checks if the specified AID bytes in bArray are the same as those encapsulated in this AID object. The result is true if and only if the bArray argument is not null and the AID bytes encapsulated in this AID object are equal to the specified AID bytes in bArray.

This method does not throw NullPointerException.

Parameters:

> bArray—containing the AID bytes
>
> offset—within bArray to begin
>
> length—of AID bytes in bArray

Returns: true if equal, false otherwise.

equals(Object)

```
public boolean equals(Object anObject)
```

Compares the AID bytes in this AID instance to the AID bytes in the specified object. The result is true if and only if the argument is not null and is an AID object that encapsulates the same AID bytes as this object.

This method does not throw NullPointerException.

Overrides: equals(Object) in class Object

Parameters:

> anObject—the object to compare this AID against.

Returns: true if the AID byte values are equal, false otherwise.

getBytes(byte[], short)

```
public byte getBytes(byte[] dest, short offset)
```

Called to get the AID bytes encapsulated within AID object.

Parameters:

> dest—byte array to copy the AID bytes.

> offset—within dest where the AID bytes begin.

Returns: the length of the AID bytes.

partialEquals(byte[], short, byte)

```
public boolean partialEquals(byte[] bArray, short offset,
            byte length)
```

Checks if the specified partial AID byte sequence matches the first length bytes of the encapsulated AID bytes within this AID object. The result is true if and only if the bArray argument is not null and the input length is less than or equal to the length of the encapsulated AID bytes within this AID object and the specified bytes match.

This method does not throw NullPointerException.

Parameters:

> bArray—containing the partial AID byte sequence

> offset—within bArray to begin

> length—of partial AID bytes in bArray

Returns: true if equal, false otherwise.

RIDEquals(AID)

```
public boolean RIDEquals(AID otherAID)
```

Checks if the RID (National Registered Application provider identifier) portion of the encapsulated AID bytes within the otherAID object matches that of this AID object. The first 5 bytes of an AID byte sequence is the RID. See ISO 7816-5 for details. The result is true if and only if the argument is not null and is an AID object that encapsulates the same RID bytes as this object.

This method does not throw NullPointerException.

Parameters:

> otherAID—the AID to compare against.

Returns: true if the RID bytes match, false otherwise.

javacard.framework
APDU

Syntax

```
public final class APDU
```

```
Object
 |
 +--javacard.framework.APDU
```

Description

Application Protocol Data Unit (APDU) is the communication format between the card and the off-card applications. The format of the APDU is defined in ISO specification 7816-4.

This class only supports messages which conform to the structure of command and response defined in ISO 7816-4. The behavior of messages which use proprietary structure of messages (for example with header CLA byte in range 0xD0-0xFE) is undefined. This class does not support extended length fields.

The APDU object is owned by the JCRE. The APDU class maintains a byte array buffer which is used to transfer incoming APDU header and data bytes as well as outgoing data. The buffer length must be at least 37 bytes (5 bytes of header and 32 bytes of data). The JCRE must zero out the APDU buffer before each new message received from the CAD.

The JCRE designates the APDU object as a temporary JCRE Entry Point Object (See *Java Card Runtime Environment (JCRE) 2.1 Specification* for details). A temporary JCRE Entry Point Object can be accessed from any applet context. References to these temporary objects cannot be stored in class variables or instance variables or array components.

The JCRE similarly marks the APDU buffer as a global array (See *Java Card Runtime Environment (JCRE) 2.1 Specification* for details). A global array can be accessed from any applet context. References to global arrays cannot be stored in class variables or instance variables or array components.

The applet receives the APDU instance to process from the JCRE in the Applet.process(APDU) method, and the first five bytes [CLA, INS, P1, P2, P3] are available in the APDU buffer.

The APDU class API is designed to be transport protocol independent. In other words, applets can use the same APDU methods regardless of whether the underlying protocol in use is T=0 or T=1 (as defined in ISO 7816-3).

The incoming APDU data size may be bigger than the APDU buffer size and may therefore need to be read in portions by the applet. Similarly, the outgoing response APDU data size may be bigger than the APDU buffer size and may need to be written in portions by the applet. The APDU class has methods to facilitate this.

For sending large byte arrays as response data, the APDU class provides a special method sendBytesLong() which manages the APDU buffer.

```
// The purpose of this example is to show most of the methods
// in use and not to depict any particular APDU processing

public void process(APDU apdu){
  // ...
  byte[] buffer = apdu.getBuffer();
  byte cla = buffer[ISO7816.OFFSET_CLA];
  byte ins = buffer[ISO7816.OFFSET_INS];
  ...
  // assume this command has incoming data
  // Lc tells us the incoming apdu command length
  short bytesLeft = (short) (buffer[ISO7816.OFFSET_LC] & 0x00FF);

  if (bytesLeft < (short)55) ISOException.throwIt
                                  ( ISO7816.SW_WRONG_LENGTH );

  short readCount = apdu.setIncomingAndReceive();
  while ( bytesLeft > 0){
      // process bytes in buffer[5] to buffer[readCount+4];
      bytesLeft -= readCount;
      readCount = apdu.receiveBytes ( ISO7816.OFFSET_CDATA );
  }

  //...
  // Note that for a short response as in the case illustrated
  // here, the three APDU method calls shown:
  // setOutgoing(),setOutgoingLength() & sendBytes()
  // could be replaced by one APDU method call:
  // setOutgoingAndSend().

  // construct the reply APDU
  short le = apdu.setOutgoing();
  if (le < (short)2) ISOException.throwIt
                  ( ISO7816.SW_WRONG_LENGTH );
  apdu.setOutgoingLength( (short)3 );
```

```
// build response data in apdu.buffer[ 0.. outCount-1 ];
buffer[0] = (byte)1; buffer[1] = (byte)2; buffer[3] = (byte)3;
apdu.sendBytes ( (short)0 , (short)3 );
// return good complete status 90 00
}
```

See Also: APDUException, ISOException

Fields

PROTOCOL_T0

public static final byte PROTOCOL_T0

ISO 7816 transport protocol type T=0

PROTOCOL_T1

public static final byte PROTOCOL_T1

ISO 7816 transport protocol type T=1

Methods

getBuffer()

public byte[] getBuffer()

Returns the APDU buffer byte array.

Notes:

- *References to the APDU buffer byte array cannot be stored in class variables or instance variables or array components. See Java Card Runtime Environment (JCRE) 2.1 Specification for details.*

Returns: byte array containing the APDU buffer

getInBlockSize()

public static short getInBlockSize()

Returns the configured incoming block size. In T=1 protocol, this corresponds to IFSC (information field size for ICC), the maximum size of incoming data blocks into the card. In T=0 protocol, this method returns 1. IFSC is defined in ISO 7816-3.

This information may be used to ensure that there is enough space remaining in the APDU buffer when `receiveBytes()` is invoked.

Notes:

- *On* `receiveBytes()` *the* `bOff` *param should account for this potential blocksize.*

Returns: incoming block size setting.

See Also: `receiveBytes(short)`

getNAD()

```
public byte getNAD()
```

In T=1 protocol, this method returns the Node Address byte, NAD. In T=0 protocol, this method returns 0. This may be used as additional information to maintain multiple contexts.

Returns: NAD transport byte as defined in ISO 7816-3.

getOutBlockSize()

```
public static short getOutBlockSize()
```

Returns the configured outgoing block size. In T=1 protocol, this corresponds to IFSD (information field size for interface device), the maximum size of outgoing data blocks to the CAD. In T=0 protocol, this method returns 258 (accounts for 2 status bytes). IFSD is defined in ISO 7816-3.

This information may be used prior to invoking the `setOutgoingLength()` method, to limit the length of outgoing messages when BLOCK CHAINING is not allowed.

Notes:

- *On* `setOutgoingLength()` *the* `len` *param should account for this potential blocksize.*

Returns: outgoing block size setting.

See Also: `setOutgoingLength(short)`

getProtocol()

```
public static byte getProtocol()
```

Returns the ISO 7816 transport protocol type, T=1 or T=0 in progress.

Returns: the protocol type in progress. One of `PROTOCOL_T0`, `PROTOCOL_T1` listed above.

receiveBytes(short)

```
public short receiveBytes(short bOff)
```

Gets as many data bytes as will fit without APDU buffer overflow, at the specified offset bOff. Gets all the remaining bytes if they fit.

Notes:

- *The space in the buffer must allow for incoming block size.*
- *In T=1 protocol, if all the remaining bytes do not fit in the buffer, this method may return less bytes than the maximum incoming block size (IFSC).*
- *In T=0 protocol, if all the remaining bytes do not fit in the buffer, this method may return less than a full buffer of bytes to optimize and reduce protocol overhead.*
- *In T=1 protocol, if this method throws an* APDUException *with* T1_IFD_ABORT *reason code, the JCRE will restart APDU command processing using the newly received command. No more input data can be received. No output data can be transmitted. No error status response can be returned.*

Parameters:

bOff—the offset into APDU buffer.

Returns: number of bytes read. Returns 0 if no bytes are available.

Throws: APDUException—with the following reason codes:

- APDUException.ILLEGAL_USE if setIncomingAndReceive() not called or if setOutgoing() or setOutgoingNoChaining() previously invoked.
- APDUException.BUFFER_BOUNDS if not enough buffer space for incoming block size.
- APDUException.IO_ERROR on I/O error.
- APDUException.T1_IFD_ABORT if T=1 protocol is in use and the CAD sends in an ABORT S-Block command to abort the data transfer.

See Also: getInBlockSize()

sendBytes(short, short)

```
public void sendBytes(short bOff, short len)
```

Sends len more bytes from APDU buffer at specified offset bOff.

If the last part of the response is being sent by the invocation of this method, the APDU buffer must not be altered. If the data is altered, incorrect output may be sent to the CAD. Requiring that the buffer not be altered allows the implementation to reduce protocol overhead by transmitting the last part of the response along with the status bytes.

Notes:

- *If* `setOutgoingNoChaining()` *was invoked, output block chaining must not be used.*
- *In T=0 protocol, if* `setOutgoingNoChaining()` *was invoked, Le bytes must be transmitted before response status is returned.*
- *In T=0 protocol, if this method throws an* `APDUException` *with* `NO_T0_GETRESPONSE` *reason code, the JCRE will restart APDU command processing using the newly received command. No more output data can be transmitted. No error status response can be returned.*
- *In T=1 protocol, if this method throws an* `APDUException` *with* `T1_IFD_ABORT` *reason code, the JCRE will restart APDU command processing using the newly received command. No more output data can be transmitted. No error status response can be returned.*

Parameters:

`bOff`—the offset into APDU buffer.

`len`—the length of the data in bytes to send.

Throws: `APDUException`—with the following reason codes:

- `APDUException.ILLEGAL_USE` if `setOutgoingLen()` not called or `setOutgoingAndSend()` previously invoked or response byte count exceeded or if `APDUException.NO_T0_GETRESPONSE` previously thrown.
- `APDUException.BUFFER_BOUNDS` if the sum of `bOff` and `len` exceeds the buffer size.
- `APDUException.IO_ERROR` on I/O error.
- `APDUException.NO_T0_GETRESPONSE` if T=0 protocol is in use and the CAD does not respond to response status with GET RESPONSE command.
- `APDUException.T1_IFD_ABORT` if T=1 protocol is in use and the CAD sends in an ABORT S-Block command to abort the data transfer.

See Also: `setOutgoing()`, `setOutgoingNoChaining()`

sendBytesLong(byte[], short, short)

`public void sendBytesLong(byte[] outData, short bOff, short len)`

Sends `len` more bytes from `outData` byte array starting at specified offset `bOff`.

If the last of the response is being sent by the invocation of this method, the APDU buffer must not be altered. If the data is altered, incorrect output may be sent to the CAD. Requiring that the buffer not be altered allows the implementation to reduce protocol overhead by transmitting the last part of the response along with the status bytes.

The JCRE may use the APDU buffer to send data to the CAD.

Notes:

- *If* setOutgoingNoChaining() *was invoked, output block chaining must not be used.*
- *In T=0 protocol, if* setOutgoingNoChaining() *was invoked, Le bytes must be transmitted before response status is returned.*
- *In T=0 protocol, if this method throws an* APDUException *with NO_T0_GETRESPONSE reason code, the JCRE will restart APDU command processing using the newly received command. No more output data can be transmitted. No error status response can be returned.*
- *In T=1 protocol, if this method throws an* APDUException *with T1_IFD_ABORT reason code, the JCRE will restart APDU command processing using the newly received command. No more output data can be transmitted. No error status response can be returned.*

Parameters:

outData—the source data byte array.

bOff—the offset into OutData array.

len—the bytelength of the data to send.

Throws: APDUException—with the following reason codes:

- APDUException.ILLEGAL_USE if setOutgoingLen() not called or setOutgoingAndSend() previously invoked or response byte count exceeded or if APDUException.NO_T0_GETRESPONSE previously thrown.
- APDUException.IO_ERROR on I/O error.
- APDUException.NO_T0_GETRESPONSE if T=0 protocol is in use and CAD does not respond to response status with GET RESPONSE command.
- APDUException.T1_IFD_ABORT if T=1 protocol is in use and the CAD sends in an ABORT S-Block command to abort the data transfer.

See Also: setOutgoing(), setOutgoingNoChaining()

setIncomingAndReceive()

```
public short setIncomingAndReceive()
```

This is the primary receive method. Calling this method indicates that this APDU has incoming data. This method gets as many bytes as will fit without buffer overflow in the APDU buffer following the header. It gets all the incoming bytes if they fit.

Notes:

- *In T=0 (Case 3&4) protocol, the P3 param is assumed to be Lc.*
- *Data is read into the buffer at offset 5.*
- *In T=1 protocol, if all the incoming bytes do not fit in the buffer, this method may return less bytes than the maximum incoming block size (IFSC).*

- *In T=0 protocol, if all the incoming bytes do not fit in the buffer, this method may return less than a full buffer of bytes to optimize and reduce protocol overhead.*
- *This method sets the transfer direction to be inbound and calls* receive-Bytes(5).
- *This method may only be called once in a* Applet.process() *method.*

Returns: number of bytes read. Returns 0 if no bytes are available.

Throws: APDUException—with the following reason codes:
- APDUException.ILLEGAL_USE if setIncomingAndReceive() already invoked or if setOutgoing() or setOutgoingNoChaining() previously invoked.
- APDUException.IO_ERROR on I/O error.
- APDUException.T1_IFD_ABORT if T=1 protocol is in use and the CAD sends in an ABORT S-Block command to abort the data transfer.

setOutgoing()

```
public short setOutgoing()
```

This method is used to set the data transfer direction to outbound and to obtain the expected length of response (Le).

Notes.

- *Any remaining incoming data will be discarded.*
- *In T=0 (Case 4) protocol, this method will return 256.*

Returns: Le, the expected length of response.

Throws: APDUException—with the following reason codes:
- APDUException.ILLEGAL_USE if this method or setOutgoingNoChaining() method already invoked.
- APDUException.IO_ERROR on I/O error.

setOutgoingAndSend(short, short)

```
public void setOutgoingAndSend(short bOff, short len)
```

This is the "convenience" send method. It provides for the most efficient way to send a short response which fits in the buffer and needs the least protocol overhead. This method is a combination of setOutgoing(), setOutgoingLength(len) followed by sendBytes(bOff, len). In addition, once this method is invoked, sendBytes() and sendBytesLong() methods cannot be invoked and the APDU buffer must not be altered.

Sends len byte response from the APDU buffer at starting specified offset bOff.

Notes:

- *No other* APDU *send methods can be invoked.*
- *The APDU buffer must not be altered. If the data is altered, incorrect output may be sent to the CAD.*
- *The actual data transmission may only take place on return from* Applet.process()

Parameters:

bOff—the offset into APDU buffer.

len—the bytelength of the data to send.

Throws: APDUException—with the following reason codes:

- APDUException.ILLEGAL_USE if setOutgoing() or setOutgoingAndSend() previously invoked or response byte count exceeded.
- APDUException.IO_ERROR on I/O error.

setOutgoingLength(short)

public void setOutgoingLength(short len)

Sets the actual length of response data. Default is 0.

Note:

- *In T=0 (Case 2&4) protocol, the length is used by the JCRE to prompt the CAD for GET RESPONSE commands.*

Parameters:

len—the length of response data.

Throws: APDUException—with the following reason codes:

- APDUException.ILLEGAL_USE if setOutgoing() not called or this method already invoked.
- APDUException.BAD_LENGTH if len is greater than 256 or if non BLOCK CHAINED data transfer is requested and len is greater than (IFSD-2), where IFSD is the Outgoing Block Size. The -2 accounts for the status bytes in T=1.
- APDUException.IO_ERROR on I/O error.

See Also: getOutBlockSize()

setOutgoingNoChaining()

public short setOutgoingNoChaining()

This method is used to set the data transfer direction to outbound without using BLOCK CHAINING(See ISO 7816-3/4) and to obtain the expected length of response (Le). This method should be used in place of the setOutgoing() method by applets which need to be compatible with legacy CAD/terminals which do not support ISO 7816-3/4 defined block chaining. See *Java Card Runtime Environment (JCRE) 2.1 Specification* for details.

Notes.

- *Any remaining incoming data will be discarded.*
- *In T=0 (Case 4) protocol, this method will return 256.*
- *When this method is used, the* waitExtension() *method cannot be used.*
- *In T=1 protocol, retransmission on error may be restricted.*
- *In T=0 protocol, the outbound transfer must be performed without using response status chaining.*
- *In T=1 protocol, the outbound transfer must not set the More(M) Bit in the PCB of the I block. See ISO 7816-3.*

Returns: Le, the expected length of response data.

Throws: APDUException—with the following reason codes:
- APDUException.ILLEGAL_USE if this method or setOutgoing() method already invoked.
- APDUException.IO_ERROR on I/O error.

waitExtension()

```
public static void waitExtension()
```

Requests additional processing time from CAD. The implementation should ensure that this method needs to be invoked only under unusual conditions requiring excessive processing times.

Notes:

- *In T=0 protocol, a NULL procedure byte is sent to reset the work waiting time (see ISO 7816-3).*
- *In T=1 protocol, the implementation needs to request the same T=0 protocol work waiting time quantum by sending a T=1 protocol request for wait time extension(see ISO 7816-3).*
- *If the implementation uses an automatic timer mechanism instead, this method may do nothing.*

Throws: APDUException—with the following reason codes:
- APDUException.ILLEGAL_USE if setOutgoingNoChaining() previously invoked.
- APDUException.IO_ERROR on I/O error.

javacard.framework
APDUException

Syntax

```
public class APDUException extends CardRuntimeException

Object
  |
  +--Throwable
       |
       +--Exception
            |
            +--RuntimeException
                 |
                 +--CardRuntimeException
                      |
                      +--javacard.framework.APDUException
```

Description

APDUException represents an APDU related exception.

The APDU class throws JCRE owned instances of APDUException.

JCRE owned instances of exception classes are temporary JCRE Entry Point Objects and can be accessed from any applet context. References to these temporary objects cannot be stored in class variables or instance variables or array components. See *Java Card Runtime Environment (JCRE) 2.1 Specification* for details.

See Also: APDU

Fields

BAD_LENGTH

```
public static final short BAD_LENGTH
```

This reason code is used by the APDU.setOutgoingLength() method to indicate that the length parameter is greater that 256 or if non BLOCK CHAINED data transfer is requested and len is greater than (IFSD-2), where IFSD is the Outgoing Block Size.

BUFFER_BOUNDS

```
public static final short BUFFER_BOUNDS
```

This reason code is used by the APDU.sendBytes() method to indicate that the sum of buffer offset parameter and the byte length parameter exceeds the APDU buffer size.

ILLEGAL_USE

```
public static final short ILLEGAL_USE
```

This APDUException reason code indicates that the method should not be invoked based on the current state of the APDU.

IO_ERROR

```
public static final short IO_ERROR
```

This reason code indicates that an unrecoverable error occurred in the I/O transmission layer.

NO_T0_GETRESPONSE

```
public static final short NO_T0_GETRESPONSE
```

This reason code indicates that during T=0 protocol, the CAD did not return a GET RESPONSE command in response to a <61xx> response status to send additional data. The outgoing transfer has been aborted. No more data or status can be sent to the CAD in this APDU.process() method.

T1_IFD_ABORT

```
public static final short T1_IFD_ABORT
```

This reason code indicates that during T=1 protocol, the CAD returned an ABORT S-Block command and aborted the data transfer. The incoming or outgoing transfer has been aborted. No more data can be received from the CAD. No more data or status can be sent to the CAD in this APDU.process() method.

Constructors

APDUException(short)

```
public APDUException(short reason)
```

Constructs an APDUException. To conserve on resources use throwIt() to use the JCRE owned instance of this class.

Parameters:

> reason—the reason for the exception.

Methods

getReason()

> public short getReason()

Get reason code

Overrides: getReason() in class CardRuntimeException

Returns: the reason for the exception

setReason(short)

> public void setReason(short reason)

Set reason code

Overrides: setReason(short) in class CardRuntimeException

Parameters:

> reason—the reason for the exception

throwIt(short)

> public static void throwIt(short reason)

Throws the JCRE owned instance of APDUException with the specified reason.

JCRE owned instances of exception classes are temporary JCRE Entry Point Objects and can be accessed from any applet context. References to these temporary objects cannot be stored in class variables or instance variables or array components. See *Java Card Runtime Environment (JCRE) 2.1 Specification* for details.

Parameters:

> reason—the reason for the exception.

Throws: APDUException—always.

javacard.framework
Applet

Syntax
```
public abstract class Applet

Object
  |
  +--javacard.framework.Applet
```

Description

This abstract class defines an applet in Java Card.

The Applet class should be extended by any applet that is intended to be loaded onto, installed into and executed on a Java Card compliant smart card.

Example usage of Applet

```
public class MyApplet extends javacard.framework.Applet{

    static byte someByteArray[];

    public static void install(byte[] bArray, short bOffset,
                               byte bLength) throws ISOException {

        // make all my allocations here, so I do not run
        // out of memory later
        MyApplet theApplet = new MyApplet();

        // check incoming parameter
        byte bLen = bArray[bOffset];
        if ( bLen!=0 ) {
            someByteArray = new byte[bLen];
            theApplet.register();
            return;
        }else
            ISOException.throwIt(ISO7816.SW_FUNC_NOT_SUPPORTED);
    }

    public boolean select(){
        // selection initialization
        someByteArray[17] = 42; // set selection state
        return true;
    }
```

```
public void process(APDU apdu) throws ISOException{
    byte[] buffer = apdu.getBuffer();
    //process the incoming data and reply
    if ( buffer[ISO7816.OFFSET_CLA] == (byte)0 ) {
        switch ( buffer[ISO7816.OFFSET_INS] ) {
            case ISO.INS_SELECT:
                ...
                // send response data to select command
                short Le = apdu.setOutgoing();
                // assume data containing response bytes in
                // replyData[] array.
                if ( Le < ..) ISOException.throwIt
                                ( ISO7816.SW_WRONG_LENGTH);
                apdu.setOutgoingLength( (short)replyData.length );
                apdu.sendBytesLong(replyData, (short) 0,
                                (short)replyData.length);
                break;
            case ...
        }
    }
}
```

See Also: SystemException, JCSystem

Constructors

Applet()

```
protected Applet()
```

Only this class's install() method should create the applet object.

Methods

deselect()

```
public void deselect()
```

Called by the JCRE to inform this currently selected applet that another (or the same) applet will be selected. It is called when a SELECT APDU command is received by the JCRE. This method is invoked prior to another applets or this very applets `select()` method being invoked.

A subclass of `Applet` should override this method if it has any cleanup or book-keeping work to be performed before another applet is selected.

The default implementation of this method provided by `Applet` class does nothing.

Notes:

- *Unchecked exceptions thrown by this method are caught by the JCRE but the applet is deselected.*
- *Transient objects of* `JCSystem.CLEAR_ON_DESELECT` *clear event type are cleared to their default value by the JCRE after this method.*
- *This method is NOT called on reset or power loss.*

getShareableInterfaceObject(AID, byte)

```
public Shareable getShareableInterfaceObject(AID clientAID,
            byte parameter)
```

Called by the JCRE to obtain a shareable interface object from this server applet, on behalf of a request from a client applet. This method executes in the applet context of `this` applet instance. The client applet initiated this request by calling the `JCSystem.getAppletShareableInterfaceObject()` method. See *Java Card Runtime Environment (JCRE) 2.1 Specification* for details.

Parameters:

clientAID—the AID object of the client applet.

parameter—optional parameter byte. The parameter byte may be used by the client to specify which shareable interface object is being requested.

Returns: the shareable interface object or `null`.

Note:

- *The* `clientAID` *parameter is a JCRE owned* AID *instance. JCRE owned instances of AID are permanent JCRE Entry Point Objects and can be accessed from any applet context. References to these permanent objects can be stored and re-used.*

See Also: `getAppletShareableInterfaceObject(AID, byte)`

install(byte[], short, byte)

```
public static void install(byte[] bArray, short bOffset,
            byte bLength)
```

To create an instance of the `Applet` subclass, the JCRE will call this static method first.

The applet should perform any necessary initializations and must call one of the register() methods. The installation is considered successful when the call to register() completes without an exception. The installation is deemed unsuccessful if the install method does not call a register() method, or if an exception is thrown from within the install method prior to the call to a register() method, or if the register() method throws an exception. If the installation is unsuccessful, the JCRE must perform all the necessary clean up when it receives control. Successful installation makes the applet instance capable of being selected via a SELECT APDU command.

Installation parameters are supplied in the byte array parameter and must be in a format defined by the applet. The bArray object is a global array. If the applet desires to preserve any of this data, it should copy the data into its own object.

bArray is zeroed by the JCRE after the return from the install() method.

References to the bArray object cannot be stored in class variables or instance variables or array components. See *Java Card Runtime Environment (JCRE) 2.1 Specification* for details.

The implementation of this method provided by Applet class throws an ISOException with reason code = ISO7816.SW_FUNC_NOT_SUPPORTED.

Note:

- *Exceptions thrown by this method after successful installation are caught by the JCRE and processed by the Installer.*

Parameters:

    bArray—the array containing installation parameters.

    bOffset—the starting offset in bArray.

    bLength—the length in bytes of the parameter data in bArray. The maximum value of bLength is 32.

Throws: ISOException

process(APDU)

```
public abstract void process(APDU apdu)
```

Called by the JCRE to process an incoming APDU command. An applet is expected to perform the action requested and return response data if any to the terminal.

Upon normal return from this method the JCRE sends the ISO 7816-4 defined success status (90 00) in APDU response. If this method throws an ISOException the JCRE sends the associated reason code as the response status instead.

The JCRE zeroes out the APDU buffer before receiving a new APDU command from the CAD. The five header bytes of the APDU command are available in APDU buffer[0..4] at the time this method is called.

The APDU object parameter is a temporary JCRE Entry Point Object. A temporary JCRE Entry Point Object can be accessed from any applet context. References to these temporary objects cannot be stored in class variables or instance variables or array components.

Notes:

- *APDU buffer[5..] is undefined and should not be read or written prior to invoking the* APDU.setIncomingAndReceive() *method if incoming data is expected. Altering the APDU buffer[5..] could corrupt incoming data.*

Parameters:

apdu—the incoming APDU object

Throws: ISOException—with the response bytes per ISO 7816-4

See Also: APDU

register()

```
protected final void register()
```

This method is used by the applet to register this applet instance with the JCRE and to assign the Applet subclass AID bytes as its instance AID bytes. One of the register() methods must be called from within install() to be registered with the JCRE. See *Java Card Runtime Environment (JCRE) 2.1 Specification* for details.

Throws: SystemException—with the following reason codes:
- SystemException.ILLEGAL_AID if the Applet subclass AID bytes are in use or if the applet instance has previously called one of the register() methods.

register(byte[], short, byte)

```
protected final void register(byte[] bArray, short bOffset,
            byte bLength)
```

This method is used by the applet to register this applet instance with the JCRE and assign the specified AID bytes as its instance AID bytes. One of the register() methods must be called from within install() to be registered with the JCRE. See *Java Card Runtime Environment (JCRE) 2.1 Specification* for details.

Parameters:

bArray—the byte array containing the AID bytes.

bOffset—the start of AID bytes in bArray.

bLength—the length of the AID bytes in bArray.

Throws: APDUException—with the following reason codes:

SystemException—with the following reason code:

- SystemException.ILLEGAL_VALUE if the bLength parameter is less than 5 or greater than 16.
- SystemException.ILLEGAL_AID if the specified instance AID bytes are in use or if the RID portion of the AID bytes in the bArray parameter does not match the RID portion of the Applet subclass AID bytes or if the applet instance has previously called one of the register() methods.

select()

public boolean select()

Called by the JCRE to inform this applet that it has been selected.

It is called when a SELECT APDU command is received and before the applet is selected. SELECT APDU commands use instance AID bytes for applet selection. See *Java Card Runtime Environment (JCRE) 2.1 Specification* for details.

A subclass of Applet should override this method if it should perform any initialization that may be required to process APDU commands that may follow. This method returns a boolean to indicate that it is ready to accept incoming APDU commands via its process() method. If this method returns false, it indicates to the JCRE that this Applet declines to be selected.

The implementation of this method provided by Applet class returns true.

Returns: true to indicate success, false otherwise.

selectingApplet()

protected final boolean selectingApplet()

This method is used by the applet process() method to distinguish the SELECT APDU command which selected this applet, from all other other SELECT APDU commands which may relate to file or internal applet state selection.

Returns: true if this applet is being selected.

javacard.framework
CardException

Syntax
```
public class CardException extends Exception
```

```
Object
  |
  +--Throwable
        |
        +--Exception
              |
              +--javacard.framework.CardException
```

Direct Known Subclasses: UserException

Description
The CardException class defines a field reason and two accessor methods getReason() and setReason(). The reason field encapsulates exception cause identifier in Java Card. All Java Card checked Exception classes should extend CardException. This class also provides a resource-saving mechanism (throwIt() method) for using a JCRE owned instance of this class.

Constructors

CardException(short)
```
public CardException(short reason)
```

Construct a CardException instance with the specified reason. To conserve on resources, use the throwIt() method to use the JCRE owned instance of this class.

Parameters:

reason—the reason for the exception

Methods

getReason()

```
public short getReason()
```

Get reason code

Returns: the reason for the exception

setReason(short)

```
public void setReason(short reason)
```

Set reason code

Parameters:

> reason—the reason for the exception

throwIt(short)

```
public static void throwIt(short reason)
```

Throw the JCRE owned instance of `CardException` class with the specified reason.

JCRE owned instances of exception classes are temporary JCRE Entry Point Objects and can be accessed from any applet context. References to these temporary objects cannot be stored in class variables or instance variables or array components. See *Java Card Runtime Environment (JCRE) 2.1 Specification* for details.

Parameters:

> reason—the reason for the exception

Throws: `CardException`—always.

javacard.framework
CardRuntimeException

Syntax

`public class CardRuntimeException extends RuntimeException`

```
Object
  |
  +--Throwable
        |
        +--Exception
              |
              +--RuntimeException
                    |
                    +--javacard.framework.CardRuntimeException
```

Direct Known Subclasses: `APDUException, CryptoException, ISOException,` `PINException, SystemException, TransactionException`

Description

The `CardRuntimeException` class defines a field `reason` and two accessor methods `getReason()` and `setReason()`. The `reason` field encapsulates exception cause identifier in Java Card. All Java Card unchecked Exception classes should extend `CardRuntimeException`. This class also provides a resource-saving mechanism (`throwIt()` method) for using a JCRE owned instance of this class.

Constructors

CardRuntimeException(short)

`public CardRuntimeException(short reason)`

Construct a CardRuntimeException instance with the specified reason. To conserve on resources, use `throwIt()` method to use the JCRE owned instance of this class.

Parameters:

> `reason`—the reason for the exception

Methods

getReason()

```
public short getReason()
```

Get reason code

Returns: the reason for the exception

setReason(short)

```
public void setReason(short reason)
```

Set reason code

Parameters:

> reason—the reason for the exception

throwIt(short)

```
public static void throwIt(short reason)
```

Throw the JCRE owned instance of the `CardRuntimeException` class with the specified reason.

JCRE owned instances of exception classes are temporary JCRE Entry Point Objects and can be accessed from any applet context. References to these temporary objects cannot be stored in class variables or instance variables or array components. See *Java Card Runtime Environment (JCRE) 2.1 Specification* for details.

Parameters:

> reason—the reason for the exception

Throws: `CardRuntimeException`—always.

javacard.framework
ISO7816

Syntax
```
public interface ISO7816
```

Description
ISO7816 encapsulates constants related to ISO 7816-3 and ISO 7816-4. ISO7816 interface contains only static fields.

The static fields with SW_ prefixes define constants for the ISO 7816-4 defined response status word. The fields which use the _00 suffix require the low order byte to be customized appropriately e.g (ISO7816.SW_CORRECT_LENGTH_00 + (0x0025 & 0xFF)).

The static fields with OFFSET_ prefixes define constants to be used to index into the APDU buffer byte array to access ISO 7816-4 defined header information.

Fields

CLA_ISO7816

```
public static final byte CLA_ISO7816
```

APDU command CLA : ISO 7816 = 0x00

INS_EXTERNAL_AUTHENTICATE

```
public static final byte INS_EXTERNAL_AUTHENTICATE
```

APDU command INS : EXTERNAL AUTHENTICATE = 0x82

INS_SELECT

```
public static final byte INS_SELECT
```

APDU command INS : SELECT = 0xA4

OFFSET_CDATA

```
public static final byte OFFSET_CDATA
```

APDU command data offset : CDATA = 5

OFFSET_CLA

```
public static final byte OFFSET_CLA
```

APDU header offset : CLA = 0

OFFSET_INS

```
public static final byte OFFSET_INS
```

APDU header offset : INS = 1

OFFSET_LC

```
public static final byte OFFSET_LC
```

APDU header offset : LC = 4

OFFSET_P1

```
public static final byte OFFSET_P1
```

APDU header offset : P1 = 2

OFFSET_P2

```
public static final byte OFFSET_P2
```

APDU header offset : P2 = 3

SW_APPLET_SELECT_FAILED

```
public static final short SW_APPLET_SELECT_FAILED
```

Response status : Applet selection failed = 0x6999;

SW_BYTES_REMAINING_00

```
public static final short SW_BYTES_REMAINING_00
```

Response status : Response bytes remaining = 0x6100

SW_CLA_NOT_SUPPORTED

```
public static final short SW_CLA_NOT_SUPPORTED
```

Response status : CLA value not supported = 0x6E00

SW_COMMAND_NOT_ALLOWED

```
public static final short SW_COMMAND_NOT_ALLOWED
```

Response status : Command not allowed (no current EF) = 0x6986

SW_CONDITIONS_NOT_SATISFIED

public static final short SW_CONDITIONS_NOT_SATISFIED

Response status : Conditions of use not satisfied = 0x6985

SW_CORRECT_LENGTH_00

public static final short SW_CORRECT_LENGTH_00

Response status : Correct Expected Length (Le) = 0x6C00

SW_DATA_INVALID

public static final short SW_DATA_INVALID

Response status : Data invalid = 0x6984

SW_FILE_FULL

public static final short SW_FILE_FULL

Response status : Not enough memory space in the file = 0x6A84

SW_FILE_INVALID

public static final short SW_FILE_INVALID

Response status : File invalid = 0x6983

SW_FILE_NOT_FOUND

public static final short SW_FILE_NOT_FOUND

Response status : File not found = 0x6A82

SW_FUNC_NOT_SUPPORTED

public static final short SW_FUNC_NOT_SUPPORTED

Response status : Function not supported = 0x6A81

SW_INCORRECT_P1P2

public static final short SW_INCORRECT_P1P2

Response status : Incorrect parameters (P1,P2) = 0x6A86

SW_INS_NOT_SUPPORTED

`public static final short SW_INS_NOT_SUPPORTED`

Response status : INS value not supported = 0x6D00

SW_NO_ERROR

`public static final short SW_NO_ERROR`

Response status : No Error = (short)0x9000

SW_RECORD_NOT_FOUND

`public static final short SW_RECORD_NOT_FOUND`

Response status : Record not found = 0x6A83

SW_SECURITY_STATUS_NOT_SATISFIED

`public static final short SW_SECURITY_STATUS_NOT_SATISFIED`

Response status : Security condition not satisfied = 0x6982

SW_UNKNOWN

`public static final short SW_UNKNOWN`

Response status : No precise diagnosis = 0x6F00

SW_WRONG_DATA

`public static final short SW_WRONG_DATA`

Response status : Wrong data = 0x6A80

SW_WRONG_LENGTH

`public static final short SW_WRONG_LENGTH`

Response status : Wrong length = 0x6700

SW_WRONG_P1P2

`public static final short SW_WRONG_P1P2`

Response status : Incorrect parameters (P1,P2) = 0x6B00

javacard.framework
ISOException

Syntax

```
public class ISOException extends CardRuntimeException
```

```
Object
  |
  +--Throwable
        |
        +--Exception
              |
              +--RuntimeException
                    |
                    +--CardRuntimeException
                          |
                          +--javacard.framework.ISOException
```

Description

ISOException class encapsulates an ISO 7816-4 response status word as its reason code.

The APDU class throws JCRE owned instances of ISOException.

JCRE owned instances of exception classes are temporary JCRE Entry Point Objects and can be accessed from any applet context. References to these temporary objects cannot be stored in class variables or instance variables or array components. See *Java Card Runtime Environment (JCRE) 2.1 Specification* for details.

Constructors

ISOException(short)

```
public ISOException(short sw)
```

Constructs an ISOException instance with the specified status word. To conserve on resources use throwIt() to use the JCRE owned instance of this class.

Parameters:

sw—the ISO 7816-4 defined status word

Methods

getReason()

`public short getReason()`

Get reason code

Overrides: `getReason()` in class `CardRuntimeException`

Returns: the reason for the exception

setReason(short)

`public void setReason(short sw)`

Set reason code

Overrides: `setReason(short)` in class `CardRuntimeException`

Parameters:

`reason`—the reason for the exception

throwIt(short)

`public static void throwIt(short sw)`

Throws the JCRE owned instance of the ISOException class with the specified status word.

JCRE owned instances of exception classes are temporary JCRE Entry Point Objects and can be accessed from any applet context. References to these temporary objects cannot be stored in class variables or instance variables or array components. See *Java Card Runtime Environment (JCRE) 2.1 Specification* for details.

Parameters:

`sw`—ISO 7816-4 defined status word

Throws: `ISOException`—always.

javacard.framework
JCSystem

Syntax
```
public final class JCSystem
```

```
Object
  |
  +--javacard.framework.JCSystem
```

Description

The JCSystem class includes a collection of methods to control applet execution, resource management, atomic transaction management and inter-applet object sharing in Java Card. All methods in JCSystem class are static methods.

The JCSystem class also includes methods to control the persistence and transience of objects. The term *persistent* means that objects and their values persist from one CAD session to the next, indefinitely. Persistent object values are updated atomically using transactions.

The makeTransient...Array() methods can be used to create *transient* arrays with primitive data components. Transient array data is lost (in an undefined state, but the real data is unavailable) immediately upon power loss, and is reset to the default value at the occurrence of certain events such as card reset or deselect. Updates to the values of transient arrays are not atomic and are not affected by transactions.

The JCRE maintains an atomic transaction commit buffer which is initialized on card reset (or power on). When a transaction is in progress, the JCRE journals all updates to persistent data space into this buffer so that it can always guarantee, at commit time, that everything in the buffer is written or nothing at all is written. The JCSystem includes methods to control an atomic transaction. See *Java Card Runtime Environment (JCRE) 2.1 Specification* for details.

See Also: SystemException, TransactionException, Applet

Fields

CLEAR_ON_DESELECT

```
public static final byte CLEAR_ON_DESELECT
```

This event code indicates that the contents of the transient object are cleared to the default value on applet deselection event or in CLEAR_ON_RESET cases.

Notes:

- CLEAR_ON_DESELECT *transient objects can be accessed only when the applet which created the object is the currently the selected applet.*
- *The JCRE will throw a* SecurityException *if a* CLEAR_ON_DESELECT *transient object is accessed when the currently selected applet is not the applet which created the object.*

CLEAR_ON_RESET

```
public static final byte CLEAR_ON_RESET
```

This event code indicates that the contents of the transient object are cleared to the default value on card reset (or power on) event.

NOT_A_TRANSIENT_OBJECT

```
public static final byte NOT_A_TRANSIENT_OBJECT
```

This event code indicates that the object is not transient.

Methods

abortTransaction()

```
public static native void abortTransaction()
```

Aborts the atomic transaction. The contents of the commit buffer is discarded.

Notes:

- *Do not call this method from within a transaction which creates new objects because the JCRE may not recover the heap space used by the new object instances.*
- *The JCRE ensures that any variable of reference type which references an object instantiated from within this aborted transaction is equivalent to a* null *reference.*

Throws: TransactionException—with the following reason codes:

- TransactionException.NOT_IN_PROGRESS if a transaction is not in progress.

See Also: beginTransaction(), commitTransaction()

beginTransaction()

```
public static native void beginTransaction()
```

Begins an atomic transaction. If a transaction is already in progress (transaction-Depth != 0), a TransactionException is thrown.

Throws: TransactionException—with the following reason codes:
  • TransactionException.IN_PROGRESS if a transaction is already in progress.

See Also: commitTransaction(), abortTransaction()

commitTransaction()

```
public static native void commitTransaction()
```

Commits an atomic transaction. The contents of commit buffer is atomically committed. If a transaction is not in progress (transactionDepth == 0) then a TransactionException is thrown.

Throws: TransactionException—with the following reason codes:
  • TransactionException.NOT_IN_PROGRESS if a transaction is not in progress.

See Also: beginTransaction(), abortTransaction()

getAID()

```
public static AID getAID()
```

Returns the JCRE owned instance of the AID object associated with the current applet context. Returns null if the Applet.register() method has not yet been invoked.

JCRE owned instances of AID are permanent JCRE Entry Point Objects and can be accessed from any applet context. References to these permanent objects can be stored and re-used.

See *Java Card Runtime Environment (JCRE) 2.1 Specification* for details.

Returns: the AID object.

getAppletShareableInterfaceObject(AID, byte)

```
public static Shareable getAppletShareableInterfaceObject(AID
            serverAID, byte parameter)
```

This method is called by a client applet to get a server applet's shareable interface object.

This method returns null if the Applet.register() has not yet been invoked or if the server does not exist or if the server returns null.

Parameters:

serverAID—the AID of the server applet.

parameter—optional parameter data.

Returns: the shareable interface object or null.

See Also: getShareableInterfaceObject(AID, byte)

getMaxCommitCapacity()

public static native short getMaxCommitCapacity()

Returns the total number of bytes in the commit buffer. This is approximately the maximum number of bytes of persistent data which can be modified during a transaction. However, the transaction subsystem requires additional bytes of overhead data to be included in the commit buffer, and this depends on the number of fields modified and the implementation of the transaction subsystem. The application cannot determine the actual maximum amount of data which can be modified during a transaction without taking these overhead bytes into consideration.

Returns: the total number of bytes in the commit buffer

See Also: getUnusedCommitCapacity()

getPreviousContextAID()

public static AID getPreviousContextAID()

This method is called to obtain the JCRE owned instance of the AID object associated with the previously active applet context. This method is typically used by a server applet, while executing a shareable interface method to determine the identity of its client and thereby control access privileges.

JCRE owned instances of AID are permanent JCRE Entry Point Objects and can be accessed from any applet context. References to these permanent objects can be stored and re-used.

See *Java Card Runtime Environment (JCRE) 2.1 Specification* for details.

Returns: the AID object of the previous context, or null if JCRE.

getTransactionDepth()

public static native byte getTransactionDepth()

Returns the current transaction nesting depth level. At present, only 1 transaction can be in progress at a time.

Returns: 1 if transaction in progress, 0 if not.

getUnusedCommitCapacity()

```
public static native short getUnusedCommitCapacity()
```

Returns the number of bytes left in the commit buffer.

Returns: the number of bytes left in the commit buffer

See Also: `getMaxCommitCapacity()`

getVersion()

```
public static short getVersion()
```

Returns the current major and minor version of the Java Card API.

Returns: version number as byte.byte (major.minor)

isTransient(Object)

```
public static native byte isTransient(Object theObj)
```

Used to check if the specified object is transient.

Notes: *This method returns* `NOT_A_TRANSIENT_OBJECT` *if the specified object is null or is not an array type.*

Parameters:

theObj—the object being queried.

Returns: `NOT_A_TRANSIENT_OBJECT`, `CLEAR_ON_RESET`, or `CLEAR_ON_DESELECT`.

See Also: `makeTransientBooleanArray(short, byte)`,
`makeTransientByteArray(short, byte)`,
`makeTransientShortArray(short, byte)`,
`makeTransientObjectArray(short, byte)`

lookupAID(byte[], short, byte)

```
public static AID lookupAID(byte[] buffer, short offset,
            byte length)
```

Returns the JCRE owned instance of the AID object, if any, encapsulating the specified AID bytes in the buffer parameter if there exists a successfully installed applet on the card whose instance AID exactly matches that of the specified AID bytes.

JCRE owned instances of AID are permanent JCRE Entry Point Objects and can be accessed from any applet context. References to these permanent objects can be stored and re-used.

See *Java Card Runtime Environment (JCRE) 2.1 Specification* for details.

Parameters:

buffer—byte array containing the AID bytes.

offset—offset within buffer where AID bytes begin.

length—length of AID bytes in buffer.

Returns: the AID object, if any; null otherwise. A VM exception is thrown if buffer is null, or if offset or length are out of range.

makeTransientBooleanArray(short, byte)

```
public static native boolean[] makeTransientBooleanArray(short
          length, byte event)
```

Create a transient boolean array with the specified array length.

Parameters:

length—the length of the boolean array.

event—the CLEAR_ON... event which causes the array elements to be cleared.

Throws: SystemException—with the following reason codes:
- SystemException.ILLEGAL_VALUE if event is not a valid event code.
- SystemException.NO_TRANSIENT_SPACE if sufficient transient space is not available.
- SystemException.ILLEGAL_TRANSIENT if the current applet context is not the currently selected applet context and CLEAR_ON_DESELECT is specified.

makeTransientByteArray(short, byte)

```
public static native byte[] makeTransientByteArray(short length,
          byte event)
```

Create a transient byte array with the specified array length.

Parameters:

length—the length of the byte array.

event—the CLEAR_ON... event which causes the array elements to be cleared.

Throws: SystemException—with the following reason codes:
- SystemException.ILLEGAL_VALUE if event is not a valid event code.
- SystemException.NO_TRANSIENT_SPACE if sufficient transient space is not available.
- SystemException.ILLEGAL_TRANSIENT if the current applet context is not the currently selected applet context and CLEAR_ON_DESELECT is specified.

makeTransientObjectArray(short, byte)

```
public static native Object[] makeTransientObjectArray(short
          length, byte event)
```

Create a transient array of Object with the specified array length.

Parameters:

length—the length of the Object array.

event—the CLEAR_ON... event which causes the array elements to be cleared.

Throws: SystemException—with the following reason codes:
- SystemException.ILLEGAL_VALUE if event is not a valid event code.
- SystemException.NO_TRANSIENT_SPACE if sufficient transient space is not available.
- SystemException.ILLEGAL_TRANSIENT if the current applet context is not the currently selected applet context and CLEAR_ON_DESELECT is specified.

makeTransientShortArray(short, byte)

```
public static native short[] makeTransientShortArray(short length,
          byte event)
```

Create a transient short array with the specified array length.

Parameters:

length—the length of the short array.

event—the CLEAR_ON... event which causes the array elements to be cleared.

Throws: SystemException—with the following reason codes:
- SystemException.ILLEGAL_VALUE if event is not a valid event code.
- SystemException.NO_TRANSIENT_SPACE if sufficient transient space is not available.
- SystemException.ILLEGAL_TRANSIENT if the current applet context is not the currently selected applet context and CLEAR_ON_DESELECT is specified.

javacard.framework
OwnerPIN

Syntax

```
public class OwnerPIN implements PIN
```

```
Object
  |
  +--javacard.framework.OwnerPIN
```

All Implemented Interfaces: PIN

Description

This class represents an Owner PIN. It implements Personal Identification Number functionality as defined in the PIN interface. It provides the ability to update the PIN and thus owner functionality.

The implementation of this class must protect against attacks based on program flow prediction.Even if a transaction is in progress, internal state such as the try counter, the validated flag and the blocking state must not be conditionally updated during PIN presentation.

If an implementation of this class creates transient arrays, it must ensure that they are CLEAR_ON_RESET transient objects.

The protected methods getValidatedFlag and setValidatedFlag allow a subclass of this class to optimize the storage for the validated boolean state.

Some methods of instances of this class are only suitable for sharing when there exists a trust relationship among the applets. A typical shared usage would use a proxy PIN interface which implements both the PIN interface and the Shareable interface.

Any of the methods of the OwnerPIN may be called with a transaction in progress. None of the methods of OwnerPIN class initiate or alter the state of the transaction if one is in progress.

See Also: PINException, PIN, Shareable, JCSystem

Constructors

OwnerPIN(byte, byte)

```
public OwnerPIN(byte tryLimit, byte maxPINSize)
```

Constructor. Allocates a new PIN instance with validated flag set to false.

Parameters:

> tryLimit—the maximum number of times an incorrect PIN can be presented.

> maxPINSize—the maximum allowed PIN size. maxPINSize must be >=1.

Throws: PINException—with the following reason codes:
- PINException.ILLEGAL_VALUE if maxPINSize parameter is less than 1.

Methods

check(byte[], short, byte)

```
public boolean check(byte[] pin, short offset, byte length)
```

Compares pin against the PIN value. If they match and the PIN is not blocked, it sets the validated flag and resets the try counter to its maximum. If it does not match, it decrements the try counter and, if the counter has reached zero, blocks the PIN. Even if a transaction is in progress, internal state such as the try counter, the validated flag and the blocking state must not be conditionally updated.

Notes:

- *If* NullPointerException *or* ArrayIndexOutOfBoundsException *is thrown, the validated flag must be set to false, the try counter must be decremented and, the PIN blocked if the counter reaches zero.*
- *If* offset *or* length *parameter is negative an* ArrayIndexOutOfBounds- Exception *exception is thrown.*
- *If* offset+length *is greater than* pin.length, *the length of the* pin *array, an* ArrayIndexOutOfBoundsException *exception is thrown.*
- *If* pin *parameter is* null *a* NullPointerException *exception is thrown.*

Specified By: check(byte[], short, byte) in interface PIN

Parameters:

> pin—the byte array containing the PIN value being checked

> offset—the starting offset in the pin array

> length—the length of pin.

Returns: true if the PIN value matches; false otherwise

Throws: ArrayIndexOutOfBoundsException—if the check operation would cause access of data outside array bounds.

NullPointerException—if pin is null

getTriesRemaining()

```
public byte getTriesRemaining()
```

Returns the number of times remaining that an incorrect PIN can be presented before the PIN is blocked.

Specified By: getTriesRemaining() in interface PIN

Returns: the number of times remaining

getValidatedFlag()

```
protected boolean getValidatedFlag()
```

This protected method returns the validated flag. This method is intended for sub-class of this OwnerPIN to access or override the internal PIN state of the OwnerPIN.

Returns: the boolean state of the PIN validated flag.

isValidated()

```
public boolean isValidated()
```

Returns true if a valid PIN has been presented since the last card reset or last call to reset().

Specified By: isValidated() in interface PIN

Returns: true if validated; false otherwise

reset()

```
public void reset()
```

If the validated flag is set, this method resets it. If the validated flag is not set, this method does nothing.

Specified By: reset() in interface PIN

resetAndUnblock()

```
public void resetAndUnblock()
```

This method resets the validated flag and resets the PIN try counter to the value of the PIN try limit. This method is used by the owner to re-enable the blocked PIN.

setValidatedFlag(boolean)

```
protected void setValidatedFlag(boolean value)
```

This protected method sets the value of the validated flag. This method is intended for subclass of this OwnerPIN to control or override the internal PIN state of the OwnerPIN.

Parameters:

value—the new value for the validated flag.

update(byte[], short, byte)

```
public void update(byte[] pin, short offset, byte length)
```

This method sets a new value for the PIN and resets the PIN try counter to the value of the PIN try limit. It also resets the validated flag.

This method copies the input pin parameter into an internal representation. If a transaction is in progress, the new pin and try counter update must be conditional i.e the copy operation must use the transaction facility.

Parameters:

pin—the byte array containing the new PIN value

offset—the starting offset in the pin array

length—the length of the new PIN.

Throws: PINException—with the following reason codes:
* PINException.ILLEGAL_VALUE if length is greater than configured maximum PIN size.

See Also: beginTransaction()

javacard.framework
PIN

Syntax
```
public interface PIN
```

All Known Implementing Classes: OwnerPIN

Description

This interface represents a PIN. An implementation must maintain these internal values:

- PIN value
- try limit, the maximum number of times an incorrect PIN can be presented before the PIN is blocked. When the PIN is blocked, it cannot be validated even on valid PIN presentation.
- max PIN size, the maximum length of PIN allowed
- try counter, the remaining number of times an incorrect PIN presentation is permitted before the PIN becomes blocked.
- validated flag, true if a valid PIN has been presented. This flag is reset on every card reset.

This interface does not make any assumptions about where the data for the PIN value comparison is stored.

An owner implementation of this interface must provide a way to initialize/update the PIN value. The owner implementation of the interface must protect against attacks based on program flow prediction. Even if a transaction is in progress, internal state such as the try counter, the validated flag and the blocking state must not be conditionally updated during PIN presentation.

A typical card global PIN usage will combine an instance of OwnerPIN class and a a a Proxy PIN interface which implements both the PIN and the Shareable interfaces. The OwnerPIN instance would be manipulated only by the owner who has update privilege. All others would access the global PIN functionality via the proxy PIN interface.

See Also: OwnerPIN, Shareable

Methods

check(byte[], short, byte)

```
public boolean check(byte[] pin, short offset, byte length)
```

Compares pin against the PIN value. If they match and the PIN is not blocked, it sets the validated flag and resets the try counter to its maximum. If it does not match, it decrements the try counter and, if the counter has reached zero, blocks the PIN. Even if a transaction is in progress, internal state such as the try counter, the validated flag and the blocking state must not be conditionally updated.

Notes:

- *If* NullPointerException *or* ArrayIndexOutOfBoundsException *is thrown, the validated flag must be set to false, the try counter must be decremented and, the PIN blocked if the counter reaches zero.*
- *If* offset *or* length *parameter is negative an* ArrayIndexOutOfBoundsException *exception is thrown.*
- *If* offset+length *is greater than* pin.length, *the length of the* pin *array, an* ArrayIndexOutOfBoundsException *exception is thrown.*
- *If* pin *parameter is* null *a* NullPointerException *exception is thrown.*

Parameters:

pin—the byte array containing the PIN value being checked

offset—the starting offset in the pin array

length—the length of pin.

Returns: true if the PIN value matches; false otherwise

Throws: ArrayIndexOutOfBoundsException—if the check operation would cause access of data outside array bounds.

NullPointerException—if pin is null

getTriesRemaining()

```
public byte getTriesRemaining()
```

Returns the number of times remaining that an incorrect PIN can be presented before the PIN is blocked.

Returns: the number of times remaining

isValidated()

```
public boolean isValidated()
```

Returns `true` if a valid PIN value has been presented since the last card reset or last call to `reset()`.

Returns: `true` if validated; `false` otherwise

reset()

```
public void reset()
```

If the validated flag is set, this method resets it. If the validated flag is not set, this method does nothing.

javacard.framework
PINException

Syntax

```
public class PINException extends CardRuntimeException
```

```
Object
  |
  +--Throwable
        |
        +--Exception
              |
              +--RuntimeException
                    |
                    +--CardRuntimeException
                          |
                          +--javacard.framework.PINException
```

Description

PINException represents a OwnerPIN class access-related exception.

The OwnerPIN class throws JCRE owned instances of PINException.

JCRE owned instances of exception classes are temporary JCRE Entry Point Objects and can be accessed from any applet context. References to these temporary objects cannot be stored in class variables or instance variables or array components. See *Java Card Runtime Environment (JCRE) 2.1 Specification* for details.

See Also: OwnerPIN

Fields

ILLEGAL_VALUE

```
public static final short ILLEGAL_VALUE
```

This reason code is used to indicate that one or more input parameters is out of allowed bounds.

Constructors

PINException(short)

```
public PINException(short reason)
```

Constructs a PINException. To conserve on resources use throwIt() to use the JCRE owned instance of this class.

Parameters:

reason—the reason for the exception.

Methods

throwIt(short)

```
public static void throwIt(short reason)
```

Throws the JCRE owned instance of PINException with the specified reason.

JCRE owned instances of exception classes are temporary JCRE Entry Point Objects and can be accessed from any applet context. References to these temporary objects cannot be stored in class variables or instance variables or array components. See *Java Card Runtime Environment (JCRE) 2.1 Specification* for details.

Parameters:

reason—the reason for the exception.

Throws: PINException—always.

javacard.framework
Shareable

Syntax
```
public interface Shareable
```

Description
The Shareable interface serves to identify all shared objects. Any object that needs to be shared through the applet firewall must directly or indirectly implement this interface. Only those methods specified in a shareable interface are available through the firewall. Implementation classes can implement any number of shareable interfaces and can extend other shareable implementation classes.

javacard.framework
SystemException

Syntax

```
public class SystemException extends CardRuntimeException

Object
  |
  +--Throwable
        |
        +--Exception
              |
              +--RuntimeException
                    |
                    +--CardRuntimeException
                          |
                          +--javacard.framework.SystemException
```

Description

SystemException represents a JCSystem class related exception. It is also thrown by the javacard.framework.Applet.register() methods and by the AID class constructor.

These API classes throw JCRE owned instances of SystemException.

JCRE owned instances of exception classes are temporary JCRE Entry Point Objects and can be accessed from any applet context. References to these temporary objects cannot be stored in class variables or instance variables or array components. See *Java Card Runtime Environment (JCRE) 2.1 Specification* for details.

See Also: JCSystem, Applet, AID

Fields

ILLEGAL_AID

    public static final short ILLEGAL_AID

This reason code is used by the javacard.framework.Applet.register() method to indicate that the input AID parameter is not a legal AID value.

ILLEGAL_TRANSIENT

```
public static final short ILLEGAL_TRANSIENT
```

This reason code is used to indicate that the request to create a transient object is not allowed in the current applet context. See *Java Card Runtime Environment (JCRE) 2.1 Specification* for details.

ILLEGAL_VALUE

```
public static final short ILLEGAL_VALUE
```

This reason code is used to indicate that one or more input parameters is out of allowed bounds.

NO_RESOURCE

```
public static final short NO_RESOURCE
```

This reason code is used to indicate that there is insufficient resource in the Card for the request.

For example, the Java Card Virtual Machine may throw this exception reason when there is insufficient heap space to create a new instance.

NO_TRANSIENT_SPACE

```
public static final short NO_TRANSIENT_SPACE
```

This reason code is used by the makeTransient..() methods to indicate that no room is available in volatile memory for the requested object.

Constructors

SystemException(short)

```
public SystemException(short reason)
```

Constructs a SystemException. To conserve on resources use throwIt() to use the JCRE owned instance of this class.

Parameters:

reason—the reason for the exception.

Methods

throwIt(short)

```
public static void throwIt(short reason)
```

Throws the JCRE owned instance of SystemException with the specified reason.

JCRE owned instances of exception classes are temporary JCRE Entry Point Objects and can be accessed from any applet context. References to these temporary objects cannot be stored in class variables or instance variables or array components. See *Java Card Runtime Environment (JCRE) 2.1 Specification* for details.

Parameters:

reason—the reason for the exception.

Throws: SystemException—always.

javacard.framework
TransactionException

Syntax

```
public class TransactionException extends CardRuntimeException
```

```
Object
   |
 +--Throwable
      |
      +--Exception
           |
           +--RuntimeException
                |
                +--CardRuntimeException
                     |
                     +--javacard.framework.TransactionException
```

Description

TransactionException represents an exception in the transaction subsystem. The methods referred to in this class are in the JCSystem class.

The JCSystem class and the transaction facility throw JCRE owned instances of TransactionException.

JCRE owned instances of exception classes are temporary JCRE Entry Point Objects and can be accessed from any applet context. References to these temporary objects cannot be stored in class variables or instance variables or array components. See *Java Card Runtime Environment (JCRE) 2.1 Specification* for details.

See Also: JCSystem

Fields

BUFFER_FULL

```
public static final short BUFFER_FULL
```

This reason code is used during a transaction to indicate that the commit buffer is full.

IN_PROGRESS

```
public static final short IN_PROGRESS
```

This reason code is used by the beginTransaction method to indicate a transaction is already in progress.

INTERNAL_FAILURE

```
public static final short INTERNAL_FAILURE
```

This reason code is used during a transaction to indicate an internal JCRE problem (fatal error).

NOT_IN_PROGRESS

```
public static final short NOT_IN_PROGRESS
```

This reason code is used by the abortTransaction and commitTransaction methods when a transaction is not in progress.

Constructors

TransactionException(short)

```
public TransactionException(short reason)
```

Constructs a TransactionException with the specified reason. To conserve on resources use throwIt() to use the JCRE owned instance of this class.

Methods

throwIt(short)

```
public static void throwIt(short reason)
```

Throws the JCRE owned instance of TransactionException with the specified reason.

JCRE owned instances of exception classes are temporary JCRE Entry Point Objects and can be accessed from any applet context. References to these temporary objects cannot be stored in class variables or instance variables or array components. See *Java Card Runtime Environment (JCRE) 2.1 Specification* for details.

Throws: TransactionException—always.

javacard.framework
UserException

Syntax
```
public class UserException extends CardException

Object
  |
  +--Throwable
        |
        +--Exception
              |
              +--CardException
                    |
                    +--javacard.framework.UserException
```

Description

`UserException` represents a User exception. This class also provides a resource-saving mechanism (the `throwIt()` method) for user exceptions by using a JCRE owned instance.

JCRE owned instances of exception classes are temporary JCRE Entry Point Objects and can be accessed from any applet context. References to these temporary objects cannot be stored in class variables or instance variables or array components. See *Java Card Runtime Environment (JCRE) 2.1 Specification* for details.

Constructors

UserException()

```
public UserException()
```

Constructs a `UserException` with reason = 0. To conserve on resources use `throwIt()` to use the JCRE owned instance of this class.

UserException(short)

```
public UserException(short reason)
```

Constructs a `UserException` with the specified reason. To conserve on resources use `throwIt()` to use the JCRE owned instance of this class.

Parameters:

reason—the reason for the exception.

Methods

throwIt(short)

```
public static void throwIt(short reason)
```

Throws the JCRE owned instance of UserException with the specified reason.

JCRE owned instances of exception classes are temporary JCRE Entry Point Objects and can be accessed from any applet context. References to these temporary objects cannot be stored in class variables or instance variables or array components. See *Java Card Runtime Environment (JCRE) 2.1 Specification* for details.

Parameters:

reason—the reason for the exception.

Throws: UserException—always.

javacard.framework
Util

Syntax
```
public class Util
```

```
Object
  |
  +--javacard.framework.Util
```

Description

The Util class contains common utility functions. Some of the methods may be implemented as native functions for performance reasons. All methods in Util, class are static methods.

Some methods of Util namely arrayCopy(), arrayCopyNonAtomic(), array-FillNonAtomic() and setShort(), refer to the persistence of array objects. The term *persistent* means that arrays and their values persist from one CAD session to the next, indefinitely. The JCSystem class is used to control the persistence and transience of objects.

See Also: JCSystem

Methods

arrayCompare(byte[], short, byte[], short, short)

```
public static final native byte arrayCompare(byte[] src,
           short srcOff, byte[] dest, short destOff,
           short length)
```

Compares an array from the specified source array, beginning at the specified position, with the specified position of the destination array from left to right. Returns the ternary result of the comparison : less than(-1), equal(0) or greater than(1).

Notes:

- *If* srcOff *or* destOff *or* length *parameter is negative an* ArrayIndex-OutOfBoundsException *exception is thrown.*
- *If* srcOff+length *is greater than* src.length, *the length of the* src *array a* ArrayIndexOutOfBoundsException *exception is thrown.*

- *If* destOff+length *is greater than* dest.length, *the length of the* dest *array an* ArrayIndexOutOfBoundsException *exception is thrown.*
- *If* src *or* dest *parameter is* null *a* NullPointerException *exception is thrown.*

Parameters:

> src—source byte array.
>
> srcOff—offset within source byte array to start compare.
>
> dest—destination byte array.
>
> destOff—offset within destination byte array to start compare.
>
> length—byte length to be compared.

Returns: the result of the comparison as follows:
- 0 if identical
- -1 if the first miscomparing byte in source array is less than that in destination array,
- 1 if the first miscomparing byte in source array is greater that that in destination array.

Throws: ArrayIndexOutOfBoundsException—if comparing all bytes would cause access of data outside array bounds.

> NullPointerException—if either src or dest is null.

arrayCopy(byte[], short, byte[], short, short)

```
public static final native short arrayCopy(byte[] src,
        short srcOff, byte[] dest, short destOff,
        short length)
```

Copies an array from the specified source array, beginning at the specified position, to the specified position of the destination array.

Notes:

- *If* srcOff *or* destOff *or* length *parameter is negative an* ArrayIndexOutOfBoundsException *exception is thrown.*
- *If* srcOff+length *is greater than* src.length, *the length of the* src *array a* ArrayIndexOutOfBoundsException *exception is thrown and no copy is performed.*
- *If* destOff+length *is greater than* dest.length, *the length of the* dest *array an* ArrayIndexOutOfBoundsException *exception is thrown and no copy is performed.*
- *If* src *or* dest *parameter is* null *a* NullPointerException *exception is thrown.*

- *If the src and dest arguments refer to the same array object, then the copying is performed as if the components at positions* srcOff *through* srcOff+length-1 *were first copied to a temporary array with length components and then the contents of the temporary array were copied into positions* destOff *through* destOff+length-1 *of the argument array.*
- *If the destination array is persistent, the entire copy is performed atomically.*
- *The copy operation is subject to atomic commit capacity limitations. If the commit capacity is exceeded, no copy is performed and a* TransactionException *exception is thrown.*

Parameters:

> src—source byte array.
>
> srcOff—offset within source byte array to start copy from.
>
> dest—destination byte array.
>
> destOff—offset within destination byte array to start copy into.
>
> length—byte length to be copied.

Returns: destOff+length

Throws: ArrayIndexOutOfBoundsException—if copying would cause access of data outside array bounds.

> NullPointerException—if either src or dest is null.
>
> TransactionException—if copying would cause the commit capacity to be exceeded.

See Also: getUnusedCommitCapacity()

arrayCopyNonAtomic(byte[], short, byte[], short, short)

```
public static final native short arrayCopyNonAtomic(byte[] src,
        short srcOff, byte[] dest, short destOff,
        short length)
```

Copies an array from the specified source array, beginning at the specified position, to the specified position of the destination array (non-atomically).

This method does not use the transaction facility during the copy operation even if a transaction is in progress. Thus, this method is suitable for use only when the contents of the destination array can be left in a partially modified state in the event of a power loss in the middle of the copy operation.

Notes:

- *If* srcOff *or* destOff *or* length *parameter is negative an* ArrayIndexOutOfBoundsException *exception is thrown.*

- *If* srcOff+length *is greater than* src.length, *the length of the* src *array a* ArrayIndexOutOfBoundsException *exception is thrown and no copy is performed.*
- *If* destOff+length *is greater than* dest.length, *the length of the* dest *array an* ArrayIndexOutOfBoundsException *exception is thrown and no copy is performed.*
- *If* src *or* dest *parameter is* null *a* NullPointerException *exception is thrown.*
- *If the src and dest arguments refer to the same array object, then the copying is performed as if the components at positions* srcOff *through* srcOff+length-1 *were first copied to a temporary array with length components and then the contents of the temporary array were copied into positions* destOff *through* destOff+length-1 *of the argument array.*
- *If power is lost during the copy operation and the destination array is persistent, a partially changed destination array could result.*
- *The copy* length *parameter is not constrained by the atomic commit capacity limitations.*

Parameters:

> src—source byte array.

> srcOff—offset within source byte array to start copy from.

> dest—destination byte array.

> destOff—offset within destination byte array to start copy into.

> length—byte length to be copied.

Returns: destOff+length

Throws: ArrayIndexOutOfBoundsException—if copying would cause access of data outside array bounds.

> NullPointerException—if either src or dest is null.

See Also: getUnusedCommitCapacity()

arrayFillNonAtomic(byte[], short, short, byte)

```
public static final native short arrayFillNonAtomic(byte[] bArray,
          short bOff, short bLen, byte bValue)
```

Fills the byte array (non-atomically) beginning at the specified position, for the specified length with the specified byte value.

This method does not use the transaction facility during the fill operation even if a transaction is in progress. Thus, this method is suitable for use only when the contents of the byte array can be left in a partially filled state in the event of a power loss in the middle of the fill operation.

Notes:

- *If* bOff *or* bLen *parameter is negative an* ArrayIndexOutOfBoundsException *exception is thrown.*
- *If* bOff+bLen *is greater than* bArray.length, *the length of the* bArray *array an* ArrayIndexOutOfBoundsException *exception is thrown.*
- *If* bArray *parameter is* null *a* NullPointerException *exception is thrown.*
- *If power is lost during the copy operation and the byte array is persistent, a partially changed byte array could result.*
- *The* bLen *parameter is not constrained by the atomic commit capacity limitations.*

Parameters:

bArray—the byte array.

bOff—offset within byte array to start filling bValue into.

bLen—byte length to be filled.

bValue—the value to fill the byte array with.

Returns: bOff+bLen

Throws: ArrayIndexOutOfBoundsException—if the fill operation would cause access of data outside array bounds.

NullPointerException—if bArray is null

See Also: getUnusedCommitCapacity()

getShort(byte[], short)

```
public static final short getShort(byte[] bArray, short bOff)
```

Concatenates two bytes in a byte array to form a short value.

Parameters:

bArray—byte array.

bOff—offset within byte array containing first byte (the high order byte).

Returns: the short value—the concatenated result

makeShort(byte, byte)

```
public static final short makeShort(byte b1, byte b2)
```

Concatenates the two parameter bytes to form a short value.

Parameters:

> b1—the first byte (high order byte).

> b2—the second byte (low order byte).

Returns: the short value—the concatenated result

setShort(byte[], short, short)

```
public static final native short setShort(byte[] bArray,
        short bOff, short sValue)
```

Deposits the short value as two successive bytes at the specified offset in the byte array.

Parameters:

> bArray—byte array.

> bOff—offset within byte array to deposit the first byte (the high order byte).

> sValue—the short value to set into array.

Returns: bOff+2

Note:

- *If the byte array is persistent, this operation is performed atomically. If the commit capacity is exceeded, no operation is performed and a* Transaction-Exception *exception is thrown.*

Throws: TransactionException—if the operation would cause the commit capacity to be exceeded.

See Also: getUnusedCommitCapacity()

package
javacard.security

Description
Provides the classes and interfaces for the Java Card security framework.

Class Summary	
Interfaces	
DESKey	DESKey contains an 8/16/24 byte key for single/2 key triple DES/3 key triple DES operations.
DSAKey	The DSAKey interface is the base interface for the DSA algorithms private and public key implementations.
DSAPrivateKey	The DSAPrivateKey interface is used to sign data using the DSA algorithm.
DSAPublicKey	The DSAPublicKey interface is used to verify signatures on signed data using the DSA algorithm.
Key	The Key interface is the base interface for all keys.
PrivateKey	The PrivateKey class is the base class for private keys used in asymmetric algorithms.
PublicKey	The PublicKey class is the base class for public keys used in asymmetric algorithms.
RSAPrivateCrtKey	The RSAPrivateCrtKey interface is used to sign data using the RSA algorithm in its Chinese Remainder Theorem form.
RSAPrivateKey	The RSAPrivateKey class is used to sign data using the RSA algorithm in its modulus/exponent form.
RSAPublicKey	The RSAPublicKey is used to verify signatures on signed data using the RSA algorithm.
SecretKey	The SecretKey class is the base interface for keys used in symmetric algorithms (e.g. DES).
Classes	
KeyBuilder	The KeyBuilder class is a key object factory.
MessageDigest	The MessageDigest class is the base class for hashing algorithms.
RandomData	The RandomData abstract class is the base class for random number generation.
Signature	The Signature class is the base class for Signature algorithms.
Exceptions	
CryptoException	CryptoException represents a cryptography-related exception.

javacard.security
CryptoException

Syntax

```
public class CryptoException extends CardRuntimeException
```

```
Object
  |
  +--Throwable
        |
        +--Exception
              |
              +--RuntimeException
                    |
                    +--CardRuntimeException
                          |
                          +--javacard.security.CryptoException
```

Description

CryptoException represents a cryptography-related exception.

The API classes throw JCRE owned instances of SystemException.

JCRE owned instances of exception classes are temporary JCRE Entry Point Objects and can be accessed from any applet context. References to these temporary objects cannot be stored in class variables or instance variables or array components.

See Also: KeyBuilder, MessageDigest, Signature, RandomData, Cipher

Fields

ILLEGAL_USE

```
public static final short ILLEGAL_USE
```

This reason code is used to indicate that the signature or cipher algorithm does not pad the incoming message and the input message is not block aligned.

ILLEGAL_VALUE

```
public static final short ILLEGAL_VALUE
```

This reason code is used to indicate that one or more input parameters is out of allowed bounds.

INVALID_INIT

`public static final short INVALID_INIT`

This reason code is used to indicate that the signature or cipher object has not been correctly initialized for the requested operation.

NO_SUCH_ALGORITHM

`public static final short NO_SUCH_ALGORITHM`

This reason code is used to indicate that the requested algorithm or key type is not supported.

UNINITIALIZED_KEY

`public static final short UNINITIALIZED_KEY`

This reason code is used to indicate that the key is uninitialized.

Constructors

CryptoException(short)

`public CryptoException(short reason)`

Constructs a `CryptoException` with the specified reason. To conserve on resources use `throwIt()` to use the JCRE owned instance of this class.

Parameters:

> reason—the reason for the exception.

Methods

throwIt(short)

`public static void throwIt(short reason)`

Throws the JCRE owned instance of `CryptoException` with the specified reason.

JCRE owned instances of exception classes are temporary JCRE Entry Point Objects and can be accessed from any applet context. References to these temporary objects cannot be stored in class variables or instance variables or array components. See *Java Card Runtime Environment (JCRE) 2.1 Specification* for details.

Parameters:

> reason—the reason for the exception.

Throws: `CryptoException`—always.

javacard.security
DESKey

Syntax
```
public interface DESKey extends SecretKey
```

All Superinterfaces: Key, SecretKey

Description
DESKey contains an 8/16/24 byte key for single/2 key triple DES/3 key triple DES operations.

When the key data is set, the key is initialized and ready for use.

See Also: KeyBuilder, Signature, Cipher, KeyEncryption

Methods

getKey(byte[], short)

```
public byte getKey(byte[] keyData, short kOff)
```

Returns the Key data in plain text. The length of output key data is 8 bytes for DES, 16 bytes for 2 key triple DES and 24 bytes for 3 key triple DES. The data format is big-endian and right-aligned (the least significant bit is the least significant bit of last byte).

Parameters:

keyData—byte array to return key data

kOff—offset within keyData to start.

Returns: the byte length of the key data returned.

setKey(byte[], short)

```
public void setKey(byte[] keyData, short kOff)
```

Sets the Key data. The plaintext length of input key data is 8 bytes for DES, 16 bytes for 2 key triple DES and 24 bytes for 3 key triple DES. The data format is big-endian and right-aligned (the least significant bit is the least significant bit of last byte). Input key data is copied into the internal representation.

Parameters:

keyData—byte array containing key initialization data

kOff—offset within keyData to start

Throws: CryptoException—with the following reason code:

- CryptoException.ILLEGAL_VALUE if the input key data length is inconsistent with the implementation or if input data decryption is required and fails.

Note:

- *If the key object implements the* javacardx.crypto.KeyEncryption *interface and the* Cipher *object specified via* setKeyCipher() *is not* null, keyData *is decrypted using the* Cipher *object.*

javacard.security
DSAKey

Syntax
```
public interface DSAKey
```

All Known Subinterfaces: DSAPrivateKey, DSAPublicKey

Description
The DSAKey interface is the base interface for the DSA algorithms private and public key implementations. A DSA private key implementation must also implement the DSAPrivateKey interface methods. A DSA public key implementation must also implement the DSAPublicKey interface methods.

When all four components of the key (X or Y, P, Q, G) are set, the key is initialized and ready for use.

See Also: DSAPublicKey, DSAPrivateKey, KeyBuilder, Signature, KeyEncryption

Methods

getG(byte[], short)
```
public short getG(byte[] buffer, short offset)
```
Returns the subprime parameter value of the key in plain text. The data format is big-endian and right-aligned (the least significant bit is the least significant bit of last byte).

Parameters:

buffer—the output buffer

offset—the offset into the output buffer at which the subprime parameter value begins

Returns: the byte length of the subprime parameter value returned

getP(byte[], short)

```
public short getP(byte[] buffer, short offset)
```

Returns the base parameter value of the key in plain text. The data format is big-endian and right-aligned (the least significant bit is the least significant bit of last byte).

Parameters:

> buffer—the output buffer
>
> offset—the offset into the output buffer at which the base parameter value starts

Returns: the byte length of the base parameter value returned

getQ(byte[], short)

```
public short getQ(byte[] buffer, short offset)
```

Returns the prime parameter value of the key in plain text. The data format is big-endian and right-aligned (the least significant bit is the least significant bit of last byte).

Parameters:

> buffer—the output buffer
>
> offset—the offset into the output buffer at which the prime parameter value begins

Returns: the byte length of the prime parameter value returned

setG(byte[], short, short)

```
public void setG(byte[] buffer, short offset, short length)
```

Sets the subprime parameter value of the key. The plaintext data format is big-endian and right-aligned (the least significant bit is the least significant bit of last byte). Input subprime parameter data is copied into the internal representation.

Parameters:

> buffer—the input buffer
>
> offset—the offset into the input buffer at which the subprime parameter value begins
>
> length—the length of the subprime parameter value

Throws: CryptoException—with the following reason code:

- CryptoException.ILLEGAL_VALUE if the input parameter data length is inconsistent with the implementation or if input data decryption is required and fails.

Note:

- *If the key object implements the* javacardx.crypto.KeyEncryption *interface and the* Cipher *object specified via* setKeyCipher() *is not* null, *the subprime parameter value is decrypted using the* Cipher *object.*

setP(byte[], short, short)

```
public void setP(byte[] buffer, short offset, short length)
```

Sets the base parameter value of the key. The plaintext data format is big-endian and right-aligned (the least significant bit is the least significant bit of last byte). Input base parameter data is copied into the internal representation.

Parameters:

buffer—the input buffer

offset—the offset into the input buffer at which the base parameter value begins

length—the length of the base parameter value

Throws: CryptoException—with the following reason code:

- CryptoException.ILLEGAL_VALUE if the input parameter data length is inconsistent with the implementation or if input data decryption is required and fails.

Note:

- *If the key object implements the* javacardx.crypto.KeyEncryption *interface and the* Cipher *object specified via* setKeyCipher() *is not* null, *the base parameter value is decrypted using the* Cipher *object.*

setQ(byte[], short, short)

```
public void setQ(byte[] buffer, short offset, short length)
```

Sets the prime parameter value of the key. The plaintext data format is big-endian and right-aligned (the least significant bit is the least significant bit of last byte). Input prime parameter data is copied into the internal representation.

Parameters:

buffer—the input buffer

offset—the offset into the input buffer at which the prime parameter value begins

length—the length of the prime parameter value

Throws: CryptoException—with the following reason code:
- CryptoException.ILLEGAL_VALUE if the input parameter data length is inconsistent with the implementation or if input data decryption is required and fails.

Note:
- *If the key object implements the* javacardx.crypto.KeyEncryption *interface and the* Cipher *object specified via* setKeyCipher() *is not* null, *the prime parameter value is decrypted using the* Cipher *object.*

javacard.security
DSAPrivateKey

Syntax
```
public interface DSAPrivateKey extends PrivateKey, DSAKey
```

All Superinterfaces: DSAKey, Key, PrivateKey

Description

The DSAPrivateKey interface is used to sign data using the DSA algorithm. An implementation of DSAPrivateKey interface must also implement the DSAKey interface methods.

When all four components of the key (X,P,Q,G) are set, the key is initialized and ready for use.

See Also: DSAPublicKey, KeyBuilder, Signature, KeyEncryption

Methods

getX(byte[], short)

```
public short getX(byte[] buffer, short offset)
```

Returns the value of the key in plain text. The data format is big-endian and right-aligned (the least significant bit is the least significant bit of last byte).

Parameters:

buffer—the output buffer

offset—the offset into the output buffer at which the key value starts

Returns: the byte length of the key value returned

setX(byte[], short, short)

```
public void setX(byte[] buffer, short offset, short length)
```

Sets the value of the key. When the base, prime and subprime parameters are initialized and the key value is set, the key is ready for use. The plaintext data format is big-endian and right-aligned (the least significant bit is the least significant bit of last byte). Input key data is copied into the internal representation.

Parameters:

> buffer—the input buffer
>
> offset—the offset into the input buffer at which the modulus value begins
>
> length—the length of the modulus

Throws: CryptoException—with the following reason code:

- CryptoException.ILLEGAL_VALUE if the input key data length is inconsistent with the implementation or if input data decryption is required and fails.

Note:
- *If the key object implements the* javacardx.crypto.KeyEncryption *interface and the* Cipher *object specified via* setKeyCipher() *is not* null, *the key value is decrypted using the* Cipher *object.*

javacard.security
DSAPublicKey

Syntax

```
public interface DSAPublicKey extends PublicKey, DSAKey
```

All Superinterfaces: DSAKey, Key, PublicKey

Description

The DSAPublicKey interface is used to verify signatures on signed data using the DSA algorithm. An implementation of DSAPublicKey interface must also implement the DSAKey interface methods.

When all four components of the key (Y,P,Q,G) are set, the key is initialized and ready for use.

See Also: DSAPrivateKey, KeyBuilder, Signature, KeyEncryption

Methods

getY(byte[], short)

```
public short getY(byte[] buffer, short offset)
```

Returns the value of the key in plain text. The data format is big-endian and right-aligned (the least significant bit is the least significant bit of last byte).

Parameters:

buffer—the output buffer

offset—the offset into the input buffer at which the key value starts

Returns: the byte length of the key value returned

setY(byte[], short, short)

```
public void setY(byte[] buffer, short offset, short length)
```

Sets the value of the key. When the base, prime and subprime parameters are initialized and the key value is set, the key is ready for use. The plaintext data format is big-endian and right-aligned (the least significant bit is the least significant bit of last byte). Input key data is copied into the internal representation.

Parameters:

> `buffer`—the input buffer
>
> `offset`—the offset into the input buffer at which the key value begins
>
> `length`—the length of the key value

Throws: `CryptoException`—with the following reason code:

- `CryptoException.ILLEGAL_VALUE` if the input key data length is inconsistent with the implementation or if input data decryption is required and fails.

Note:

- *If the key object implements the* `javacardx.crypto.KeyEncryption` *interface and the* `Cipher` *object specified via* `setKeyCipher()` *is not* `null`*, the key value is decrypted using the* `Cipher` *object.*

javacard.security
Key

Syntax
```
public interface Key
```

All Known Subinterfaces: DESKey, DSAPrivateKey, DSAPublicKey,
PrivateKey, PublicKey, RSAPrivateCrtKey, RSAPrivateKey, RSAPublicKey,
SecretKey

Description
The Key interface is the base interface for all keys.

See Also: KeyBuilder

Methods

clearKey()
```
public void clearKey()
```
Clears the key and sets its initialized state to false.

getSize()
```
public short getSize()
```
Returns the key size in number of bits.

Returns: the key size in number of bits.

getType()
```
public byte getType()
```
Returns the key interface type.

Returns: the key interface type.

See Also: KeyBuilder

isInitialized()

```
public boolean isInitialized()
```

Reports the initialized state of the key. Keys must be initialized before being used.

A Key object sets its initialized state to true only when all the associated set methods have been invoked at least once since the time the initialized state was set to false.

A newly created Key object sets its initialized state to false. Invocation of the clearKey() method sets the initialized state to false. A key with transient key data sets its initialized state to false on the associated clear events.

Returns: true if the key has been initialized.

javacard.security
KeyBuilder

Syntax

```
public class KeyBuilder
```

```
Object
   |
   +--javacard.security.KeyBuilder
```

Description

The KeyBuilder class is a key object factory.

Fields

LENGTH_DES

> public static final short LENGTH_DES

> DES Key Length LENGTH_DES = 64.

LENGTH_DES3_2KEY

> public static final short LENGTH_DES3_2KEY

> DES Key Length LENGTH_DES3_2KEY = 128.

LENGTH_DES3_3KEY

> public static final short LENGTH_DES3_3KEY

> DES Key Length LENGTH_DES3_3KEY = 192.

LENGTH_DSA_1024

> public static final short LENGTH_DSA_1024

> DSA Key Length LENGTH_DSA_1024 = 1024.

LENGTH_DSA_512

```
public static final short LENGTH_DSA_512
```

DSA Key Length LENGTH_DSA_512 = 512.

LENGTH_DSA_768

```
public static final short LENGTH_DSA_768
```

DSA Key Length LENGTH_DSA_768 = 768.

LENGTH_RSA_1024

```
public static final short LENGTH_RSA_1024
```

RSA Key Length LENGTH_RSA_1024 = 1024.

LENGTH_RSA_2048

```
public static final short LENGTH_RSA_2048
```

RSA Key Length LENGTH_RSA_2048 = 2048.

LENGTH_RSA_512

```
public static final short LENGTH_RSA_512
```

RSA Key Length LENGTH_RSA_512 = 512.

LENGTH_RSA_768

```
public static final short LENGTH_RSA_768
```

RSA Key Length LENGTH_RSA_768 = 768.

TYPE_DES

```
public static final byte TYPE_DES
```

Key object which implements interface type DESKey with persistent key data.

TYPE_DES_TRANSIENT_DESELECT

```
public static final byte TYPE_DES_TRANSIENT_DESELECT
```

Key object which implements interface type DESKey with CLEAR_ON_DESE-LECT transient key data.

This Key object implicitly performs a clearKey() on power on, card reset and applet deselection.

TYPE_DES_TRANSIENT_RESET

`public static final byte TYPE_DES_TRANSIENT_RESET`

Key object which implements interface type DESKey with CLEAR_ON_RESET transient key data.

This Key object implicitly performs a `clearKey()` on power on or card reset.

TYPE_DSA_PRIVATE

`public static final byte TYPE_DSA_PRIVATE`

Key object which implements the interface type DSAPrivateKey for the DSA algorithm.

TYPE_DSA_PUBLIC

`public static final byte TYPE_DSA_PUBLIC`

Key object which implements the interface type DSAPublicKey for the DSA algorithm.

TYPE_RSA_CRT_PRIVATE

`public static final byte TYPE_RSA_CRT_PRIVATE`

Key object which implements interface type RSAPrivateCrtKey which uses Chinese Remainder Theorem.

TYPE_RSA_PRIVATE

`public static final byte TYPE_RSA_PRIVATE`

Key object which implements interface type RSAPrivateKey which uses modulus/exponent form.

TYPE_RSA_PUBLIC

`public static final byte TYPE_RSA_PUBLIC`

Key object which implements interface type RSAPublicKey.

Methods

buildKey(byte, short, boolean)

```
public static Key buildKey(byte keyType, short keyLength,
            boolean keyEncryption)
```

Creates cryptographic keys for signature and cipher algorithms. Instances created by this method may be the only key objects used to initialize instances of Signature and Cipher. Note that the object returned must be cast to their appropriate key type interface.

Parameters:

keyType—the type of key to be generated. Valid codes listed in TYPE.. constants.

keyLength—the key size in bits. The valid key bit lengths are key type dependent. See above.

keyEncryption—if true this boolean requests a key implementation which implements the javacardx.cipher.KeyEncryption interface.

Returns: the key object instance of the requested key type, length and encrypted access.

Throws: CryptoException—with the following reason codes:

- CryptoException.NO_SUCH_ALGORITHM if the requested algorithm associated with the specified type, size of key and key encryption interface is not supported.

javacard.security
MessageDigest

Syntax
```
public abstract class MessageDigest
```
```
Object
  |
  +--javacard.security.MessageDigest
```

Description
The MessageDigest class is the base class for hashing algorithms. Implementations of MessageDigest algorithms must extend this class and implement all the abstract methods.

Fields

ALG_MD5
```
public static final byte ALG_MD5
```
Message Digest algorithm MD5.

ALG_RIPEMD160
```
public static final byte ALG_RIPEMD160
```
Message Digest algorithm RIPE MD-160.

ALG_SHA
```
public static final byte ALG_SHA
```
Message Digest algorithm SHA.

Constructors

MessageDigest()

```
protected MessageDigest()
```

Protected Constructor

Methods

doFinal(byte[], short, short, byte[], short)

```
public abstract short doFinal(byte[] inBuff, short inOffset,
            short inLength, byte[] outBuff, short outOffset)
```

Generates a hash of all/last input data. Completes and returns the hash computation after performing final operations such as padding. The MessageDigest object is reset after this call is made.

The input and output buffer data may overlap.

Parameters:

> inBuff—the input buffer of data to be hashed
>
> inOffset—the offset into the input buffer at which to begin hash generation
>
> inLength—the byte length to hash
>
> outBuff—the output buffer, may be the same as the input buffer
>
> outOffset—the offset into the output buffer where the resulting hash value begins

Returns: number of bytes of hash output in outBuff

getAlgorithm()

```
public abstract byte getAlgorithm()
```

Gets the Message digest algorithm.

Returns: the algorithm code defined above.

getInstance(byte, boolean)

```
public static final MessageDigest getInstance(byte algorithm,
            boolean externalAccess)
```

Creates a MessageDigest object instance of the selected algorithm.

Parameters:

> algorithm—the desired message digest algorithm. Valid codes listed in ALG_.. constants. See above.

> externalAccess—if true indicates that the instance will be shared among multiple applet instances and that the MessageDigest instance will also be accessed (via a Shareable interface) when the owner of the MessageDigest instance is not the currently selected applet.

Returns: the MessageDigest object instance of the requested algorithm.

Throws: CryptoException—with the following reason codes:
- CryptoException.NO_SUCH_ALGORITHM if the requested algorithm is not supported.

getLength()

```
public abstract byte getLength()
```

Returns the byte length of the hash.

Returns: hash length

reset()

```
public abstract void reset()
```

Resets the MessageDigest object to the initial state for further use.

update(byte[], short, short)

```
public abstract void update(byte[] inBuff, short inOffset,
            short inLength)
```

Accumulates a hash of the input data. When this method is used temporary storage of intermediate results is required. This method should only be used if all the input data required for the hash is not available in one byte array. The doFinal() method is recommended whenever possible.

Parameters:

> inBuff—the input buffer of data to be hashed

> inOffset—the offset into the input buffer at which to begin hash generation

> inLength—the byte length to hash

See Also: doFinal(byte[], short, short, byte[], short)

javacard.security
PrivateKey

Syntax

```
public interface PrivateKey extends Key
```

All Known Subinterfaces: DSAPrivateKey, RSAPrivateCrtKey, RSAPrivateKey

All Superinterfaces: Key

Description

The PrivateKey class is the base class for private keys used in asymmetric algorithms.

javacard.security
PublicKey

Syntax

```
public interface PublicKey extends Key
```

All Known Subinterfaces: DSAPublicKey, RSAPublicKey

All Superinterfaces: Key

Description

The PublicKey class is the base class for public keys used in asymmetric algorithms.

javacard.security
RandomData

Syntax
```
public abstract class RandomData
```
```
Object
  |
  +--javacard.security.RandomData
```

Description
The RandomData abstract class is the base class for random number generation. Implementations of RandomData algorithms must extend this class and implement all the abstract methods.

Fields

ALG_PSEUDO_RANDOM
```
public static final byte ALG_PSEUDO_RANDOM
```
Utility pseudo random number generation algorithms.

ALG_SECURE_RANDOM
```
public static final byte ALG_SECURE_RANDOM
```
Cryptographically secure random number generation algorithms.

Constructors

RandomData()
```
protected RandomData()
```
Protected constructor for subclassing.

Methods

generateData(byte[], short, short)

```
public abstract void generateData(byte[] buffer, short offset,
            short length)
```

Generates random data.

Parameters:

> buffer—the output buffer

> offset—the offset into the output buffer

> length—the length of random data to generate

getInstance(byte)

```
public static final RandomData getInstance(byte algorithm)
```

Creates a RandomData instance of the selected algorithm. The pseudo random RandomData instance's seed is initialized to a internal default value.

Parameters:

> algorithm—the desired random number algorithm. Valid codes listed in ALG_.. constants. See above.

Returns: the RandomData object instance of the requested algorithm.

Throws: CryptoException—with the following reason codes:
- CryptoException.NO_SUCH_ALGORITHM if the requested algorithm is not supported.

setSeed(byte[], short, short)

```
public abstract void setSeed(byte[] buffer, short offset,
            short length)
```

Seeds the random data generator.

Parameters:

> buffer—the input buffer

> offset—the offset into the input buffer

> length—the length of the seed data

javacard.security
RSAPrivateCrtKey

Syntax
```
public interface RSAPrivateCrtKey extends PrivateKey
```

All Superinterfaces: Key, PrivateKey

Description

The RSAPrivateCrtKey interface is used to sign data using the RSA algorithm in its Chinese Remainder Theorem form. It may also be used by the javacardx.crypto.Cipher class to encrypt/decrypt messages.

Let $S = m^d$ mod n, where m is the data to be signed, d is the private key exponent, and n is private key modulus composed of two prime numbers p and q. The following names are used in the initializer methods in this interface:

P, the prime factor p

Q, the prime factor q.

PQ = q^{-1} mod p

DP1 = d mod $(p—1)$

DQ1 = d mod $(q—1)$

When all five components (P,Q,PQ,DP1,DQ1) of the key are set, the key is initialized and ready for use.

See Also: RSAPrivateKey, RSAPublicKey, KeyBuilder, Signature, Cipher, KeyEncryption

Methods

getDP1(byte[], short)

```
public short getDP1(byte[] buffer, short offset)
```

Returns the value of the DP1 parameter in plain text. The data format is big-endian and right-aligned (the least significant bit is the least significant bit of last byte).

Parameters:

> buffer—the output buffer

> offset—the offset into the output buffer at which the parameter value begins

Returns: the byte length of the DP1 parameter value returned

getDQ1(byte[], short)

```
public short getDQ1(byte[] buffer, short offset)
```

Returns the value of the DQ1 parameter in plain text. The data format is big-endian and right-aligned (the least significant bit is the least significant bit of last byte).

Parameters:

> buffer—the output buffer

> offset—the offset into the output buffer at which the parameter value begins

Returns: the byte length of the DQ1 parameter value returned

getP(byte[], short)

```
public short getP(byte[] buffer, short offset)
```

Returns the value of the P parameter in plain text. The data format is big-endian and right-aligned (the least significant bit is the least significant bit of last byte).

Parameters:

> buffer—the output buffer

> offset—the offset into the output buffer at which the parameter value begins

Returns: the byte length of the P parameter value returned

getPQ(byte[], short)

```
public short getPQ(byte[] buffer, short offset)
```

Returns the value of the PQ parameter in plain text. The data format is big-endian and right-aligned (the least significant bit is the least significant bit of last byte).

Parameters:

> buffer—the output buffer

> offset—the offset into the output buffer at which the parameter value begins

Returns: the byte length of the PQ parameter value returned

getQ(byte[], short)

```
public short getQ(byte[] buffer, short offset)
```

Returns the value of the Q parameter in plain text. The data format is big-endian and right-aligned (the least significant bit is the least significant bit of last byte).

Parameters:

buffer—the output buffer

offset—the offset into the output buffer at which the parameter value begins

Returns: the byte length of the Q parameter value returned

setDP1(byte[], short, short)

```
public void setDP1(byte[] buffer, short offset, short length)
```

Sets the value of the DP1 parameter. The plaintext data format is big-endian and right-aligned (the least significant bit is the least significant bit of last byte). Input DP1 parameter data is copied into the internal representation.

Parameters:

buffer—the input buffer

offset—the offset into the input buffer at which the parameter value begins

length—the length of the parameter

Throws: CryptoException—with the following reason code:
- CryptoException.ILLEGAL_VALUE if the input parameter data length is inconsistent with the implementation or if input data decryption is required and fails.

Note:
- *If the key object implements the* javacardx.crypto.KeyEncryption *interface and the* Cipher *object specified via* setKeyCipher() *is not* null, *the DP1 parameter value is decrypted using the* Cipher *object.*

setDQ1(byte[], short, short)

```
public void setDQ1(byte[] buffer, short offset, short length)
```

Sets the value of the DQ1 parameter. The plaintext data format is big-endian and right-aligned (the least significant bit is the least significant bit of last byte). Input DQ1 parameter data is copied into the internal representation.

Parameters:

> buffer—the input buffer
>
> offset—the offset into the input buffer at which the parameter value begins
>
> length—the length of the parameter

Throws: CryptoException—with the following reason code:

- CryptoException.ILLEGAL_VALUE if the input parameter data length is inconsistent with the implementation or if input data decryption is required and fails.

Note:

- *If the key object implements the* javacardx.crypto.KeyEncryption *interface and the* Cipher *object specified via* setKeyCipher() *is not* null, *the DQ1 parameter value is decrypted using the* Cipher *object.*

setP(byte[], short, short)

```
public void setP(byte[] buffer, short offset, short length)
```

Sets the value of the P parameter. The plaintext data format is big-endian and right-aligned (the least significant bit is the least significant bit of last byte). Input P parameter data is copied into the internal representation.

Parameters:

> buffer—the input buffer
>
> offset—the offset into the input buffer at which the parameter value begins
>
> length—the length of the parameter

Throws: CryptoException—with the following reason code:

- CryptoException.ILLEGAL_VALUE if the input parameter data length is inconsistent with the implementation or if input data decryption is required and fails.

Note:

- *If the key object implements the* javacardx.crypto.KeyEncryption *interface and the* Cipher *object specified via* setKeyCipher() *is not* null, *the P parameter value is decrypted using the* Cipher *object.*

setPQ(byte[], short, short)

```
public void setPQ(byte[] buffer, short offset, short length)
```

Sets the value of the PQ parameter. The plaintext data format is big-endian and right-aligned (the least significant bit is the least significant bit of last byte). Input PQ parameter data is copied into the internal representation.

Parameters:

buffer—the input buffer

offset—the offset into the input buffer at which the parameter value begins

length—the length of the parameter

Throws: CryptoException—with the following reason code:

- CryptoException.ILLEGAL_VALUE if the input parameter data length is inconsistent with the implementation or if input data decryption is required and fails.

Note:

- *If the key object implements the* javacardx.crypto.KeyEncryption *interface and the* Cipher *object specified via* setKeyCipher() *is not* null, *the PQ parameter value is decrypted using the* Cipher *object.*

setQ(byte[], short, short)

```
public void setQ(byte[] buffer, short offset, short length)
```

Sets the value of the Q parameter. The plaintext data format is big-endian and right-aligned (the least significant bit is the least significant bit of last byte). Input Q parameter data is copied into the internal representation.

Parameters:

buffer—the input buffer

offset—the offset into the input buffer at which the parameter value begins

length—the length of the parameter

Throws: CryptoException—with the following reason code:

- CryptoException.ILLEGAL_VALUE if the input parameter data length is inconsistent with the implementation or if input data decryption is required and fails.

Note:

- *If the key object implements the* javacardx.crypto.KeyEncryption *interface and the* Cipher *object specified via* setKeyCipher() *is not* null, *the Q parameter value is decrypted using the* Cipher *object.*

javacard.security
RSAPrivateKey

Syntax
```
public interface RSAPrivateKey extends PrivateKey
```

All Superinterfaces: `Key, PrivateKey`

Description
The `RSAPrivateKey` class is used to sign data using the RSA algorithm in its modulus/exponent form. It may also be used by the `javacardx.crypto.Cipher` class to encrypt/decrypt messages.

When both the modulus and exponent of the key are set, the key is initialized and ready for use.

See Also: `RSAPublicKey, RSAPrivateCrtKey, KeyBuilder, Signature, Cipher, KeyEncryption`

Methods

getExponent(byte[], short)
```
public short getExponent(byte[] buffer, short offset)
```
Returns the private exponent value of the key in plain text. The data format is big-endian and right-aligned (the least significant bit is the least significant bit of last byte).

Parameters:

buffer—the output buffer

offset—the offset into the output buffer at which the exponent value begins

Returns: the byte length of the private exponent value returned

getModulus(byte[], short)
```
public short getModulus(byte[] buffer, short offset)
```

Returns the modulus value of the key in plain text. The data format is big-endian and right-aligned (the least significant bit is the least significant bit of last byte).

Parameters:

> buffer—the output buffer

> offset—the offset into the output buffer at which the modulus value starts

Returns: the byte length of the modulus value returned

setExponent(byte[], short, short)

```
public void setExponent(byte[] buffer, short offset, short length)
```

Sets the private exponent value of the key. The plaintext data format is big-endian and right-aligned (the least significant bit is the least significant bit of last byte). Input exponent data is copied into the internal representation.

Parameters:

> buffer—the input buffer

> offset—the offset into the input buffer at which the exponent value begins

> length—the length of the exponent

Throws: CryptoException—with the following reason code:

- CryptoException.ILLEGAL_VALUE if the input exponent data length is inconsistent with the implementation or if input data decryption is required and fails.

Note:

- *If the key object implements the* javacardx.crypto.KeyEncryption *interface and the* Cipher *object specified via* setKeyCipher() *is not* null, *the exponent value is decrypted using the* Cipher *object.*

setModulus(byte[], short, short)

```
public void setModulus(byte[] buffer, short offset, short length)
```

Sets the modulus value of the key. The plaintext data format is big-endian and right-aligned (the least significant bit is the least significant bit of last byte). Input modulus data is copied into the internal representation.

Parameters:

buffer—the input buffer

offset—the offset into the input buffer at which the modulus value begins

length—the length of the modulus

Throws: CryptoException—with the following reason code:

- CryptoException.ILLEGAL_VALUE if the input modulus data length is inconsistent with the implementation or if input data decryption is required and fails.

Note:

- *If the key object implements the* javacardx.crypto.KeyEncryption *interface and the* Cipher *object specified via* setKeyCipher() *is not* null, *the modulus value is decrypted using the* Cipher *object.*

javacard.security

RSAPublicKey

Syntax

```
public interface RSAPublicKey extends PublicKey
```

All Superinterfaces: Key, PublicKey

Description

The RSAPublicKey is used to verify signatures on signed data using the RSA algorithm. It may also used by the javacardx.crypto.Cipher class to encrypt/decrypt messages.

When both the modulus and exponent of the key are set, the key is initialized and ready for use.

See Also: RSAPrivateKey, RSAPrivateCrtKey, KeyBuilder, Signature, Cipher, KeyEncryption

Methods

getExponent(byte[], short)

```
public short getExponent(byte[] buffer, short offset)
```

Returns the private exponent value of the key in plain text. The data format is big-endian and right-aligned (the least significant bit is the least significant bit of last byte).

Parameters:

buffer—the output buffer

offset—the offset into the output buffer at which the exponent value begins

Returns: the byte length of the public exponent returned

getModulus(byte[], short)

```
public short getModulus(byte[] buffer, short offset)
```

Returns the modulus value of the key in plain text. The data format is big-endian and right-aligned (the least significant bit is the least significant bit of last byte).

Parameters:

> buffer—the output buffer

> offset—the offset into the input buffer at which the modulus value starts

Returns: the byte length of the modulus value returned

setExponent(byte[], short, short)

```
public void setExponent(byte[] buffer, short offset, short length)
```

Sets the public exponent value of the key. The plaintext data format is big-endian and right-aligned (the least significant bit is the least significant bit of last byte). Input exponent data is copied into the internal representation.

Parameters:

> buffer—the input buffer

> offset—the offset into the input buffer at which the exponent value begins

> length—the byte length of the exponent

Throws: CryptoException—with the following reason code:

- CryptoException.ILLEGAL_VALUE if the input exponent data length is inconsistent with the implementation or if input data decryption is required and fails.

> Note:
> - *If the key object implements the* javacardx.crypto.KeyEncryption *interface and the* Cipher *object specified via* setKeyCipher() *is not* null, *the exponent value is decrypted using the* Cipher *object.*

setModulus(byte[], short, short)

```
public void setModulus(byte[] buffer, short offset, short length)
```

Sets the modulus value of the key. The plaintext data format is big-endian and right-aligned (the least significant bit is the least significant bit of last byte). Input modulus data is copied into the internal representation.

Parameters:

buffer—the input buffer

offset—the offset into the input buffer at which the modulus value begins

length—the byte length of the modulus

Throws: CryptoException—with the following reason code:

- CryptoException.ILLEGAL_VALUE if the input modulus data length is inconsistent with the implementation or if input data decryption is required and fails.

Note:

- *If the key object implements the* javacardx.crypto.KeyEncryption *interface and the* Cipher *object specified via* setKeyCipher() *is not* null, *the modulus value is decrypted using the* Cipher *object.*

javacard.security
SecretKey

Syntax

```
public interface SecretKey extends Key
```

All Known Subinterfaces: DESKey

All Superinterfaces: Key

Description

The SecretKey class is the base interface for keys used in symmetric algorithms (e.g. DES).

javacard.security
Signature

Syntax

```
public abstract class Signature
```

```
Object
  |
  +--javacard.security.Signature
```

Description

The Signature class is the base class for Signature algorithms. Implementations of Signature algorithms must extend this class and implement all the abstract methods.

The term "pad" is used in the public key signature algorithms below to refer to all the operations specified in the referenced scheme to transform the message digest into the encryption block size.

Fields

ALG_DES_MAC4_ISO9797_M1

```
public static final byte ALG_DES_MAC4_ISO9797_M1
```

Signature algorithm ALG_DES_MAC4_ISO9797_M1 generates a 4 byte MAC (most significant 4 bytes of encrypted block) using DES or triple DES in CBC mode. This algorithm uses outer CBC for triple DES. Input data is padded according to the ISO 9797 method 1 scheme.

ALG_DES_MAC4_ISO9797_M2

```
public static final byte ALG_DES_MAC4_ISO9797_M2
```

Signature algorithm ALG_DES_MAC4_ISO9797_M2 generates a 4 byte MAC (most significant 4 bytes of encrypted block) using DES or triple DES in CBC mode. This algorithm uses outer CBC for triple DES. Input data is padded according to the ISO 9797 method 2 (ISO 7816-4, EMV'96) scheme.

ALG_DES_MAC4_NOPAD

`public static final byte ALG_DES_MAC4_NOPAD`

Signature algorithm `ALG_DES_MAC4_NOPAD` generates a 4 byte MAC (most significant 4 bytes of encrypted block) using DES or triple DES in CBC mode. This algorithm uses outer CBC for triple DES. This algorithm does not pad input data. If the input data is not (8 byte) block aligned it throws `CryptoException` with the reason code `ILLEGAL_USE`.

ALG_DES_MAC4_PKCS5

`public static final byte ALG_DES_MAC4_PKCS5`

Signature algorithm `ALG_DES_MAC4_PKCS5` generates a 4 byte MAC (most significant 4 bytes of encrypted block) using DES or triple DES in CBC mode. This algorithm uses outer CBC for triple DES. Input data is padded according to the PKCS#5 scheme.

ALG_DES_MAC8_ISO9797_M1

`public static final byte ALG_DES_MAC8_ISO9797_M1`

Signature algorithm `ALG_DES_MAC8_ISO9797_M1` generates a 8 byte MAC using DES or triple DES in CBC mode. This algorithm uses outer CBC for triple DES. Input data is padded according to the ISO 9797 method 1 scheme.

Note:
- *This algorithm must not be implemented if export restrictions apply.*

ALG_DES_MAC8_ISO9797_M2

`public static final byte ALG_DES_MAC8_ISO9797_M2`

Signature algorithm `ALG_DES_MAC8_ISO9797_M2` generates a 8 byte MAC using DES or triple DES in CBC mode. This algorithm uses outer CBC for triple DES. Input data is padded according to the ISO 9797 method 2 (ISO 7816-4, EMV'96) scheme.

Note:
- *This algorithm must not be implemented if export restrictions apply.*

ALG_DES_MAC8_NOPAD

`public static final byte ALG_DES_MAC8_NOPAD`

Signature algorithm `ALG_DES_MAC_8_NOPAD` generates a 8 byte MAC using DES or triple DES in CBC mode. This algorithm uses outer CBC for triple DES. This algorithm does not pad input data. If the input data is not (8 byte) block aligned it throws `CryptoExeption` with the reason code `ILLEGAL_USE`.

Note:
  • *This algorithm must not be implemented if export restrictions apply.*

ALG_DES_MAC8_PKCS5

`public static final byte ALG_DES_MAC8_PKCS5`

Signature algorithm ALG_DES_MAC8_PKCS5 generates a 8 byte MAC using DES or triple DES in CBC mode. This algorithm uses outer CBC for triple DES. Input data is padded according to the PKCS#5 scheme.

Note:
  • *This algorithm must not be implemented if export restrictions apply.*

ALG_DSA_SHA

`public static final byte ALG_DSA_SHA`

Signature algorithm `ALG_DSA_SHA` signs/verifies the 20 byte SHA digest using DSA.

ALG_RSA_MD5_PKCS1

`public static final byte ALG_RSA_MD5_PKCS1`

Signature algorithm `ALG_RSA_MD5_PKCS1` encrypts the 16 byte MD5 digest using RSA. The digest is padded according to the PKCS#1 (v1.5) scheme.

ALG_RSA_MD5_RFC2409

`public static final byte ALG_RSA_MD5_RFC2409`

Signature algorithm `ALG_RSA_MD5_RFC2409` encrypts the 16 byte MD5 digest using RSA. The digest is padded according to the RFC2409 scheme.

ALG_RSA_RIPEMD160_ISO9796

```
public static final byte ALG_RSA_RIPEMD160_ISO9796
```

Signature algorithm `ALG_RSA_RIPEMD160_ISO9796` encrypts the 20 byte RIPE MD-160 digest using RSA. The digest is padded according to the ISO 9796 scheme.

ALG_RSA_RIPEMD160_PKCS1

```
public static final byte ALG_RSA_RIPEMD160_PKCS1
```

Signature algorithm `ALG_RSA_RIPEMD160_PKCS1` encrypts the 20 byte RIPE MD-160 digest using RSA. The digest is padded according to the PKCS#1 (v1.5) scheme.

ALG_RSA_SHA_ISO9796

```
public static final byte ALG_RSA_SHA_ISO9796
```

Signature algorithm `ALG_RSA_SHA_ISO9796` encrypts the 20 byte SHA digest using RSA. The digest is padded according to the ISO 9796 (EMV'96) scheme.

ALG_RSA_SHA_PKCS1

```
public static final byte ALG_RSA_SHA_PKCS1
```

Signature algorithm `ALG_RSA_SHA_PKCS1` encrypts the 20 byte SHA digest using RSA. The digest is padded according to the PKCS#1 (v1.5) scheme.

ALG_RSA_SHA_RFC2409

```
public static final byte ALG_RSA_SHA_RFC2409
```

Signature algorithm `ALG_RSA_SHA_RFC2409` encrypts the 20 byte SHA digest using RSA. The digest is padded according to the RFC2409 scheme.

MODE_SIGN

```
public static final byte MODE_SIGN
```

Used in `init()` methods to indicate signature sign mode.

MODE_VERIFY

```
public static final byte MODE_VERIFY
```

Used in `init()` methods to indicate signature verify mode.

Constructors

Signature()

```
protected Signature()
```

Protected Constructor

Methods

getAlgorithm()

```
public abstract byte getAlgorithm()
```

Gets the Signature algorithm.

Returns: the algorithm code defined above.

getInstance(byte, boolean)

```
public static final Signature getInstance(byte algorithm,
                boolean externalAccess)
```

Creates a Signature object instance of the selected algorithm.

Parameters:

> algorithm—the desired Signature algorithm. See above.

> externalAccess—if true indicates that the instance will be shared among multiple applet instances and that the Signature instance will also be accessed (via a Shareable interface) when the owner of the Signature instance is not the currently selected applet.

Returns: the Signature object instance of the requested algorithm.

Throws: CryptoException—with the following reason codes:
- CryptoException.NO_SUCH_ALGORITHM if the requested algorithm is not supported.

getLength()

```
public abstract short getLength()
```

Returns the byte length of the signature data.

Returns: the byte length of the signature data.

init(Key, byte)

```
public abstract void init(Key theKey, byte theMode)
```

Initializes the Signature object with the appropriate Key. This method should be used for algorithms which do not need initialization parameters or use default parameter values.

Note:

- *DES and triple DES algorithms in CBC mode will use 0 for initial vector(IV) if this method is used.*

Parameters:

> theKey—the key object to use for signing or verifying
>
> theMode—one of MODE_SIGN or MODE_VERIFY

Throws: CryptoException—with the following reason codes:
- CryptoException.ILLEGAL_VALUE if theMode option is an undefined value or if the Key is inconsistent with theMode or with the Signature implementation.

init(Key, byte, byte[], short, short)

```
public abstract void init(Key theKey, byte theMode, byte[] bArray,
            short bOff, short bLen)
```

Initializes the Signature object with the appropriate Key and algorithm specific parameters.

Note:

- *DES and triple DES algorithms in outer CBC mode expect an 8 byte parameter value for the initial vector(IV) in* bArray.
- *RSA and DSA algorithms throw* CryptoException.ILLEGAL_VALUE.

Parameters:

> theKey—the key object to use for signing
>
> theMode—one of MODE_SIGN or MODE_VERIFY
>
> bArray—byte array containing algorithm specific initialization info.
>
> bOff—offset within bArray where the algorithm specific data begins.
>
> bLen—byte length of algorithm specific parameter data

Throws: CryptoException—with the following reason codes:

- CryptoException.ILLEGAL_VALUE if theMode option is an undefined value or if a byte array parameter option is not supported by the algorithm or if the bLen is an incorrect byte length for the algorithm specific data or if the Key is inconsistent with theMode or with the Signature implementation.

sign(byte[], short, short, byte[], short)

```
public abstract short sign(byte[] inBuff, short inOffset,
              short inLength, byte[] sigBuff, short sigOffset)
```

Generates the signature of all/last input data. A call to this method also resets this Signature object to the state it was in when previously initialized via a call to init(). That is, the object is reset and available to sign another message.

The input and output buffer data may overlap.

Parameters:

inBuff—the input buffer of data to be signed

inOffset—the offset into the input buffer at which to begin signature generation

inLength—the byte length to sign

sigBuff—the output buffer to store signature data

sigOffset—the offset into sigBuff at which to begin signature data

Returns: number of bytes of signature output in sigBuff

Throws: CryptoException—with the following reason codes:

- CryptoException.UNINITIALIZED_KEY if key not initialized.
- CryptoException.INVALID_INIT if this Signature object is not initialized or initialized for signature verify mode.
- CryptoException.ILLEGAL_USE if this Signature algorithm does not pad the message and the message is not block aligned.

update(byte[], short, short)

```
public abstract void update(byte[] inBuff, short inOffset,
              short inLength)
```

Accumulates a signature of the input data. When this method is used temporary storage of intermediate results is required. This method should only be used if all the input data required for the signature is not available in one byte array. The sign() or verify() method is recommended whenever possible.

Parameters:

    inBuff—the input buffer of data to be signed

    inOffset—the offset into the input buffer at which to begin signature generation

    inLength—the byte length to sign

Throws: CryptoException—with the following reason codes:
- CryptoException.UNINITIALIZED_KEY if key not initialized.

See Also: sign(byte[], short, short, byte[], short), verify(byte[], short, short, byte[], short, short)

verify(byte[], short, short, byte[], short, short)

```
public abstract boolean verify(byte[] inBuff, short inOffset,
            short inLength, byte[] sigBuff, short sigOffset,
            short sigLength)
```

Verifies the signature of all/last input data against the passed in signature. A call to this method also resets this Signature object to the state it was in when previously initialized via a call to init(). That is, the object is reset and available to verify another message.

Parameters:

    inBuff—the input buffer of data to be verified

    inOffset—the offset into the input buffer at which to begin signature generation

    inLength—the byte length to sign

    sigBuff—the input buffer containing signature data

    sigOffset—the offset into sigBuff where signature data begins.

    sigLength—the byte length of the signature data

Returns: true if signature verifies false otherwise.

Throws: CryptoException—with the following reason codes:
- CryptoException.UNINITIALIZED_KEY if key not initialized.
- CryptoException.INVALID_INIT if this Signature object is not initialized or initialized for signature sign mode.
- CryptoException.ILLEGAL_USE if this Signature algorithm does not pad the message and the message is not block aligned.

package
javacardx.crypto

Description

Extension package containing security classes and interfaces for export-controlled functionality.

Class Summary	
Interfaces	
KeyEncryption	KeyEncryption interface defines the methods used to enable encrypted key data access to a key implementation.
Classes	
Cipher	The Cipher class is the abstract base class for Cipher algorthims.

javacardx.crypto
Cipher

Syntax

```
public abstract class Cipher
```

```
Object
  |
  +--javacardx.crypto.Cipher
```

Description

The Cipher class is the abstract base class for Cipher algorthims. Implementations of Cipher algorithms must extend this class and implement all the abstract methods.

The term "pad" is used in the public key cipher algorithms below to refer to all the operations specified in the referenced scheme to transform the message block into the cipher block size.

Fields

ALG_DES_CBC_ISO9797_M1

```
public static final byte ALG_DES_CBC_ISO9797_M1
```

Cipher algorithm ALG_DES_CBC_ISO9797_M1 provides a cipher using DES in CBC mode. This algorithm uses outer CBC for triple DES. Input data is padded according to the ISO 9797 method 1 scheme.

ALG_DES_CBC_ISO9797_M2

```
public static final byte ALG_DES_CBC_ISO9797_M2
```

Cipher algorithm ALG_DES_CBC_ISO9797_M2 provides a cipher using DES in CBC mode. This algorithm uses outer CBC for triple DES. Input data is padded according to the ISO 9797 method 2 (ISO 7816-4, EMV'96) scheme.

ALG_DES_CBC_NOPAD

```
public static final byte ALG_DES_CBC_NOPAD
```

Cipher algorithm ALG_DES_CBC_NOPAD provides a cipher using DES in CBC mode. This algorithm uses outer CBC for triple DES. This algorithm does not pad input data. If the input data is not (8 byte) block aligned it throws `CryptoExeption` with the reason code `ILLEGAL_USE`.

ALG_DES_CBC_PKCS5

```
public static final byte ALG_DES_CBC_PKCS5
```

Cipher algorithm ALG_DES_CBC_PKCS5 provides a cipher using DES in CBC mode. This algorithm uses outer CBC for triple DES. Input data is padded according to the PKCS#5 scheme.

ALG_DES_ECB_ISO9797_M1

```
public static final byte ALG_DES_ECB_ISO9797_M1
```

Cipher algorithm `ALG_DES_ECB_ISO9797_M1` provides a cipher using DES in ECB mode. Input data is padded according to the ISO 9797 method 1 scheme.

ALG_DES_ECB_ISO9797_M2

```
public static final byte ALG_DES_ECB_ISO9797_M2
```

Cipher algorithm `ALG_DES_ECB_ISO9797_M2` provides a cipher using DES in ECB mode. Input data is padded according to the ISO 9797 method 2 (ISO 7816-4, EMV'96) scheme.

ALG_DES_ECB_NOPAD

```
public static final byte ALG_DES_ECB_NOPAD
```

Cipher algorithm `ALG_DES_ECB_NOPAD` provides a cipher using DES in ECB mode. This algorithm does not pad input data. If the input data is not (8 byte) block aligned it throws `CryptoExeption` with the reason code `ILLEGAL_USE`.

ALG_DES_ECB_PKCS5

```
public static final byte ALG_DES_ECB_PKCS5
```

Cipher algorithm `ALG_DES_ECB_PKCS5` provides a cipher using DES in ECB mode. Input data is padded according to the PKCS#5 scheme.

ALG_RSA_ISO14888

```
public static final byte ALG_RSA_ISO14888
```

Cipher algorithm `ALG_RSA_ISO14888` provides a cipher using RSA. Input data is padded according to the ISO 14888 scheme.

ALG_RSA_ISO9796

```
public static final byte ALG_RSA_ISO9796
```

Cipher algorithm `ALG_RSA_ISO9796` provides a cipher using RSA. Input data is padded according to the ISO 9796 (EMV'96) scheme.

Note:

- *This algorithm is only suitable for messages of limited length. The total number of input bytes processed may not be more than k/2, where k is the RSA key's modulus size in bytes.*

ALG_RSA_PKCS1

```
public static final byte ALG_RSA_PKCS1
```

Cipher algorithm `ALG_RSA_PKCS1` provides a cipher using RSA. Input data is padded according to the PKCS#1 (v1.5) scheme.

Note:

- *This algorithm is only suitable for messages of limited length. The total number of input bytes processed may not be more than k-11, where k is the RSA key's modulus size in bytes.*

MODE_DECRYPT

```
public static final byte MODE_DECRYPT
```

Used in `init()` methods to indicate decryption mode.

MODE_ENCRYPT

```
public static final byte MODE_ENCRYPT
```

Used in `init()` methods to indicate encryption mode.

Constructors

Cipher()

```
protected Cipher()
```

Protected Constructor

Methods

doFinal(byte[], short, short, byte[], short)

```
public abstract short doFinal(byte[] inBuff, short inOffset,
            short inLength, byte[] outBuff, short outOffset)
```

Generates encrypted/decrypted output from all/last input data. A call to this method also resets this Cipher object to the state it was in when previously initialized via a call to init(). That is, the object is reset and available to encrypt or decrypt (depending on the operation mode that was specified in the call to init()) more data.

The input and output buffer data may overlap.

Notes:

- *On decryption operations (except when ISO 9797 method 1 padding is used), the padding bytes are not written to* outBuff.
- *On encryption operations, the number of bytes output into* outBuff *may be larger than* inLength.

Parameters:

inBuff—the input buffer of data to be encrypted/decrypted.

inOffset—the offset into the input buffer at which to begin encryption/decryption.

inLength—the byte length to be encrypted/decrypted.

outBuff—the output buffer, may be the same as the input buffer

outOffset—the offset into the output buffer where the resulting hash value begins

Returns: number of bytes output in outBuff

Throws: CryptoException—with the following reason codes:

- CryptoException.UNINITIALIZED_KEY if key not initialized.
- CryptoException.INVALID_INIT if this Cipher object is not initialized.
- CryptoException.ILLEGAL_USE if this Cipher algorithm does not pad the message and the message is not block aligned or if the input message length is not supported.

getAlgorithm()

```
public abstract byte getAlgorithm()
```

Gets the Cipher algorithm.

Returns: the algorithm code defined above.

getInstance(byte, boolean)

```
public static final Cipher getInstance(byte algorithm,
            boolean externalAccess)
```

Creates a `Cipher` object instance of the selected algorithm.

Parameters:

algorithm—the desired Cipher algorithm. See above.

externalAccess—if `true` indicates that the instance will be shared among multiple applet instances and that the `Cipher` instance will also be accessed (via a `Shareable` interface) when the owner of the `Cipher` instance is not the currently selected applet.

Returns: the `Cipher` object instance of the requested algorithm.

Throws: `CryptoException`—with the following reason codes:
- `CryptoException.NO_SUCH_ALGORITHM` if the requested algorithm is not supported.

init(Key, byte)

```
public abstract void init(Key theKey, byte theMode)
```

Initializes the `Cipher` object with the appropriate `Key`. This method should be used for algorithms which do not need initialization parameters or use default parameter values.

Note:

- *DES and triple DES algorithms in CBC mode will use 0 for initial vector(IV) if this method is used.*

Parameters:

theKey—the key object to use for signing or verifying

theMode—one of `MODE_DECRYPT` or `MODE_ENCRYPT`

Throws: `CryptoException`—with the following reason codes:
- `CryptoException.ILLEGAL_VALUE` if theMode option is an undefined value or if the Key is inconsistent with the `Cipher` implementation.

init(Key, byte, byte[], short, short)

```
public abstract void init(Key theKey, byte theMode, byte[] bArray,
            short bOff, short bLen)
```

Initializes the `Cipher` object with the appropriate `Key` and algorithm specific parameters.

Note:

- *DES and triple DES algorithms in outer CBC mode expect an 8 byte parameter value for the initial vector(IV) in* bArray.
- *RSA and DSA algorithms throw* CryptoException.ILLEGAL_VALUE.

Parameters:

theKey—the key object to use for signing

theMode—one of MODE_DECRYPT or MODE_ENCRYPT

bArray—byte array containing algorithm specific initialization info.

bOff—offset withing bArray where the algorithm specific data begins.

bLen—byte length of algorithm specific parameter data

Throws: CryptoException—with the following reason codes:

- CryptoException.ILLEGAL_VALUE if theMode option is an undefined value or if a byte array parameter option is not supported by the algorithm or if the bLen is an incorrect byte length for the algorithm specific data or if the Key is inconsistent with the Cipher implementation.

update(byte[], short, short, byte[], short)

```
public abstract short update(byte[] inBuff, short inOffset,
            short inLength, byte[] outBuff, short outOffset)
```

Generates encrypted/decrypted output from input data. When this method is used temporary storage of intermediate results is required. This method should only be used if all the input data required for the cipher is not available in one byte array. The doFinal() method is recommended whenever possible.

The input and output buffer data may overlap.

Notes:

- *On decryption operations(except when ISO 9797 method 1 padding is used), the padding bytes are not written to* outBuff.
- *On encryption operations, the number of bytes output into* outBuff *may be larger than* inLength.
- *On encryption and decryption operations(except when ISO 9797 method 1 padding is used), block alignment considerations may require that the number of bytes output into* outBuff *be smaller than* inLength *or even 0.*

Parameters:

> inBuff—the input buffer of data to be encrypted/decrypted.

> inOffset—the offset into the input buffer at which to begin encryption/decryption.

> inLength—the byte length to be encrypted/decrypted.

> outBuff—the output buffer, may be the same as the input buffer

> outOffset—the offset into the output buffer where the resulting hash value begins

Returns: number of bytes output in outBuff

Throws: CryptoException—with the following reason codes:
- CryptoException.UNINITIALIZED_KEY if key not initialized.
- CryptoException.INVALID_INIT if this Cipher object is not initialized.
- CryptoException.ILLEGAL_USE if the input message length is not supported.

javacardx.crypto
KeyEncryption

Syntax
`public interface KeyEncryption`

Description
`KeyEncryption` interface defines the methods used to enable encrypted key data access to a key implementation.

See Also: `KeyBuilder`, `Cipher`

Methods

getKeyCipher()

> `public Cipher getKeyCipher()`
>
> Returns the `Cipher` object to be used to decrypt the input key data and key parameters in the set methods.
>
> Default is `null`—no decryption performed.
>
> **Returns:**   keyCipher the decryption `Cipher` object to decrypt the input key data. `null` return indicates that no decryption is performed.

setKeyCipher(Cipher)

> `public void setKeyCipher(Cipher keyCipher)`
>
> Sets the `Cipher` object to be used to decrypt the input key data and key parameters in the set methods.
>
> Default `Cipher` object is `null`—no decryption performed.
>
> **Parameters:**
>
> > keyCipher—the decryption `Cipher` object to decrypt the input key data. `null` parameter indicates that no decryption is required.

Glossary

AID (application identifier)—Unique number assigned to an applet instance or a Java package.

APDU (application protocol data unit)—Data unit exchanged between a smart card and a terminal at the application layer. An APDU contains either a command or a response.

Applet firewall—Protection mechanism that enforces applet isolation and separates the system space from the applet space. In the firewall scheme, each applet runs within a context (object space). Applets cannot access each other's objects unless they are defined in the same package (and thus share the same context) or through well-defined and secure object-sharing mechanisms supported by the Java card platform.

API (application programming interface)—It defines calling conventions by which an application program accesses the operating system and other services.

Atomicity—Term referring to any update to a persistent object field, a class field, or a persistent array element that is guaranteed to either complete successfully, or else be restored to its original value.

ATR (answer to reset)—String of bytes sent by a smart card after a reset condition.

CAD (card acceptance device)—Device that is used to communicate with a smart card. It may also provide power and timing to the smart card.

CAD session—Period from the time the card is inserted into the card acceptance device (CAD) and is powered up until the time the card is removed from the CAD is called a CAD session.

CAP (converted applet) file—The standard file format for the binary compatibility of the Java Card platform. A CAP file contains an executable binary representation of the classes in a Java package.

Context—Protected object space into which the applet firewall partitions the Java Card object system. Applets from the same package share one context. The JCRE resides in the JCRE context.

EEPROM (electrically erasable programmable read-only memory)—Typical persistent storage medium used in smart cards.

Export file—File containing public API information for an entire package of classes.

Garbage collection—Process by which dynamically allocated storage is automatically reclaimed during the execution of a program.

Global arrays—Primitive array that can be accessed by any applet and the JCRE. A global array is a special type of JCRE entry point object.

ISO 7816—Document that sets the standard for the smart card industry.

Java Card applet—Smart card application written in the Java language that can be downloaded and executed in the JCRE.

Java Card application framework—It defines the application programming interfaces. The framework consists of four core and extension API packages.

Java Card virtual machine—It consists of the converter running off card on a PC or a workstation and the interpreter running inside a card. Together, they implement the virtual machine functions—loading Java class files and executing them with a particular set of semantics.

Java Card converter—Off-card component of the Java Card virtual machine. The converter preprocesses all the class files that make up a Java package and creates a CAP file and an export file for the package being converted.

Java Card interpreter—On-card component of the Java Card virtual machine. The interpreter executes bytecode instructions and enforces runtime security. In this book, the terms Java Card interpreter and Java Card virtual machine are used synonymously unless otherwise stated.

Java Card installer—Module in the JCRE for downloading and installing a CAP file.

JCRE (Java card runtime environment)—Runtime environment for executing Java Card applets.

JCRE entry point objects—Objects owned by the JCRE. Public methods of such objects can be invoked by any applets.

Java smart card—Smart card that supports Java Card technology.

Persistent objects—Objects that are created using the `new` operator. Persistent objects hold states and values across CAD sessions.

SI (shareable interface)—Interface that extends, either directly or indirectly, the tagging interface `javacard.framework.Shareable`.

SIO (shareable interface object)—Object of a class that implements a shareable interface. The methods defined in the shareable interface of such an object are accessible across by any applets.

Transaction—An atomic operation in which either all updates take place correctly and consistently or all persistent fields are restored to their previous values.

Transient objects—Objects created by invoking the Java Card APIs. Transient objects do not hold states and values across CAD sessions.

Bibliography

[1] W. Rankl and W. Effing. *Smart Card Handbook*. John Wiley & Sons, New York, 1997.

[2] S. B. Guthery and T. M. Jurgensen. *Smart Card Developer's Kit*. Macmillan Technical Publishing, Indianapolis, 1998.

[3] Robin C. Townend. *Finance: History, Development & Market Overview*, Smart Card News Ltd. http://www.smartcard.co.uk/

[4] Java Card Forum, http://www.javacardforum.org/

[5] OpenCard consortium, http://www.opencard.org/

[6] International Organization for Standards, http://www.iso.ch/

[7] PC/SC Workgroup, http://www.pcscworkgroup.com/

[8] European Telecommunications Standards Institute, http://www.etsi.org/

[9] GlobalPlatform, http://www.globalplatform.org/

[10] Li Gong. *Inside Java™ 2 Platform Security, Architecture, API Design and Implementation*. Addison-Wesley, Reading, MA, 1999.

[11] Java 2.1 Cryptography Architecture API Specification & Reference. http://java.sun.com/products/jdk/1.2/docs/guide/security/CryptoSpec.html

[12] Bruce Schneier. *Applied Cryptography, Protocols, Algorithms, and Source Code in C*. John Wiley & Sons, New York, 1996.

[13] Mike Hendry. *Smart Card Security and Applications*. Artech House, Norwood, MA, 1997.

[14] Java Card Technology Home Page. http://java.sun.com/products/javacard/

[15] Frank Yellin. "Low-Level Security in Java." http://www.javasoft.com/sfaq/verifier.html/

[16] Tim Lindholm and Frank Yellin. *The Java Virtual Machine Specification, Second Edition*. Addison-Wesley, Reading, MA, 1999.

[17] Henry Dreifus and J. Thomas Monk. *Smart Cards, A Guide to Building and Managing Smart Card Applications*. John Wiley & Sons, 1998.

[18] Catherine Allen and William J. Barr. *Smart Cards, Seizing Strategic Business Opportunities*. IRWIN Professional Publishing, 1997.

[19] Uwe Hansmann, Martin S. Nicklous, Thomas Schack, and Frank Seliger. *Smart Card Application Development Using Java*. Springer, 2000.

[20] Ken Arnold and James Gosling. *The Java Programming Language, Second Edition*. Addison-Wesley, Reading, MA, 1998.

Index

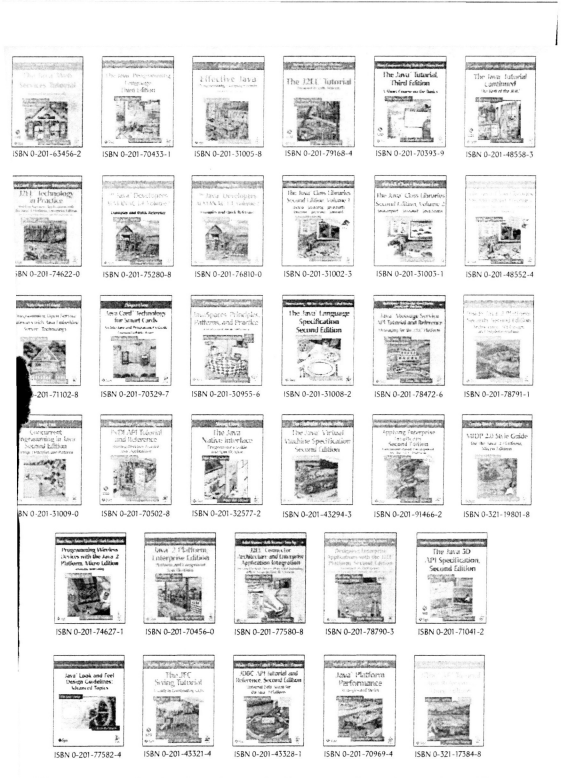

ISBN 0-201-63456-2   ISBN 0-201-70433-1   ISBN 0-201-31005-8   ISBN 0-201-79168-4   ISBN 0-201-70393-9   ISBN 0-201-48558-3

ISBN 0-201-74622-0   ISBN 0-201-75280-8   ISBN 0-201-76810-0   ISBN 0-201-31002-3   ISBN 0-201-31003-1   ISBN 0-201-48552-4

ISBN 0-201-71102-8   ISBN 0-201-70329-7   ISBN 0-201-30955-6   ISBN 0-201-31008-2   ISBN 0-201-78472-6   ISBN 0-201-78791-1

ISBN 0-201-31009-0   ISBN 0-201-70502-8   ISBN 0-201-32577-2   ISBN 0-201-43294-3   ISBN 0-201-91466-2   ISBN 0-321-19801-8

ISBN 0-201-74627-1   ISBN 0-201-70456-0   ISBN 0-201-77580-8   ISBN 0-201-78790-3   ISBN 0-201-71041-2

ISBN 0-201-77582-4   ISBN 0-201-43321-4   ISBN 0-201-43328-1   ISBN 0-201-70969-4   ISBN 0-321-17384-8

Visit www.awprofessional.com/javaseries for more information on these titles.

Register
Your Book
at www.awprofessional.com/register

You may be eligible to receive:
- Advance notice of forthcoming editions of the book
- Related book recommendations
- Chapter excerpts and supplements of forthcoming titles
- Information about special contests and promotions throughout the year
- Notices and reminders about author appearances, tradeshows, and online chats with special guests

Contact us

If you are interested in writing a book or reviewing manuscripts prior to publication, please write to us at:

Editorial Department
Addison-Wesley Professional
75 Arlington Street, Suite 300
Boston, MA 02116 USA
Email: AWPro@aw.com

Visit us on the Web: http://www.awprofessional.com